Haya de la Torre
and the Pursuit of Power
in Twentieth-Century Peru
and Latin America

Haya de la Torre and the Pursuit of Power in Twentieth-Century Peru and Latin America

Iñigo García-Bryce

The University of North Carolina Press CHAPEL HILL

This book was published with the assistance of the Anniversary Fund of the University of North Carolina Press.

The University of North Carolina Press has been a member of the
Green Press Initiative since 2003.

Library of Congress Cataloging-in-Publication Data
Names: García-Bryce, Iñigo L., 1966– author.
Title: Haya de la Torre and the pursuit of power in twentieth-century Peru
    and Latin America / Iñigo García-Bryce.
Description: Chapel Hill : University of North Carolina Press, [2018] |
    Includes bibliographical references and index.
Identifiers: LCCN 2017048513 | ISBN 9781469636559 (cloth : alk. paper) |
    ISBN 9781469636573 (pbk : alk. paper) | ISBN 9781469636603 (ebook)
Subjects: LCSH: Haya de la Torre, Víctor Raúl, 1895–1979. | Haya de la Torre,
    Víctor Raúl, 1895–1979—Influence. | Politicians—Peru—Biography. | Partido Aprista
    Peruano. | Peru—Politics and government—1919–1968. | Latin America—Politics and
    government—20th century. | United States—Foreign relations—Peru.
Classification: LCC F3448.H3 G38 2018 | DDC 985.06/3092 [B]—dc23
    LC record available at https://lccn.loc.gov/2017048513

Cover illustration: Haya de la Torre giving a speech, ca. 1957 (Armando Villanueva Papers,
courtesy of Lucía Villanueva).

Small portions of chapters 1 and 5 were previously published in "Transnational Activist: Magda
Portal and the American Popular Revolutionary Alliance, 1926–1950," *The Americas* 70:4
(April 2014): 677–706. © Cambridge University Press. Reprinted with permission.

*I dedicate this book to my children, Samuel and Mateo,
who make my life much richer than it otherwise would be.*

Contents

Illustrations

Acknowledgments

With research for this book stretching back over the course of more than a decade, the list of people and institutions to thank is long.

I begin by thanking the many colleagues who have contributed to the intellectual formulation of this project and to its development over the years. José Z. García is at the top of the list. I thank him for challenging me to not shy away from an important topic, and for being a constant interlocutor over the years on the American Popular Revolutionary Alliance (APRA) and Víctor Raúl Haya de la Torre; I also forgive him for disparaging historians for their overuse of footnotes. Ray Sadler, who constantly stopped by my office to check on how the project was moving along, had encouraging words and insights into Latin American history. Peter Klaren commented on more than one conference paper and supported my project, as did Chuck Walker. The late Jeffrey Klaiber was generous with his time whenever I stopped by his office at Universidad Católica to discuss my project. Natalia Sobrevilla offered critical comments and encouragement during numerous transatlantic phone calls and conferences. Barbara Tenenbaum helped to keep me on a steady course whenever I wavered as the topic seemed to become too unmanageable: "You owe this to your colleagues," she would say, appealing to my overdeveloped sense of duty. I also thank Friedrich Schuller for his support. José Flores figured out a foolproof method for me to not miss the final deadline.

Next I thank my editor, Elaine Maisner, at the University of North Carolina Press. From the moment she accepted the manuscript, she seemed to have a feel for the topic that I had spent years researching, as well as a knack for publicity through social media—a quality that would have been much appreciated by Haya. I thank the copyeditor, Ashley Moore; the production editor, Annette Calzone; and the staff at the press for their excellent work. I also thank Danielle Swope for her assistance with editing.

The Fulbright Foundation provided generous support for a semester of research in Lima and a position as visiting professor from August to December 2009 at the Universidad Nacional Mayor de San Marcos. Special thanks to Francisco Quiroz and Teresa Vergara for their support and good humor, and to my students in the class I taught on oral history.

The following friends and colleagues commented on drafts of chapters: Cristóbal Aljovín, Sam Brunk, Sandra McGee Deutsch, José Z. García, Jon Hunner, Tim Kettelaar, Lisa Moricoli-Latham, Alison Newby, Andrea Orzoff, Neal Rosendorf, Mary Alice Scott, Natalia Sobrevilla, and Mike Zigmund. Their comments proved invaluable in improving the writing and pointing to blind spots. Natalia Sobrevilla and Alison Newby both went out of their way to offer quick turnaround on chapters as deadlines loomed. Ed Shirkey would have provided excellent comments had he been able to. I thank Bill Storey and Jamie Bronstein for their feedback.

I thank my co-panelists at the Rocky Mountain Council for Latin American Studies and at the Latin American Studies Association for their insights: Martin Bergel, Jo Crow, Ombelyne Dagicour, Geneviève Dorais, Paulo Drinot, Nils Jacobsen, and Leandro Sessa. I also thank Ulrich Mücke for publishing an early iteration of this text.

I must also take a step much further back to thank two enormously influential people in my intellectual career. Jeff Weintraub at Harvard University introduced me to the joys of social analysis and gave me the tools to begin to understand the society where I grew up. Efraín Kristal, also at Harvard, zealously drove home the point that rigor and knowledge remained important goals in a postmodern age.

I owe a debt of gratitude to the late Pedro Planas, who, before his untimely death, dedicated his first-class mind to the study of Haya. I met Pedro Planas when I was a young intern at Oiga in 1986, long before I fully understood the contributions he was making to the study of Peruvian politics.

Archivists and librarians silently make it possible for historians to do their work. I begin close to home by thanking Molly Molloy for building a strong Latin American collection at New Mexico State University: many of the secondary sources I needed were at the library; for those that weren't, the university librarians exhibited great tolerance toward my constant string of late returns of Interlibrary Loan books. I thank the archivists and librarians at the many archives and libraries that I visited to research this book in Peru, Argentina, the United States, Germany, and England.

A number of individuals in the APRA party generously contributed their time by sharing memories and experiences that helped me to better understand the workings of the party. Armando Villanueva shared not only his knowledge but also his private archive; I thank his daughter Lucy Villanueva for allowing me to continue to use this archive after his death. Tito Aguero deserves special mention for his former connection to the party and his scholarly approach to its history. Luis Alva Castro shared often-emotional memories of Haya. Alejandro Santa María told me stories of APRA in an unlikely but meaningful place: Berlin.

The following individuals gave very generously of their time and shared hours of memories of their own connection to the party and to Haya: Alfonso Aguilar, Luis Armando Sánchez, César Atala, Bársalo Burga, Manuel Chávez Vargas, Clodomiro Cueva Lujan and Graciela Zurita de Cueva, Isabel Macalopú, Juan Manuel Ontaneda, Carlos and Rosa Miranda, Juvenal Ñique, Lindomira Peirano, Germán Perez Palma, Alfredo Santa María, Consuelo Torres Tello, and Alfonso Velazquez. President Morales Bermúdez and Luis Bedoya Reyes conveyed to me the respect that Haya had earned by the end of his life from some members of the opposition.

Peruvians have not lost the art of conversation, and I have learned a great deal about APRA from numerous conversations over the course of my research. I thank in particular Tito Aguero, Carlos Aguirre, Roisida Aguila, Carlos Giesecke, Agustín Haya de la Torre, Raúl Haya de la Torre, Javier Landázuri, Scarlett O'Phelan, Richard Stoddart, Rafael Tapia, Guillermo Tirado, and Imelda Vega-Centeno.

For assistance with research, I thank my research assistant in Lima, Julio Abanto, now a historian in his own right. I also thank Luis Barraza, Loudan Downer, Gabriella Flynn, Breauna Sánchez, and Charles Savage at New Mexico State University for their assistance in scouring certain sources to help hunt down some important details.

Finally, although this paragraph should really precede all the others, I thank my family, and those friends who are like family, for their patience and encouragement throughout the whole endeavor. Special thanks go to Andrea Orzoff, who provided both encouragement and critical feedback during the many long years of research and conceptualization of this book.

Timeline

1895	February 22: Haya born in Trujillo, Peru
1922	Haya attends YMCA student camp in Piriápolis, Uruguay
	Haya travels to Argentina and Chile
1923	October 3: Haya deported from Peru by President Augusto B. Leguía
1924	Haya works with José Vasconcelos in Mexico
	Haya visits Russia
1925	Haya studies at London School of Economics and Oxford University
1926	Haya founds first American Popular Revolutionary Alliance (APRA) cell in Paris and publishes "What Is the APRA?" in *Labour Monthly*
1927	Haya attends First International Congress against Imperialism and Colonialism, Brussels
	Haya travels to the United States
1928	Haya founds APRA Mexico cell
	Haya attempts to implement "Plan de Mexico"—plan to start a revolution in Peru
	Haya writes *El antimperialismo y el APRA* in response to attack by Cuban Communist Julio Antonio Mella
1929	Haya not allowed to disembark in Panama; his ship, *Phoenicia*, takes him to Germany
1929–1931	Haya lives in Berlin
1930	September 20: Partido Aprista Peruano (PAP), Peruvian branch of APRA, founded (Haya still in Berlin)

1931	July 12: Haya returns to Peru; disembarks in Talara
	August 23: Haya gives speech at Plaza de Acho (Lima's bullring) presenting his political program (*programa mínimo*) for Peru
	October 11: Election Day—Haya loses to Colonel Luis Sánchez Cerro
1932	January 8: Emergency Law declares PAP illegal, labels it an "international party"
	May: Haya jailed in Lima's Panopticon
	July 7: Trujillo insurrection occurs
1933	March 11: Gustavo Jimenez attempts a failed insurrection in Cajamarca
	April 30: Aprista assassinates Sánchez Cerro
1933–1934	President Oscar Benavides allows APRA to operate legally
1934	Federación Aprista Juvenil (FAJ) founded
1934–1945	Haya lives in hiding
1936	Benavides holds elections but cancels them when the APRA-supported candidate Luis Eguiguren wins
	Haya publishes *El antimperialismo y el APRA* in Chile
1939	February 19: General Antonio Rodríguez attempts a failed coup
1942	PAP convention: deletion of the word *Yankee* from "Yankee imperialism" in continental party platform
	APRA renamed Partido del Pueblo
	FAJ renamed Juventud Aprista Peruana
1944	March 18: Sergeant Claudio López Lavalle takes over Base Naval Ancón
1945	APRA regains legal status and becomes part of the Frente Democrático coalition, which comes to power with President José Luís Bustamante y Rivero
	Haya still barred from running for president

1946   Haya visits Colombia

November: First National Convention of Aprista Women

1947   January 7: Francisco Graña Garland, editor of *La Prensa*, assassinated

June: Haya visits U.S. youth forum organized by *New York Herald Tribune*

Haya meets with Albert Einstein at Princeton University

1948   February: Haya visits Gabriela Mistral in California

February 6: Aprista sympathizer Major Víctor Villanueva attempts a failed armed uprising in Ancón

May 27–June 3: Second APRA party congress; Haya denies women full voting membership within the party

October 3: Callao uprising is led by APRA sympathizers in the navy

1949–1954   Haya lives in the Colombian embassy while his political asylum case delays and reaches the International Court of Justice in The Hague

1954   Insurgency against Manuel Odría fails (party leader Manuel Seoane involved)

May: Haya travels to San Miguel Allende, Mexico, after finally being allowed to leave Peru

1954–1969   Haya lives in Europe during most of these years, returning to Peru for short visits

1955   General Odría grants women the vote

1962   Allowed to run for president again, Haya returns to Peru and wins the presidential election by such a slim margin that by law the decision is in the hands of Congress; the military stages a coup before a winner can be declared

1963   Haya runs for president for the last time and loses to young reformer Fernando Belaúnde Terry

1969   Haya returns to Peru to reside at Villa Mercedes

July 7: Haya names Alan García president of the Parlamento Universitario (University Parliament)

1976   Haya speaks on the Dia de la Fraternidad to large crowds

1978   Haya elected president of the Constituent Assembly

1979   Haya travels to the United States for cancer treatment

August 2: Haya dies shortly after signing new constitution

Haya de la Torre
and the Pursuit of Power
in Twentieth-Century Peru
and Latin America

Introduction

> He has not grown between the paws of military cabalism nor has
> he been formed from the incantations of traditional fortunes.
> He comes out of the fervor of the well-digested readings and the
> masticated pain among everyday crumbs. He is the leader, par
> excellence, of the new times, the man who carries the message of
> the books to the people.... This man who frequents Shakespeare
> and can spell the names of the countryside of his land; this man is
> more than a common politician. I say that it is the arm chosen by
> history to move the airs of all America.
>
> —ALBERTO HIDALGO

> Haya was clearly the premier bigger-than-life political personage
> to have emerged since the Mexican Revolution, although later
> Fidel Castro and Ernesto "Che" Guevara would begin to eclipse
> Haya as leaders of mythic proportions.
>
> —FREDERICK PIKE

At a time when the world is entering another populist moment, Víctor Raúl
Haya de la Torre has become a timely figure. The founder of the American
Popular Revolutionary Alliance (APRA) and its leader from 1926 to his
death in 1979, Haya offered Latin America a homegrown formula for revolutionary nationalism—Aprismo—and the model of a successful political
organization that remains among Latin America's longest-lived populist
parties. Designed to challenge both the Communist International (Comintern) and the power of U.S. imperialism in Latin America, Aprismo drew
on a series of revolutionary and reformist traditions (the Mexican Revolution, the Russian Revolution, European Fascism, British Labourism, and
Chinese nationalism) to offer a political program that addressed Latin
America's problems of economic development and social injustice. Latin
America need not look to European or North American political traditions
for solutions; it needed simply to look inward to its own revolution, the
Mexican Revolution, as a homegrown model to follow. Haya masterfully
distilled what he saw as the teachings of the Mexican Revolution into a po-
litical ideology that gained widespread currency among twentieth-century

parties of the nationalist left during the interwar and early Cold War periods, from Venezuela to Costa Rica, from Cuba to Chile and Paraguay. Among others, Haya influenced the Nicaraguan Augusto Sandino, who borrowed from Haya's notion of a multiclass coalition, and Rómulo Betancourt, founder of Venezuela's Acción Democrática.

In Peru, where APRA took hold most strongly and was the country's main political party for many decades, Haya's particular brand of leftist politics generated both fervent adherence among his supporters and vehement opposition among his detractors. Still referred to today as El Jefe (the chief) by his followers, or more familiarly as El Viejo (the old man), Haya emerged as the revered quasi-messianic leader of a party almost akin to a religious movement. During the presidential campaign of 1980, one year after Haya's death, the Aprista campaign song for then-candidate Armando Villanueva proclaimed, "APRA is the way" and "Victor Raúl stayed in my heart." As intensely as his followers venerated him, his detractors hated him and accused him of having betrayed the very ideals on which he founded the party. To guarantee his party's survival, he had made, they claimed, too many political compromises with former enemies. I have personally experienced these passions in conversations, in many cases with Lima's taxi drivers, who are among the city's best conversationalists. The *taxistas* have either congratulated me for my efforts in studying APRA or treated me to icy silence when I told them about my research topic. Was I an Aprista? they wanted to know. They often followed the question with lengthy tirades against Alan García, the only Aprista leader who reached the presidency of Peru (1985–90 and 2006–11).

These passions have spilled over into the historiography and generated two views of Haya—Haya the hero and Haya the betrayer—that have made it difficult to assess his political legacy. This partisanship is also the product of a long-standing enmity between Apristas and Communists that dates back to the ideological battles in the 1920s between the founders of these two movements in Peru: Haya, who favored a multiclass revolution led by the middle class, and José Carlos Mariátegui, who saw the peasantry as the revolutionary class. In subsequent decades, APRA's ideological shift toward the center of the political spectrum as it sought to gain power made the enmity more pronounced, particularly as defectors from APRA joined the chorus of those accusing APRA of having abandoned its original revolutionary ideals. This ideological divide has had a lasting effect on the writing of APRA's history. On the one hand, Apristas have written with obvious sympathy about their own party and its founder, Haya. On the other hand, scholars on the left have been highly critical of APRA. Academic scholarship, often written by non-Peruvians, outside these two traditions has focused on a number of important themes for understanding the ideological and social origins of APRA, as well as the quasi-religious nature of its following.[1]

A revolutionary student leader whose years in exile allowed him to found a transnational political movement, Haya quickly realized the need to play by the rules of the political system once he entered the fray of Peruvian politics. Unlike the other great Latin American revolutionary figure, Fidel Castro, Haya practiced a much less glamorous brand of politics: the politics of compromise. Haya never held the reigns of executive power, nor did he lead a successful revolutionary movement. He spent decades facing political persecution and maneuvering to bring APRA to power. He made compromises that have led his detractors to accuse him of abandoning his youthful revolutionary ideas.

Unlike his intellectual rival, the Communist Mariátegui, Haya did not die young. If he had, he might have gone down in Latin American politics as a type of hero similar to Che Guevara, Mariátegui, Sandino, or José Martí—Haya the anti-imperialist crusader. Haya survived into old age. We must therefore assess his entire life, in all its messiness: a life in which the early theme of political martyrdom became intertwined with that of political compromise. Yet, as Charles Anderson points out in reference to the politics of compromise, these particular skills "are not to be despised . . . and often appear a little short of incredible."[2]

Haya's contributions were fourfold. Haya the ideologue invented a political doctrine tailored to Latin American social realities. Haya the propagandist disseminated Aprismo through his writings (as did his followers), brought Aprismo to all corners of the continent, and ensured that Aprismo had a wide impact on twentieth-century Latin American politics. Haya the institution builder created a lasting political organization with a mass following in Peru that greatly increased the legitimacy of his political ideas. Haya the pragmatist guaranteed the survival of his party against all odds thanks to his ability to practice politics as the art of compromise. That he often went too far in compromising his political ideals for the pursuit of power is undeniable. Yet by condemning him for this we cease the process of understanding him.

The vicissitudes of Haya's political life illustrate broader themes in the history of his party, of Peru, and of Latin American populism. Haya was one of many populist leaders who emerged during the middle decades of the twentieth century, a period known as that of classical populism in Latin America. Their fortunes varied. Juan Domingo Perón ruled Argentina for nine years during his first presidency and forever transformed the country. Getulio Vargas had a similarly transformative impact on Brazil. In Colombia, the assassination of Jorge Eliécer Gaitán threw the country into a political crisis that arguably still lasts today. Haya faced persecution and led his party through complicated twists and turns over the course of decades to establish political legitimacy. He never reached power—however, his party survived him and has held power twice in the years since Peru returned to democracy in 1980.

The stories of those who reached power and of those who did not constitute pieces of the larger puzzle of Latin American populism. The puzzle is not an easy one to solve. In fact, the very definition of populism has continued to elude scholars over the years. Perhaps all we can agree on is the most general definition of populists as politicians who emerge at certain critical junctures to challenge the power of elites and offer to rule in the name of the people. In 1980, Steve Stein wrote, "Existing literature on populism often contains contrasting, even contradictory arguments regarding the nature of populist movements."[3] More recently, Kenneth Roberts wrote, "Indeed, scholars have struggled even to reach a consensus on the meaning of the concept and its essential empirical properties."[4] The scholarship on populism has elucidated an important aspect of the phenomenon: the existence of "critical junctures," defined as moments in the history of a society marked by economic and political shifts that create the conditions for the emergence of a populist leader.[5] We are clearly experiencing such a moment today with the election of Donald J. Trump in the United States and Narendra Modi in India and the rise of Far Right populisms in Europe.

One way out of this definitional quagmire is to take a biographical approach that complements the notion of critical junctures. Although the critical junctures provide the historical stage, we must explore the stories of the individual populist leaders who step onto it. We must examine how their personalities affected their handling of the challenges that arose at those critical junctures. As in a theater, the scenery, plot, and characters form part of a whole. We cannot ignore the role of the individual's personal story in shaping the form and outcome of political movements.[6]

Haya de la Torre and the Pursuit of Power in Twentieth-Century Peru and Latin America takes a biographical approach. The fact that Haya was a student leader and not a military man shaped his quest for power in ways very different from Perón's. His friendships with the Scottish Presbyterian minister John Mackay and the North American teacher and internationalist Anna Melissa Graves opened up a network of contacts for Haya that influenced his relationship with the United States. His friends and his enemies in the Peruvian military played a role in determining the degree of support he received from the armed forces. Haya's alleged homosexuality influenced his life—had he married, his fate as a politician would likely have been different. His alleged homosexuality is a fact of Peruvian political life: his political enemies used it to smear him when he ran for president in 1962 and 1963, while Apristas have constantly challenged it by attempting to demonstrate that Haya had a number of romantic liaisons with women. His alleged homosexuality must have reinforced his sense of being an outsider trying to break into the Peruvian political system. The kind of exposure that he would have received as president of Peru perhaps explains why he never really sought the position wholeheartedly after his first youthful presidential run.

While Haya's story is part of the story of populism in Peru, his is also a much larger Latin American story. Haya is unique among the populist leaders of his time in that he was an internationalist. At a time of fervent nationalisms, Haya aspired to blur national borders and create a Latin American political movement. A continentalist in the tradition of Simón Bolívar and Martí, Haya was the first person to attempt to found a transnational Latin American political party. Beginning in 1926, Apristas founded "cells"—small groups of followers tasked with disseminating Aprista ideas—in cities throughout the continent, from Buenos Aires to Havana to Mexico, and even outside Latin America in New York and Paris. While APRA took root most strongly in Peru, Apristas also founded parties in Cuba and Costa Rica, albeit short-lived ones. The emergence of APRA-inspired parties has led some scholars to use the category *Aprista parties*, which includes Venezuela's Acción Democrática, Costa Rica's Partido de Liberación Nacional, Cuba's Partido Revolucionario Cubano Auténtico, the Dominican Republic's Partido Revolucionario Dominicano, and the Febreristas in Paraguay.[7] APRA also influenced the Chilean Socialist Party, as well as politics in Panama, and may have had an influence on Peronismo.[8] Charles Ameringer argues that "the APRA Movement of Haya de la Torre was the precursor of the parties of the Democratic Left."[9] In many of these cases, the influence has been difficult to trace because, as Robert Alexander has pointed out, politicians such as Rómulo Betancourt were reluctant to openly admit any Aprista influence.[10] Admitting the influence of an international political movement did not constitute good politics in the national context.

Haya continued to embrace and disseminate his continentalist ideas and to call for a united Latin America well into his later years. A new generation of scholars has begun to explore APRA's transnational dimension.[11] This transnational history of APRA presents Aprismo from an entirely new perspective: while Haya did not reach the presidency in Peru, Aprismo took root not only in Peru but also in the political programs of parties that came to power in Venezuela, Costa Rica, Chile, and perhaps even Argentina and Brazil.

Haya the propagandist offers another key to understanding classical populism in Latin America: its connection to the Mexican Revolution. Haya is the most important propagandist of populism: by distilling Mexico's Constitution of 1917 into a simple political doctrine, Aprismo, he offered Latin America a model of non-Communist revolution, driven by an international capitalist economy, tempered by the guiding hand of the anti-imperialist state, and capable of representing the interests of the working, peasant, and middle classes. This "political formula," as Tulio Halperín has pointed out, "was destined to echo throughout Latin America following the Second World War."[12] The twenty-first-century radical populists Hugo Chávez, Evo Morales, and Rafael Correa belong to a political tradition that began with Aprismo and the Mexican Revolution.

Thus, Haya connects classical populism to the first great revolution of the twentieth century: the Mexican Revolution. At a time when Latin Americans were rejecting European and North American cultural models, Aprismo proposed Latin American solutions to Latin American problems. It offered much more than a political theory: it had a concrete revolution to draw on. From the messy experience of the Mexican Revolution, Haya managed to distill a simple political program for Latin American political and economic development. Latin America did not need to follow foreign examples (the Russian Revolution being the main one) as it had its own model of revolution, which could be exported to the rest of Latin America. Haya did see parallels between Peru and China. The closest foreign model that Haya admired was Sun Yat-sen's nationalist revolution in China (1911–12)—in fact, the name of APRA was derived from the Chinese movement, T'ung Meng Hui (Revolutionary Alliance), founded by Sun, which gave birth to the Kuomintang. Aprismo condensed the experience of the Mexican Revolution as part of its five-point program and promoted its adoption throughout the continent.

Unlike the Cuban Revolution after it, the Mexican Revolution did not attempt to export its model of revolution to the rest of Latin America, although it did seek international legitimacy through a number of propaganda campaigns.[13] It took an outsider not caught up in the postrevolutionary political battles to come up with a formula for exporting the Mexican Revolution.[14] Haya had the advantage of being able to look back on the revolution and select what he saw as its lessons to build the Aprista political program. He considered the Mexican Revolution as an improvised movement that had developed without a clear direction. By systematizing the somewhat chaotic experience of the revolution and offering a clear program, Aprismo made it possible to spread it to the rest of Latin America. Aprismo offered a precise program based on what remained an ongoing process in Mexico. Haya saw the postrevolutionary Mexican state as an incomplete step in the direction of revolution: "The new architecture of the State—of which we see only an unfulfilled attempt in Mexico, but from which we take advantage of the incomparably valuable experience for our peoples—suggests to us the foundations of the true Indo-American Anti-imperialist State."[15]

Haya can be compared to Guevara (it should be the other way around) for his role in promoting the export of a revolution—in this case, the Mexican Revolution. Intriguing parallels exist between the two men. In each case, we have a foreigner whose Latin American perspective enabled him to distill aspects of a revolutionary experience into a simple, exportable formula. The two almost met in Guatemala in January 1954 when Haya stopped at the airport on his way to a new period of exile in Mexico. Guevara apparently wanted to challenge Haya for his rapprochement with the United States. The meeting never happened between these two very different types of revolutionaries. Aprismo offered a program, albeit not a method, for taking power. As Harry Kantor has pointed out, "The Aprista ideology has its weaknesses, the most conspicuous being its neglect of a method of achieving power, but it is an impressive attempt to create a political program suitable to Latin American conditions."[16] Guevara, on the other hand, wrote an explicit handbook on his theory of the *foco* (a theory stating that a small group of guerrillas operating from the countryside can topple a government), giving other revolutionaries a method for taking power. Although Haya was not explicit on the subject, his actions prove his flexibility regarding the means of gaining power, as he was willing to pursue both armed insurgency and elections.

Given the influence of APRA and the Mexican Revolution on the development of Latin American populism, why have scholars not established more explicitly the connections between these various political movements? To begin with, influence is difficult to prove. And it is particularly difficult to prove if those influenced by a set of ideas have a great deal at stake in denying them. During a time of rising nationalism throughout the continent, any leader who claimed influence from a foreign revolution and set of ideas—albeit a Latin American one—would not have been politically popular. Robert Alexander states that Betancourt, while heavily influenced by APRA, "would never admit it."[17] The new scholarship on transnational Aprista networks is examining the personal connections between exiled Peruvian Apristas and intellectuals and politicians in their host countries, and it could help to elucidate the slippery issue of influence.

The present book is simultaneously a political biography of the man and of his party. It is not a "cradle-to-grave" biography but rather presents five main themes in Haya's life. It argues that Haya was a skillful practitioner of politics who operated in multiple arenas both national and international. Each of the book's five chapters addresses a distinct sphere of action and is organized chronologically. In a *Rashomon*-like style, the chapters sometimes revisit similar incidents in Haya's life from different perspectives. Chapter 1, "Revolution for Export: Forging a Latin American Revolution," portrays Haya operating in a transnational arena at a time when the Comintern supported the spread of Communism in Latin America. Haya's Aprismo offered a Latin American alternative to the Comintern and a concrete Latin American example to follow: that of the Mexican Revolution. It competed with the Comintern by proclaiming solidarity among the oppressed peoples of the world, in addition to joint action of Latin American countries against imperialism. Aprismo, together with the rest of the Left in Latin America, cannot be understood as separate from the influence of Communism, either in the early stages following the Russian Revolution or in the later stages during the Cold War. Much of APRA's political strategy both nationally and internationally involved distinguishing itself as a homegrown revolutionary party distinct from Communist parties. Paradoxically, Aprismo was an international political movement that called for the development of a strong national state. As Manuel Caballero points out, "For several of those countries, Marxism or even Socialism arrived wrapped in Leninism not to say Stalinism. From the beginning of the twenties, the entire Left had to define itself with regard to the Comintern, and the ideological struggle with the 'Cominternianos' presided over the birth of such important non-Communist parties as the APRA in Perú and 'Democrátic Action' of Venezuela."[18] To this day, the distinction between the Communist and non-Communist Left holds valuable lessons as we try to make sense of the latest wave of Latin American populisms, often confused with Socialism and therefore misunderstood in their true Latin American context.

Chapter 2, "Bullets and Ballots: Revolutionaries, Elections, and the Military," follows Haya as he maneuvered in the arena of national politics, although the transnational dimension never ceased to be present, as Aprista politics included its exiles, as well as some efforts to seek support from foreign governments. Following the loss of the 1931 election, Haya had to manage the insurgent wing of his own party, negotiate an increasingly hostile relationship with the Peruvian military, and push forward with his own desire to participate in democratic elections when the opportunities became available. The coexistence of insurgent and democratic leanings within APRA and Haya's fraught relationship with the military illustrate a broader theme in Latin American politics. The oscillation between democratic transitions, insurgent politics, and military coups has characterized the continent's political landscape from the outset of the national period. As Charles Anderson has argued, this process must be normalized rather than seen as an aberration; Anderson offers the concept of "power contenders" as a way of understanding that elections are only one of many ways in which individuals attempt to enter the political process.[19] APRA exemplifies this category of power contender almost to perfection. According to the political moment, Haya supported insurgent violence, elections, or a military coup as a means to gain power.

As a justification for the use of violence, Haya quoted the earlier Peruvian president and caudillo Nicolás de Piérola as having said that when the doors of legality close, the doors of violence open. In other words, under dictatorship or situations such as that faced by APRA for over two decades during which the party was stripped of its political rights and declared illegal, the recourse to violence became a legitimate road to power. This pattern connects APRA to other political movements of the time. The Cuban Revolution began when the doors of legality closed on Castro, who chose the route of armed violence after his run for the Senate was frustrated by the shutdown of democratic politics following Batista's 1952 coup. When Perón, living in exile, wrote to his followers urging them to turn to violence, he made a similar argument.

Chapter 3, "*Marinera* with the Yankees: Haya de la Torre and the United States," examines Haya's relationship with the United States—that is, his writings on the United States and his personal relations with North Americans, both with independent citizens and with others associated with the

U.S. government. The notion of an anti-imperialist who embraced the United States may on the face of it seem confusing. By referring to the *marinera*, a traditional dance from Haya's native land, Peru's northern coast, I attempt to capture the complexity of this relationship. When dancing *marinera*, the partners circle one another, approaching each other to the point that they are almost touching and then moving farther apart. The dance metaphorically captures Haya's motions as he first established distance by condemning imperialism and then moved to forge closer ties with the United States in his quest for power in Peru. Haya the pragmatist understood that he needed the United States if he was to succeed in gaining power in Peru. Haya's relationship to the United States underscores the importance of placing Latin American populism, both classic and contemporary, more broadly in the context of U.S.-Latin American relations. Examining this relationship can help to further distinguish classic populists from one another: Brazil's Vargas, who benefited from his support of the United States; Perón, who remained isolated from the United States; and Mexico's Lázaro Cárdenas, who fell somewhere in the middle. Latin America's most recent populists—the radical populists—have continued with the anti-imperialist line and challenged the United States. Foremost among them, the late Chávez engaged in rhetorical flourishes that went as far as comparing President George W. Bush to the devil.

Chapter 4, "*El Jefe y el Partido*: Party Discipline and the Cult of Personality," explores the ways in which the cult of personality and the building of a long-lasting political party reinforced one another. As Cynthia McClintock points out, "Haya was a dedicated and effective architect of political institutions."[20] His visit to Russia in 1924 and his sojourn in Berlin between 1929 and 1931 taught him the power of the cult of personality in both Fascist and Communist parties. He quickly began to encourage a similar cult of personality within APRA. The Apristas succeeded in building a long-lasting political party on a continent with traditionally weak political institutions. APRA stands with the Institutional Revolutionary Party and the Peronistas as one of the continent's longest-lasting political parties. Roberts groups Haya with other classic populists (Vargas, Perón, and Cárdenas) and writes that "these leaders served as unifying figures to help weave together the heterogeneous strands of populist coalitions, but their appeals to mass constituencies were mediated by representative institutions, even if those institutions were ultimately subordinated to the personal authority and political interests of dominant personalities."[21] Aprismo developed a strong party tradition based on solid organization and on the cult of a leader who now has risen to almost mythical proportions in the eyes of many of his followers. I once visited the house of an elderly Aprista militant, active from the earliest days of the party, who had built an altar to Haya in her home, complete with numerous images and candles. At the same time, the party from the outset had a solid organization, with committees and in some cases block-by-block organizations designed to spread propaganda. It is unusual for a Latin American political party to survive its founder. Although much weakened, APRA remains a "power contender" in Peru, a well-organized party over three decades after Haya's death.

Chapter 5, "Broken Promises: The Women of APRA," addresses the issue of women in the party and therefore, more broadly, the role of women in populist movements. It examines the important role of women in supporting the party and traces the relationship between Haya and influential women in his life. It shows how one of the first Latin American political parties to recruit women had a paradoxical position in that it did not support the process of granting women full political rights within the party. Haya continued to reinforce male-dominated hierarchies and undermined the power of one of the most powerful women both within APRA and within Latin American politics at the time, Magda Portal.

Each of the five themes deserves to be further explored and researched. In addition to its main theme, each chapter raises other topics, some explicit, others hidden ones that still need to be teased out. It is my hope that other scholars will pursue these many leads.

CHAPTER ONE

Revolution for Export

Forging a Latin American Revolution

The Mexican Revolution is our revolution.

—HAYA DE LA TORRE

The Mexican Revolution offers us a set of events whose dialectical interpretation reinforces the foundation of an Indoamerican social ideology. This ideology is on its way.

—HAYA DE LA TORRE

In Lima's port Callao, on October 3, 1923, after being briefly jailed on the island of San Lorenzo off the coast of Lima, the young student leader Víctor Raúl Haya de la Torre boarded the German merchant ship *Negada*, which took him to Panama and into exile. At twenty-eight he had already become something of a celebrity both in Peru and abroad. His magnetic personality and charisma had placed him at the forefront of student and worker movements that challenged Peru's political establishment. He had stood boldly with workers on the streets of Lima in a protest that led to legislation guaranteeing an eight-hour workday. Peru's president Augusto B. Leguía deemed Haya sufficiently dangerous to deport him from Peru, accusing him of having participated in a Communist plot against the government. The persecution by Leguía would only add to Haya's celebrity status.

His departure from Peru that year marked the beginning of an eight-year period that offered the young Peruvian activist a most remarkable international political education at some of the world's major political hotspots: Mexico City, Moscow, London, and Berlin. In postrevolutionary Mexico he briefly worked as secretary to José Vasconcelos, the secretary of education, who personally helped to forge a state-led revolutionary national culture in Mexico; in 1924 he visited Communist Russia and met with leaders of the Russian Revolution; in 1926 he studied in England, where he met leaders of the Labour Party; and between 1929 and 1931 he lived in Berlin, where he observed firsthand the rise of the Nazi Party. Before his exile, Haya had also traveled to Uruguay and Argentina shortly after the influential University Reform movement and had met many of its leaders. While he did not travel to China, he did meet members of the Kuomintang while in Europe. All of these experiences and contacts contributed to his founding of the American Popular Revolutionary Alliance (APRA), a new revolutionary political party that constituted a unique Latin American response to the global pressures of the early twentieth-century to represent the middle, working, and indigenous classes.

This chapter explores the paradoxical relationship between the party's international aspirations and its identity as a national party in Peru.[1] At a time of growing nationalism in Latin America that led to the emergence of populist regimes throughout the continent, APRA both rode the nationalist wave and attempted to build a transnational political organization. The party's program was inherently internationalist, as it aimed to export the program of the Mexican Revolution to the rest of Latin America. Haya argued that only by presenting a unified political front would nationalist governments throughout the region be able to face the challenges posed by U.S. imperialism. Yet this same internationalism would be used to ban APRA from participating in Peruvian politics. Successive Peruvian governments attempted to discredit the party by linking it to international Communism.

During his years of exile, Haya founded APRA in Paris as an international movement, a Latin American alternative to the Communist International (Comintern)—hence the lack of reference to any particular country in the name American Popular Revolutionary Alliance. His followers soon founded APRA cells in various cities in the Americas. Ideologically, APRA framed its goals in broad international terms. Haya's first public statement on APRA, published in 1926 in Britain's *Labour Monthly*, stated that "the programme of international action of the A.P.R.A. has five general points which serve as a basis for the national sections." These points were (1) joint action of the countries in Latin America against "Yankee imperialism," (2) "the political unity of Latin America," (3) "the nationalization of land and industry," (4) a demand for the internationalization of the Panama Canal, and (5) "the solidarity of all the oppressed people and classes of the world"—a direct challenge to similar efforts by the Comintern.[2] Point 3 was implicitly international in spirit, as Haya believed that such nationalizations could only take place if Latin American countries united forces against foreign imperialism.

Haya framed his ideas in the broadest international terms through reference to the world's major revolutionary movement as he sought to come up with a theory of revolution that would work for Latin America. He rejected Soviet Communism as alien to Latin America and inverted

Vladimir Lenin's view of imperialism as the highest stage of capitalism, claiming that for Latin America—or Indo-America, to use Haya's preferred terminology—imperialism in fact represented the first stage of capitalism.[3] As mentioned earlier, he found a better model in Chinese nationalism and expressed great admiration for Sun Yat-sen's nationalist revolution in China (1911–12).

However, Latin America did not need to look overseas for a model of revolution—the world's first great social revolution had taken place in the Americas: the Mexican Revolution. The Mexican example remained central to Aprismo as it addressed problems particular to Latin America, such as land reform and curtailment of the power of foreign capitalism. For Haya, the Mexican Revolution offered the best example of a homegrown revolution that could be replicated in other parts of Latin America. Aprismo synthesized the messy example of Mexico into a clear political program for the rest of Latin America. With its creation, Haya formulated a revolutionary doctrine that laid the foundations for the non-Communist Left throughout Latin America.

Haya was not alone in promoting the Mexican Revolution in Latin America. Mexican governments, beginning with that of Venustiano Carranza, had been sending out propagandists to defend the revolution, particularly in the face of U.S. attacks seeking to discredit it. Yet Mexican propaganda efforts were geared not so much at exporting a particular model of revolution to the rest of Latin America as at seeking international legitimacy for postrevolutionary governments.[4] By synthesizing what he saw as the main contributions of the revolution, Haya contributed to exporting the revolution to the rest of the continent. The writings of Haya and other Apristas take the Mexican Revolution as a starting point for the proposed continent-wide revolution, at a time when intellectuals throughout the continent had begun to see it as a model of nationalist revolution and continental unity.[5]

When Haya ended his exile and returned to Peru in 1931 to lead the Peruvian Aprista Party, he continued to embrace his international program. At a now famous political rally in Lima's colonial bullring, the Plaza de Acho, on August 23, Haya made the distinction between APRA's "maximum" and "minimum" programs—one international and one national, specific to Peru. Yet the party's international aspirations would soon be used against it when, in 1932, the Peruvian government banned APRA from legal participation in Peru for being an international party. The ban became part of the country's new constitution that was adopted in 1933 and whose Article 53 outlawed "political parties of international organization."[6] After this, Apristas

Young Haya, approximately 1931 (Armando Villanueva Papers, courtesy of Lucía Villanueva).

had to downplay the party's internationalist aspirations. In 1942 the party was officially renamed the Partido del Pueblo (People's Party) to eliminate any international references. Another factor that undermined the party's internationalist aspirations was the logistical difficulty of maintaining an international presence while trying to build a political party in Peru under very difficult conditions of political persecution. Haya anticipated these difficulties quite early in a letter from Berlin in 1930 in which he threatened to stay abroad if he did not receive the party's support for his presidential candidacy in the upcoming 1931 elections: "I will publicly give up my participation in political struggles in Peru and will continue to live as an expatriate, leading the Latin American Aprista campaign."[7]

Yet despite the political force of nationalism, Haya and other Apristas continued to push the internationalist agenda. Well into the 1950s, political persecution led the party to rely on a transnational network of exiles for important aspects of its functioning, such as political propaganda. During one of the times of the harshest persecution in Peru, exile communities even formulated party policy. After APRA gained definitive legal status in Peru after 1956, Haya remained abroad until 1969, a distant leader engaged more with issues in international politics than with Peruvian affairs, though he returned to participate in two elections, both of which he lost. Thus, while he was alive, Haya, as leader of a national party, continued to play politics on an international stage.

Latin American Transnational Networks

During its early years, APRA's existence depended on various transnational networks of exiled intellectuals. Such individuals have played an important role in Latin American politics from the earliest times. The nineteenth-century Argentine Domingo Sarmiento, who challenged dictatorship in his native Argentina from his Chilean exile, is perhaps the most famous example. During the early twentieth century, these networks became increasingly dense and visible due to the large volume of publications generated. These networks were crucial in the formation of APRA.[8] Cities such as Mexico City and San José de Costa Rica became havens for exiles persecuted by dictatorships in their own countries. These exiles were able to establish personal connections that reinforced ties across national boundaries and influenced developments in national politics. Betancourt, for example, while fleeing the dictatorship of Juan Vicente Gomez in Venezuela, met both Haya and Magda Portal. He even acknowledged that Portal's lectures on Marxism had a strong influence on his political development.[9] Julio Antonio Mella, a Cuban Communist who fled the Gerardo Machado y Morales dictatorship, was living in Mexico City. Over time, Paris, Mexico City, Buenos Aires, and Santiago all functioned as hubs for Aprista exiles and centers for the publication and dissemination of Aprista propaganda.

Apristas established connections with existing networks of intellectuals already busy founding transnational organizations and disseminating cultural and political ideas.[10] These networks consisted of personal connections among intellectuals in different countries who would embark on a common cultural or political project, such as a journal or an association. As Barry Carr describes it, "Radical print culture provided channels for communication among scattered activists and intellectuals as well as networks that were used to supply moral and material solidarity for popular struggles."[11] The personal connections forged through these networks proved crucial for exiled intellectuals to survive abroad. The connections provided economic and moral sustenance as exiled intellectuals waited to receive payment for their articles, and they afforded them a sense of community with like-minded colleagues. Considering his youth, it is perhaps surprising that Haya became one of the best-networked Latin Americans, with connections that included intellectual and political figures in Latin America, the United States, and Europe.

In Latin America, unlike Europe, cultural and linguistic affinities facilitated communication across national borders. The existence of such a Latin American public sphere is more than theoretical. Political exiles moved across national boundaries to countries that offered greater political freedom, and those countries in turn became loci for political action against dictatorial regimes, as witnessed in cities such as Santiago, Chile, and San José, Costa Rica.[12] National politics during this time can be more fully understood in a transnational context that takes exile communities into account as political actors.

These networks contributed to create what Jussi Pakkasvirta has termed a "continental consciousness."[13] The notion of continental unity had been part of the Latin American political imagination as far back as Simón Bolívar in the early nineteenth century. The Cuban José Martí, later in that century, and José Enrique Rodó, near its end, elaborated on this idea. By the early twentieth century, intellectuals exchanged ideas with one another in essays and articles and through new cultural associations, reflecting on questions of Latin American identity and modernity. They delineated a Latin American path that deliberately sought to differentiate the continent from Europe and the United States.

Those who participated in these networks came from middle-class backgrounds in their respective countries.[14] Haya descended on his mother's side from an old Trujillo landowning family that had lost lands and wealth as a result of economic transformations (including foreign investment) in the region. He had to work for a living when he was a student in Lima in the 1920s, and he taught at the Colegio Anglo-Peruano in Lima. The eventual Aprista leaders who found refuge in exile—Haya, Portal, Luis Alberto Sánchez, Manuel Seoane, and many others—possessed the necessary connections to continue their life abroad. In this, they stood apart from the majority of working-class members of the party—without the means to leave Peru, many suffered persecution and spent time in jail.

During the 1920s the transnational cultural and literary networks of Latin American intellectuals were becoming increasingly political in nature.[15] These networks helped to sustain not only individuals but also a number of internationally oriented organizations that united intellectuals in different countries. For example, the Unión Latinoamericana, founded in Buenos Aires by José Ingenieros and Alfredo Palacios, published the journal *Renovación: Boletín Mensual de Idea, Libros y Revistas de la América Latina* and promoted anti-imperialism and continental unity.[16] The Liga Antiimperialista de las Américas, formed in Mexico, first united Communists from a number of Latin American countries, including Cuba, Colombia, Guatemala, Argentina, and Chile, as well as some from the United States.[17] Its key figure, Mella, was eventually assassinated in Mexico in 1929. The organization raised consciousness across national boundaries about a number of political issues—for example, by protesting the U.S. presence in the Philippines. By creating a transnational political organization that led to the successful founding of a political party in Peru, APRA took the politicization of these cultural networks to a new level.

Early Internationalism, the YMCA, and the University Reform Movement

In 1917 Haya left his native town of Trujillo and traveled to Lima to study at the Universidad Mayor de San Marcos. Like many other provincial students who made this move, he discovered a city whose intellectuals looked down on those arriving from the provinces. Yet like other provincial intellectuals of his generation who made a similar journey, such as historian Jorge Basadre and Marxist ideologue José Carlos Mariátegui, Haya quickly rose to prominence. As a student activist he established connections with an incipient labor movement. He made a name for himself when he joined workers in the streets of Lima in protests that led to the establishment of the eight-hour workday.

Haya took his first steps in the direction of international politics after he became president of the Peruvian Student Federation (Federación de Estudiantes del Perú) in October 1919. In this post he organized the first National Student Congress in Peru, in the city of Cusco. Two years later, he and fellow students at San Marcos University in Lima founded the popular universities, a type of extension education service for workers. They were named Universidades Populares Gonzalez Prada after the Peruvian anarchist thinker.[18] Haya later acknowledged the importance of this experience for his political career: "I would not have become a revolutionary without the schooling in true proletarian discipline that I received during my three years at the popular universities."[19] At the time, Haya had already begun to establish connections with student leaders outside Peru, such as Gabriel del Mazo, president of the Argentine Student Federation and one of the leaders of the Argentine University Reform movement.[20]

That movement had a strong impact throughout Latin America. It began in 1917 when students in the city of Córdoba, Argentina, initiated a series of protests to democratize the university by giving students a greater role in university affairs and governance. Students there created a national student federation in Argentina, and eventually, in October 1918, President Hipólito Yrigoyen granted their demands and extended them beyond Córdoba to other Argentine universities. The movement set a precedent beyond Argentina's borders and became a model that inspired students in other Latin American countries to pursue similar reforms.[21]

In 1922, Haya had the opportunity to travel to Argentina and meet some of the main leaders of the University Reform movement.[22] The journey was made possible thanks to his connections to the Scottish Presbyterian minister John Mackay and to the YMCA in Peru. Mackay, an active member of the YMCA, was also founder and director of the Colegio Anglo-Peruano—supported by the Scottish Presbyterian mission—where Haya worked as a teacher.[23] Mackay would later go on to be president of the Princeton Theological Seminar from 1936 to 1959. He encouraged Haya to accept an invitation from the YMCA to participate in a camp for student leaders in Piriápolis, Uruguay, and loaned him five hundred soles for the trip. The money allowed Haya not only to attend the camp but also to visit Argentina, Bolivia, and Chile. The YMCA had formally begun its activities in Peru in 1920, encouraging physical activity and open-air events to promote physical health. It organized the sports events at the Fiesta de la Planta, a workers' festival. Haya had also given lectures in 1922 in Arequipa and Trujillo titled "Christ and Society."[24] A nominal Catholic, Haya seems not to have been bothered by the fact that the Catholic Church formally banned Catholics from partaking in YMCA activities, and he may even have taken pleasure in challenging Peru's oldest institution, traditionally tied to the government.

While in Buenos Aires, Haya met Ingenieros, a physician and essayist who publicly promoted ideas of continental unity and anti-imperialism. He also met Del Mazo, one of the leaders of the University Reform movement, with whom he would maintain a friendship for many years to come. Influenced by the writings of the Uruguayan Rodó, whose essay "Ariel" had affirmed the importance of a unified Latin American culture in opposition to the United States, these intellectuals sought to put the notion of a unified Latin American culture into practice. Through lectures, publications, and the Unión Latinoamericana, Ingenieros and others pushed the notion of Latin American cultural unity beyond elite discourse to the political sphere that would include the middle classes and workers. In Argentina, Haya lectured at the Universidad de Buenos Aires. Aprista biographer Roy Soto Rivera claims that Haya was received by President Yrigoyen in the Casa Rosada and had met the president of Uruguay, José Batlle y Ordoñez, while in that country.[25]

On his way back to Peru, Haya stopped in Chile, where he laid a wreath on the tombs of students and workers who had died in labor and student protests. This expression of solidarity with students and workers across borders came into conflict with nationalist feelings fueled by ongoing territorial tensions between Peru and Chile. These tensions were high at a time when a pending plebiscite was still expected to determine the fate of the border provinces of Tacna and Arica, which Peru had lost during the War of the Pacific (1879–83). Eventually Tacna would return to Peru in 1929, while Arica remained part of Chile. Haya continued to promote internationalist ideas after his return to Lima when, in 1923, he founded the journal *Claridad*, which was linked to the popular universities. *Claridad* expressed ideals of Latin American unity and described itself as the mouthpiece of the Free Youth of Peru. It also reflected the fact that Peruvian students were in contact not only with their neighbors to the south but also with Mexican students. Honorary editors of the journal included the Mexican intellectuals Carlos Pellicier and Daniel Cosío Villegas, and its mentors included five important figures who were working to further educational reform in Mexico under Alvaro Obregón: Vasconcelos, Antonio Caso, Chilean poet Gabriela Mistral, Alfonso Goldschmidt, and U.S. educator Anna Melissa Graves.[26]

Back in Lima, Haya became an increasingly public nuisance to the Leguía regime. On May 23, 1923, he led a demonstration in response to an announced public ceremony to consecrate Peru to the Sacred Heart of Jesus. The ceremony represented the Catholic Church's attempt to reassert its authority in the face of growing secularization, as well as Leguía's attempt to gain Catholic votes for an unconstitutional run for a second term. After successfully foiling the administration's plans to hold the ceremony, which was ultimately canceled, Haya went into hiding. He had also begun to make enemies at the university of San Marcos, where, according to one of his opponents, "he had become a kind of professional politician. . . . He remained a first year student. He did not study."[27] In October, Haya, who had been hiding in the home of his friend and employer Mackay, was arrested and deported to Panama.

Faced with Haya's arrest and deportation, the Peruvian Student Federation honored him with the presidency once again and displaced the actual winner of the election and his later rival within APRA, Seoane. A letter that he wrote to "students and workers" from the San Lorenzo prison before his deportation expressed how he had begun to see himself as having a chosen place in a continent-wide struggle: "While I am going into exile, some day I will return. I will return when my time comes, when the time of the great transformation arrives. I have said it before and I repeat it now: only death will be stronger than my decision to untiringly pursue the crusade of liberation that America expects of its youth in the name of Social Justice."[28]

The Mexican Connections

After a brief stop in Panama, the deported student leader traveled to Cuba, where he remained for only twelve days before proceeding to Mexico. His role in both the student and labor movements in Peru, and the persecution by the Leguía government, had bolstered Haya's image, and he was by this time well known in student circles throughout Latin America. The newspaper *Heraldo de Cuba*, on November 1, 1923, ran a front-page article on Haya stating that Cuban students had received Haya with great honors. The article proclaimed that "the journey of Haya de la Torre throughout America has been a great, imperishable and triumphal pilgrimage."[29] In Havana, Haya had his first radio interview with PWX, the first commercial broadcast station in Cuba.[30] He also participated in the inauguration of the Universidad Popular José Martí and met the president of the Cuban Student Federation, Mella, who was soon to be the founder of the Cuban Communist Party. Mella praised Haya and compared him to Rodó's Ariel. The adulation would not be long-lived, as Mella and Haya were soon to become ideological rivals over the issue of Communism.

After his very brief stay in Cuba, Haya moved on to Mexico, invited by the Mexican national secretary of education, Vasconcelos. The travel costs of 500 pesos were covered by the administration of President Obregón.[31] Haya was employed, according to Vasconcelos, as a lecturer on Ibero-American history.[32] His credentials as editor of the journal *Claridad* in Lima, which supported Vasconcelos's ideas and established connections to Mexican students and intellectuals, helped Haya to quickly become connected at a high level. While in Mexico he sought collaborators for *Claridad*, which was now in the hands of José Carlos Mariátegui. Mistral, the Chilean poet who many years later won the Nobel Prize, was working with Vasconcelos on his educational reform projects and helped Haya to establish connections to the Mexican government.[33] She even provided lodging for him at her home, the Finca de San Angel.

As a representative of the Peruvian Student Federation, Haya also established contact with the Mexican Student Federation. He eventually worked as secretary to Vasconcelos, who was engaged in a wide range of projects intended to disseminate art among the public and to increase literacy in rural areas. Haya participated briefly in the rural education efforts, but he did so at a time when these efforts were waning. He wrote for the magazine *El Maestro*. It was in Mexico that, by reading the Argentine writer Manuel Ugarte, Haya became aware of anti-imperialist thinking.[34] He once again experienced the novelty of speaking on the radio on Radio Mundo, at a time when radio was beginning to become a popular means of communication worldwide.[35]

As secretary of education for the Obregón government, Vasconcelos participated not only in the promotion of a nationalist culture but also in the official state-sponsored propaganda to defend and seek support abroad for the revolution among intellectuals throughout Latin America.[36] Mexican diplomacy now included a cultural component, as Vasconcelos and other Mexican intellectuals traveled to other Latin American countries to spread the revolutionary message. In 1922, Vasconcelos traveled to Brazil, Uruguay, and Argentina, where he lectured and promoted his ideas of cultural nationalism. Vasconcelos also joined forces with the student movement in Mexico to denounce dictatorships in different parts of Latin America—he contributed to promoting a critique that operated on a continental level and that promoted a new cultural nationalism. He would later express this idea in his book *La raza cósmica*, published in 1925, which rejected European notions of racial purity and celebrated *mestizaje* as central to Latin American cultural identity.[37]

As Haya participated in Mexican cultural life, one can imagine the richness of his experiences in Mexico in both the urban and rural settings. Mexico City was one of the most cosmopolitan cities in the Americas, the hub in a vast network of intellectuals and artists stretching across the continent, some seeking refuge as exiles from various Latin American dictatorships, others having left the United States to participate in the postrevolutionary scene. The list of prominent intellectuals included artists such as the muralist Diego Rivera; his wife, the painter Frida Kahlo; Italian American photographer and Communist Tina Modotti; and composers Carlos Chávez and Aaron Copland.[38] Haya met some of the intellectuals in the network, such as the U.S. Communist Bertram Wolfe.[39] Haya would later comment on the importance of visiting other Latin American countries and accused many Latin American intellectuals of going first to Europe without knowing their own continent: "The great mistake of our interpreters, excessively Europeanized, is in my opinion that they come to the Old World without having visited their America."[40] Haya himself quickly moved on to Europe but would soon return to Mexico and Central America after founding APRA.

Haya established connections to a number of intellectuals in the circle of Vasconcelos, such as Pellicier, Jaime Torres Bodet, Eduardo Villaseñor, and Moises Sáenz.[41] He developed a friendship with Rafael Carrillo Azpeitia, secretary general of the Communist Party in Mexico. Pellicier described Haya in enthusiastic terms as "the most distinguished young man of Our America."[42] The term "Our America" probably comes from the famous essay written by Martí. Other networks crisscrossed those that centered on Vasconcelos. Haya's earlier Protestant connections may have helped him to approach Sáenz, as well as Frances Toor, the latter of whom directed the magazine *Mexican Folkway*.[43] Both Mistral and Vasconcelos were also linked to theosophic groups. Haya was present in Mexico when the PEN Club of Mexico was founded and probably met the labor leader Vicente Lombardo

Toledano. There were many political divisions among intellectuals—Ricardo Melgar Bao describes it as a mined territory and in particular situates the Vasconcelos group at a distance from the radical positions of the First International Student Congress of 1921.

As an outsider, Haya navigated these complicated waters skillfully. He was able to "operate with relative autonomy in relation to the personal contradictions and factionalisms that enveloped his friends and travel companions."[44] These connections would serve him well at the next stage of his journey. For example, one of his letters of recommendation to the Comintern in Russia was from his friend Carrillo Azpeitia. He used his connections to continue promoting the ideas of continental unity associated with Vasconcelos and Ingenieros. Efforts by the Peruvian legation to discredit him backfired and marred the international image of the Leguía regime that had expelled him.[45]

While an outsider, Haya, as a Peruvian, must have found Mexico to be a very familiar environment, and the contrast between Mexico City and the heavily indigenous rural areas must have reminded him of his native country. In Morelos, he participated in a graveside ceremony on April 10, 1924, in the town of Cuatlua, commemorating the revolutionary leader Emiliano Zapata. He arrived by train with a delegation accompanying presidential candidate Plutarco Elías Calles. Armed peasants received the illustrious visitors and led them to the cemetery in a procession accompanied by large wreaths of flowers and the red-and-black flag of the agrarian movement. Here Calles spoke and declared that he would continue the revolutionary work begun by Zapata.[46] The process whereby Mexican governments co-opted the rebel and former enemy Zapata had begun. In his writing, Haya praised Zapata as one of the least-known leaders of the revolution outside Mexico. He described the armed peasants in idealized terms: "The peasant is that which is most noble in the country. With clean body and soul, the man of the countryside is the bravest soldier of the revolution."[47]

These men, Haya claimed, asked him many questions about Peru and one even announced that they needed to go to Peru to spread agrarianism—the Zapatista call for land reform. Speakers that day included Antonio Diaz Soto y Gama, an intellectual who had fought with Zapata and had founded the Partido Nacional Agrarista. Haya described him as Mexico's most famous orator.[48] During his travels through Mexico, Haya visited the ruins of Chichen Itza. He also established a connection to a Masonic lodge in Mérida.[49]

Mexico has played such an important role in the official history of APRA that it is considered the place of APRA's founding. Even scholarly literature continues to repeat this official history, which claims Haya founded APRA at a ceremony of the Mexican Student Federation on May 7, 1924.[50] Yet the date may have an even greater significance that relates to APRA's ideals of continental unity. The year marked the centennial of the Battle of Ayacucho, in which Bolívar liberated the continent from Spanish rule. In a speech to the First National Congress of the Peruvian Aprista Party in 1931, Haya refers to this coincidence: "We must not forget that in Peru the independence revolution concluded in 1824. Thus Aprismo proclaims the New Ayacucho, which represents, by means of this tribute by our generation to the patriotic legion whose eponymous hero is Bolivar, our energetic will to fully realize his unfinished ideal: to consolidate the freedom of each of the peoples of Indoamerica through the undying link of their union and by the affirmation of each one of them of true social justice."[51]

Impressions of Postrevolutionary Russia

In May 1924, after a stay of approximately six months in Mexico, Haya traveled to Russia. The trip was organized through a Protestant delegation of the YMCA. Haya departed from New York on a ship that followed a route that took him to the Baltic Sea, stopping at Libau and then Riga, the capital of Latvia, where he disembarked to travel by train to Moscow. His remarks on Riga reflect his awareness of architecture and knowledge of history: "Forty-eight hours in Riga are pleasantly spent with sunny days. There are interesting buildings to visits. An old XIII century cathedral—reconstructed in the XVI century and completely repaired in 1883—is, together with the famous House of the Blackheads Castle, a reminder of the adventurous days of the Hanseatic League.... A tour through the poorer neighborhoods leaves one with a bad impression. At dusk, we went into the orthodox churches which are full of people."[52] His observation of the poorer neighborhoods is quite cursory, which is perhaps surprising for a man who dedicated his life to achieving social justice.

He arrived in Moscow with a letter of introduction from Ricardo Cáceres, secretary general of the Federación Obrera de Lima (Worker's Federation of Lima), explaining that the federation expected Haya to inform them of events in Russia.[53] He also had a letter from the Mexican Communist Carrillo Azpeitia addressed to the Executive Committee of the Communist

International in Moscow.[54] He arrived in Russia shortly after Lenin's death, at a time when Leon Trotsky and Joseph Stalin were battling for succession with their different visions of Communism: Trotsky advocating for international revolution, Stalin for a focus on building Communism in the Soviet Union.

In Moscow Haya participated as a guest at the Fifth Congress of the Communist Party. Here he met delegates from many different countries, including those of the Chinese delegation of the Kuomintang. He also met Anatoly Lunacharsky, the first Soviet commissar of education, who expressed an interest in the popular universities. Lunacharsky later took the time to write a letter to Haya answering a questionnaire about literary and educational topics.[55] At the congress, Haya shook hands with high members of the party, including Stalin, Grigory Zinoviev, Mikhail Kalinin, and others. He later described these brief encounters as follows: "They are only useful to have the pleasure of being close to the protagonists of a great moment in history."[56] He also noted the enthusiasm of the youth in Russia and quoted Bertrand Russell, who compared Communism to a new religion.[57] Members of the World Congress of Communist Youth in Moscow also attended the congress.

His experiences in Russia would leave a deep imprint on his thought. In particular, there were two topics addressed at the congress that would influence Haya's founding of APRA two years later. The first was the call for a reorganization of Communist parties using cells to be based in factories to prepare workers for revolution. Haya would organize APRA following this cell structure. The second was the emphasis on anti-imperialism, which would reinforce Haya's interest in this topic. More generally, his growing familiarity with Marxism would leave a deep imprint on Aprismo.

Haya was an exemplar of an entire generation of Latin American intellectuals who were rejecting foreign models, attempting to think about Latin America on its own terms, and reaffirming a sense of cultural nationalism vis-à-vis other parts of the world. In this spirit, he warned of the need to draw universal lessons from the Russian experience but to adjust these to Latin American realities: "We will achieve nothing by simply copying ideas, by pursuing unconditional imitation, looking at details and stumbling on that which is artificial.... I recognize, and every day I am more convinced, that America, our America, offers the world a new reality, an extraordinary and exceptional reality."[58] Haya left Russia with very favorable impressions of the Russian Revolution. While Mexico had offered him an example, albeit messy, of a Latin American revolution, postrevolutionary Russia and

Marxism provided a theoretical challenge to formulate a more systematic revolutionary program and ideology for the entire continent.

While in Russia, he had developed a respiratory ailment that led him to seek treatment in Switzerland at the Leysin sanatorium. Here he met the pacifist and winner of the 1915 Nobel Prize for Literature, Romain Rolland, who lived in the nearby town of Villeneuve, on the shores of Lake Leman. In accordance with his internationalist and pacifist ideas, Rolland had opposed the Great War. Almost thirty years Haya's elder, Rolland developed a somewhat fatherly relationship with Haya. In a 1926 letter, after Haya had left Switzerland, Rolland wrote to him saying, "I think of you as a son or a younger brother." He also was one of the many people who helped to fuel Haya's sense of mission. He wrote in the same letter, "For men like us, happiness consists of carrying, like Cristopher, the Child Humanity on our shoulders, and to cross the river bearing this crushing burden. Although our fields of action may be different, we are animated by the same flame: the passion for truth and our active pity for humanity."[59] Rolland would publicly support Haya and the Aprista cause.

As a pacifist, Rolland also offered a very different model of politics from the Leninist model Haya had observed in Russia. To what degree Rolland's thinking may have influenced Haya is difficult to determine. In the years immediately following his contact with Rolland, Haya clearly turned to the Leninist model of revolution. However, later in his political career he wavered and seemed less convinced by the path of violent revolution, perhaps reflecting the influence of Rolland. Harassed by the Swiss police, apparently at the prompting of the Peruvian government, Haya left Switzerland for Italy, where he was received by the Peruvian painter Felipe Cossío del Pomar, who would later become a staunch party member and hagiographer of Haya.

The Oxford Years, 1925–1927

After a brief stay in Italy, Haya traveled to England and became a student once again. One of the first things he did upon his arrival in England was to visit to tomb of Karl Marx. He studied at Oxford University, where he belonged to Ruskin College, the workers' college, and at the London School of Economics. Among the topics he studied was Marxism.[60] He attended the lectures of Harold Laski, the British Socialist and political theorist, who taught at the London School of Economics. Laski was a brilliant lecturer, and he appealed particularly to students from Africa and Asia. Laski, who "lived a frantic life as a political and intellectual gadfly, pouring out books, pamphlets, and newspaper columns in an endless stream,"[61] may well have served as a model for the propagandist that Haya was on his way to becoming.

How Haya financed his stay in England remains somewhat unclear. Some studies claim that he had a scholarship and the support of his benefactress, Graves, the teacher, writer, and internationalist, whom Haya had met in Lima when they both taught at the Colegio Anglo-Peruano.[62] After the two later had a falling out, Graves angrily pointed out in a letter to another Aprista, Portal, that "other people paid all of his expenses with money—most of it—earned through hard work and personal sacrifice."[63] She did not indicate directly that she was one of these people who had helped Haya financially, however. Graves also challenged Aprista versions of Haya's life in England that linked him to famous intellectuals and politicians such as Ramsay MacDonald and Bernard Shaw, neither of whom she claimed he had never met.

Yet Haya did establish a connection to the Socialist 1917 Club located at 4–5 Gerrard Street in Soho, London. The club, founded by Leonard Woolf, included among its members such prominent intellectuals, actors, and politicians as MacDonald, Aldous Huxley, H. G. Wells, Elsa Lanchester, and Rose Macaulay.[64] The extent of his contact with some of these individuals is hard to judge. To approach Russell and Wells, he asked the Peruvian student Luis Heysen in Argentina to get the "*compañeros* of *Sagitario* to write two letters of greeting, one for Russel [sic] and the other for Wells, letters that should be attached to copies of the journal . . . and in which they will name me as the person in charge of giving them the journal and asking for an autograph, etc."[65] Haya and Heysen had known each other as students in Lima and Heysen was now living in exile and studying agriculture in La Plata. *Sagitario* was a journal published by politically active students in La Plata.[66]

Haya's connections to the Labour Party helped him to publish his article "What Is the APRA?" in the December 1926 issue of Britain's *Labour Monthly*. In this article, he publicly defined the APRA doctrine for the first time. His followers republished the Spanish version of the article in many parts of Latin America. Haya also sought financial support from the Labour Party for an Aprista publication to be titled *APRA*.[67] It is unclear whether he ever received such support. *APRA* did not appear until 1930 in Peru.

In addition to his studies and contacts with the Labour Party, in London Haya met students from other parts of the world, including India and

China. On October 11, 1926, he attended a dinner of the Kuomintang commemorating the Chinese Nationalist Revolution. He offered a toast in which he compared the struggles of Latin American and Chinese youths for independence and against imperialism. Following the event, a reporter named Chong Sgeik interviewed Haya for the *Canton Tribune*. The reporter described Haya's sitting room at Oxford as a room full of books, newspapers, magazines, a red silk flag of APRA, and a number of portraits of Peruvian and Latin American student leaders, as well as a portrait of a very beautiful woman. They ate a vegetarian lunch together and then walked along the Thames, where Haya answered the reporter's questions, comparing the situations of China and Peru as agrarian countries.[68]

The Kuomintang became an important model for Haya's development of APRA.[69] Haya wrote admiringly of Sun Yat-sen, as well as Lenin, for their ability to launch political movements that corresponded to their particular social contexts: "The admirable thing about Sun-Yat-Sen's conception of politics is his genius as a realist; as much of a genius in realism as Lenin was for Russia. . . . They created for their respective countries the political forces necessary for their particular environments."[70] In a letter to the Argentine Ugarte, whom Haya considered a forerunner of his movement, he wrote, "With APRA we want to form a great continental army. A Latin American Kuomintang." Haya acknowledged that when he read Ugarte's book *El destino de un continente* in Mexico, it had helped him define his ideas of a class-based, anti-imperialist revolution.[71] In England, Haya's ideas became more radical as he incorporated the Marxist notion of class conflict. He also commented on the poor treatment of Jews in England and expressed sympathy for them. Aprista biographer Soto Rivera describes this as a key period in Haya's intellectual and political development.[72]

APRA: A Latin American Rival to the Comintern

During the summer vacation of 1926, Haya traveled to Paris. In September 1926 he and a small group of Peruvians founded the first APRA cell at a Paris restaurant. Haya claimed that the members of the first Aprista cell could all fit on a single sofa. One of the cell's main goals was to raise political consciousness through teaching. On January 22, 1927, the Paris Apristas founded the APRA's Center for Anti-imperialist Studies. The cell may eventually have had as many as fifty people connected to it, including twenty-two from the region of Cusco in Peru. The famous Peruvian poet César Vallejo briefly belonged to the APRA Paris cell, as did the lesser-known

Edgardo Rozas, a medical student to whom Eudocio Ravines refers as "a black man from Cuzco" and who would meet a premature death soon thereafter.[73] Ravines, who later left APRA to join the Communist Party, was put in charge of the Paris APRA cell. By 1928, the members of the cell had been able to buy a mimeograph machine to print propaganda.[74] Eventually, the tension between Apristas and Communists tore the cell apart, reducing its membership. By 1930, when the Peruvian government asked the French police to track Aprista activities, the French Ministry of the Interior reported that the cell had only a tiny membership.[75]

While it was active, the APRA cell coordinated some successful activities, such as a large event on January 13, 1927, organized to promote the cause of the Nicaraguan revolutionary Augusto Sandino and protest the U.S. presence in Nicaragua. Apristas did not work alone—this event counted on the support of the Asociación General de Estudiantes Latinoamericanos, an association of Latin American students that took an active anti-imperialist stance. Association member and eventually famed Guatemalan writer Miguel Angel Asturias helped to solicit and obtain letters of support from Rolland and Miguel de Unamuno. Haya was one of various speakers at this event, which was attended by 250 people.[76] On another occasion, Apristas in Paris delivered a letter to the U.S. embassy protesting U.S. actions in Haiti.[77]

Apristas quickly proved adept at using their networks to establish a broad transnational presence. In 1927, Peruvian exiles including Seoane, Oscar Herrera, Enrique Cornejo Koster, and Heysen founded a second APRA cell, in Buenos Aires. Apristas also founded cells in Havana, La Paz, and Mexico City. These cells, while small, were able to publicize the Aprista doctrine through publications and lectures. Publicity crossed borders, and in 1930, the U.S. embassy in Costa Rica took note of the fact that the journal *APRA* (published in Peru) was criticizing two U.S. companies in Costa Rica, the Electric Bond and Share Company and the United Fruit Company.[78] Cells sought to impart a political education to members, as well as to disseminate APRA propaganda. The cells also sought connections with political organizations in the countries where they were located. The Mexico cell established contact with the Liga de Escritores Revolucionarios, the Federación Estudiantil Mexicana, and the Liga Nacional de Estudiantes in Mexico.[79] In some cases personal connections facilitated these links—Seoane, living in Buenos Aires, was general secretary of the Unión Latinoamericana from 1928 to 1930.

Apristas belonging to these cells published in well-known journals with a continental readership such as *Amauta* (Peru) and *Repertorio Americano* (Costa Rica), as well as in smaller, ephemeral "Aprista" journals such as *Indoamerica* in Mexico and *Atuei* in Cuba. In Cuba, Apristas led by Enrique Delahoza founded the Partido Aprista Cubano, which eventually merged with the Partido Revolucionario Cubano Auténtico in 1937. The publication networks allowed this small group of Apristas to magnify their impact by disseminating printed political propaganda. The networks also provided personal contacts and a crucial source of livelihood for political exiles. Apristas also began to establish closer ties to other emerging parties, such as the Venezuelan Partido Revolucionario de Venezuela.[80]

In a world still dominated by European colonial powers and in which both the United States and the Soviet Union displayed new imperialist tendencies, anti-imperialism was a concern that went well beyond Latin America. From February 5 to 15, 1927, Haya had the opportunity to meet delegates from around the world at the First International Congress against Imperialism and Colonialism in Brussels. Haya had not actually been invited to the congress, but fellow Aprista Ravines got him a last-minute invitation. The congress brought together anticolonial movements and supported struggles for national liberation across the world. In total, 174 delegates from twenty-one countries attended.

Although the congress attempted to maintain an independent image, it had the financial support of the Russian government. The Mexican government also contributed to sponsor the event. The attendees included well-known personalities from a number of different countries: George Lansbury of the British Labour Party, the French Communist and writer Henri Barbusse, the Chinese general Liau Hansin representing the Kuomintang, Madame Sun Yat-sen, Jawaharlal Nehru of the National Congress Party in India, Vasconcelos of Mexico, Albert Einstein, and the African politician Lamine Senghore. The congress, unique in the number of points of view represented and in bringing together representatives of both colonial and colonized powers, focused primarily on struggles taking place in Asia, such as that surrounding the presence of the British in China, and paid relatively little attention to Latin America.[81]

The congress marked a turning point in Haya's relationship with international Communism, as he became increasingly critical and distanced himself from the Comintern. During the 1920s, the Comintern was gradually "discovering" Latin America. Argentina was the site of the first South

American secretariat, founded in 1925. The Comintern's "discovery" of Latin America occurred relatively late—at the sixth meeting (1928). A few Latin American delegates had attended earlier congresses.[82] The 1928 meeting brought greater awareness of the diversity within the region and of the fact that its countries could no longer simply be lumped under the label of "semi-colonies."[83] Nonetheless, in the eyes of the Comintern, Latin America remained a secondary locus of revolution, after Europe and Asia.[84] It took Comintern leaders some time to realize the centrality of the agrarian issue in Latin America, which had played such a key role in the Mexican Revolution. A large part of the interest in the region that originated at the sixth congress stemmed from seeing it as a possible bulwark against the spread of U.S. imperialism. Despite the ignorance about Latin America, the Comintern influenced intellectuals throughout Latin America at the time.[85]

The dispute between Apristas and Communists very quickly became bitter and led to personal splits between Haya and both Mariátegui and Mella. In Latin America, the Liga Antiimperialista de las Américas (founded in Mexico in 1925) represented Latin American Communists. The Aprista Carlos Manuel Cox, living in Mexico in 1928, claimed that Mexico was "the center of the anti-Aprista conspiracy"; attacks were mounted there against APRA in the journals *El Machete*, which was associated with the Liga Antiimperialista, and *El Libertador*, which was associated with the Communist Party. He wrote, "The attacks by both El Machete and the League are filthy."[86] The dispute had much longer-term ramifications and initiated a century-long ideological battle between the Communist and non-Communist Left. According to Christine Hatzky, Mella used the term *populism* for the first time in his attack on APRA.[87] APRA thus lies at the origins of Latin American populism as a left-leaning political ideology separate from Communism.

Moscow's refusal to support Haya's new political party certainly contributed to his opposition to the Comintern. After the congress, when he returned to England, he wrote to Alexander Losovsky of the Comintern, seeking support for the revolution in Peru.[88] Losovsky was sympathetic to Haya, despite the fact that he did not consider APRA to be particularly revolutionary, and commented, "But while I do not believe Haya is capable of organizing an effective political party, I think he will create a very important movement. He is brave, ambitious and tenacious. Our alliance with him will fill a need, and when one supplies something that would otherwise be lacking, one is successful."[89] Yet financial support was not forthcoming, and within the Comintern, Haya soon became "persona non grata. The APRA he developed . . . became a 'problem' to be taken very seriously by the leadership in Moscow. . . . In parallel with the struggle against social-democracy (in Germany and in Europe) Haya de la Torre and his APRA, which did not yet exist in Peru, became a 'principal enemy.'"[90] Thus the split between Communists in Moscow and Social Democrats in Europe also impacted Moscow's view of APRA and Haya. Anti-Communism would soon become a signature part of Aprista identity in Peru as the party developed a connection to the Peruvian labor movement.[91]

Despite his dispute with the Comintern and its Latin American supporters, Haya remained strongly influenced by Marxism. Aprismo was cast in a Marxist-Leninist mold as an ideology based on notions of class conflict and on the need to create a revolutionary party led by an intellectual vanguard. In a letter to Esteban Pavletich, Haya lamented the absence of a Spanish translation of *Das Kapital*: "Can one call oneself a communist not knowing in the most elementary way what scientific communism is about?"[92] Marxism became part of the intellectual preparation of Apristas, as the following testimony of Ravines regarding the Paris cell reveals: "I have formed a group of five to whom I give lessons on Marxism every night and on imperialism during the morning."[93]

As Haya tailored his Marxism to Latin America realities, he rejected the idea of a proletarian revolution in favor of a coalition of working, middle, and peasant classes that would challenge ruling oligarchies. The middle class played a leading role in this revolutionary coalition.[94] Rather than call for the elimination of capitalism as Communists did, Haya demanded the formation of strong national governments to defend the interests of these classes in the face of imperialism. Mexico offered a model of just such a multiclass revolution. "The Mexican Revolution—a social but not a socialist revolution—does not represent the definitive victory of a single class," wrote Haya. "The social triumph would correspond, historically, to the peasant class; but in the Mexican Revolution other classes also benefited: the working and the middle class."[95]

Haya's originality lay in his ability to combine theory and practice and to disseminate his ideas while building an effective political organization. He followed the Leninist model of the vanguard intellectual fully engaged in politics and showed profound disdain for politically unengaged intellectuals: "What I decided to do, mainly, when I began to take action, was to put an end to the literary types at the university and to create a school for men of action. . . . I am happy because some day it will be said that I was a 'teacher of action' and this will be my greatest prize. I am sure that we will have created a gap with the traditional school of literary young men, little poets and fools."[96] This disdain also reflects Haya's own attitudes toward some of Lima's elite intellectuals, the product of class divisions in Peruvian society. As a newly arrived student from an impoverished provincial family, Haya would have been looked down on by many in Lima's high society. Haya further sums up his political objective as "agitate, agitate and agitate as well as organization and discipline."[97]

In a letter to Pavletich, Haya expressed both his admiration for Marxism-Leninism and his desire to shape it to fit Latin American reality. He compared APRA to the great Red Army: "Our A.P.R.A. will either be a great red army or it will be nothing."[98] His goal was to promote his own political movement with an organization that had all the strength of a Leninist party: "The issue is to give our movement a truly communist, Marxist, Leninist character WITHOUT SAYING SO, WITHOUT CALLING OURSELVES COMMUNISTS OR LENINISTS but acting as such." APRA needed to develop a unique Latin American approach to a Marxist-inspired revolution: "THE ONLY WAY to give our anti-imperialist movement mass strength and revolutionary strength, is to make it typically Latin American, like the Chinese movement, like the Moorish movement, if you will. The Only Way to give it strength and sympathy is to not label it as something built in Moscow and paid for in Chicago."[99] Once again, he repeats his admiration for the Chinese nationalists, whom he sees as a model for APRA. The reference to "the Moorish movement" is rare but interesting, as it demonstrates Haya's awareness of events in the Middle East that certainly offered many parallels with the Aprista project of Latin American unity. Muslim intellectuals and politicians had founded the Young Arab Society (Al-Fatat) in Paris in 1911 and the Arab Independence Party (al-Istiqlal) in 1919 to promote unity and independence in the Middle East against the colonial control of the French and the British in the region.

Haya lost some of the original supporters of APRA in the bitter public polemics with the Communist Mariátegui, founder of Peru's Communist Party, and Mella, founder of the Cuban Communist Party. The polemic and eventual break with Mariátegui was about nationalism, as Mariátegui criticized Haya for his nationalist focus when Haya unveiled a plan to take power in Peru by forming a nationalist party. Mariátegui criticized Haya for departing from the ideals of Socialism, as well as for having developed a revolutionary plan while abroad, without consulting APRA's Peruvian supporters.[100]

In a pamphlet titled "Que es el ARPA?," Mella purposefully inverted the letters in the party's name as he attacked Haya. Mella accused Haya of opportunism and of seeing himself as the only representative of the people of Latin America.[101] Mella sought to discredit APRA's attempt to position itself as a beacon of continental revolution. He took the side of the Communist Liga Antiimperialista, which opposed APRA. He also criticized Haya for departing from strict Marxist class analysis by proposing that a multiclass alliance could lead the revolution and for rejecting the notion that Communism could take hold in Latin America.[102]

Haya responded to Mella with what would be his most complete description of the Aprista doctrine and program, *El antimperialismo y el APRA*. He wrote the work in Mexico, allegedly in just three weeks in 1928, although he did not publish it until eight years later, in 1936, in Chile.[103] *El antimperialismo y el APRA* made clear Haya's commitment to his internationalist goals: "The organization of the anti-imperialist struggle in Latin America, through an international United Front of manual and intellectual workers (workers, students, peasants, intellectuals, etc.) with a common program of action—that is APRA (American Popular Revolutionary Alliance)."[104] The book also reaffirmed the extent to which Haya viewed the Mexican Revolution as a model for the rest of Latin America.

Mexico Again: Revolution for Export

Haya wrote *El antimperialismo y el APRA* during his second visit to Mexico, which began in November 1927 and lasted for six months. He had returned from England a month earlier and visited the United States, where he participated at Harvard University in a debate, organized by the Debating Union, in which he defended the position that the United States ought to give up the Monroe Doctrine.[105] Earlier that year, Haya had participated in a debate at Oxford in which he also took a position critical of the Monroe Doctrine. In both cases, it is interesting to note that he had mastered the English language well enough to participate in these debates. After the debate at Harvard, he traveled to New York, where he spoke at Columbia University. He then visited Washington, D.C., where he met with Senator William Borah, the Republican senator from Idaho known for his pro-Soviet views, then chairman of the Senate Foreign Relations Committee.[106] Describing the United States as expensive, Haya claimed, "I am very poor,"

APRA cell in Mexico. *Left to right:* unidentified, Carlos Manuel Cox, Magda Portal, Serafín Delmar, Gloria Portal, Haya, Esteban Pavletich, unidentified, and unidentified (Armando Villanueva Papers, courtesy of Lucía Villanueva).

and said that he was writing some articles in English to make a few dollars.[107] He continued his journey south and crossed the border into Mexico at El Paso, Texas.

Once in Mexico City, he joined other Peruvian exiles who now supported APRA, including Cox, Manuel Vázquez Diaz, Serafín Delmar, and Portal. Most sources claim that Haya, together with these exiles, founded the Mexican APRA cell in 1928. Yet one reference suggests that the cell may actually have been founded before Haya's second trip to Mexico, as early as October 1926.[108] The Mexican Apristas edited their own journal, titled *Indoamérica*, using the term made popular by Vasconcelos to emphasize the native roots of Latin American culture. *Indigenismo*, or the glorification of the continent's indigenous heritage through art and literature, had taken a strong hold in Latin America by the 1920s and influenced Aprismo as well.

Haya's public activities in Mexico included lecturing at the University of Mexico. While Mexico City remained an active hub of exile activity during these years, the country's political atmosphere had shifted as the pace of reform slowed under President Calles. For many, the revolutionary promises of the 1917 Constitution seemed to remain unfulfilled.

While in Europe, Haya had already pointed to the Mexican Revolution as a model for his Latin American supporters to follow. In a letter from London in 1925 to Heysen, who had recently arrived in the city of La Plata to study agriculture, Haya advised him to hold up Mexico as an example for the youth: "That should contribute so that the people know where to turn to for their guides and banner and that when talking about Mexico not to forget to say that in Peru a revolution such as that one is necessary and that it will be our task to carry it out."[109] Heysen, who had known Haya when he was a student leader in Lima, became president of the Federación Universitaria de la Plata in 1926 and supported the APRA cause in Argentina. In the first public statement of Aprismo, the *Labour Monthly* article "What Is the APRA?," Haya presented the Mexican experience as essential to his cause. He sought to learn from the failures of the revolution and claimed that only continental unity across national boundaries could combat the alliance between governing elites in Latin American and foreign capital.[110]

At times, Haya described the Mexican Revolution in very romantic terms, as an improvised movement that lacked a clear program and was born of the people, in particular the Mexican peasant: "In Mexico, we found a spontaneous revolution, with hardly a program, an instinctive revolution, without science. . . . It is a marvelous succession of improvisations, of probes and stumbles, rescued by the strength of the people, by the energetic and almost indomitable instinct of the revolutionary peasant. That is why the Mexican revolution is admirable, because it was the work of ignorant men."[111] Haya sounds prideful when he suggests that, had it only had a program, the Mexican Revolution would have influenced the entire continent: "Mexico could have fulfilled for Latin America as great a mission as or perhaps a greater one than that of Russia for the world, if its Revolution had followed a program."[112]

APRA and its vanguard intellectuals would provide that missing program to lead the rest of Latin America in the task of revolution. By systematizing the somewhat chaotic experience of the Mexican Revolution and offering a clear program, Haya hoped to facilitate the spread of revolution to the rest of Latin America. This was a crucial task because Haya saw the United States, at this point in his career, as an obstacle to political and social revolutions in Latin America; the United States would intervene violently against "any political or social attempt at transformation that, in the view of the Yankee empire, could affect its interests."[113] Haya insisted on Latin American unity as a vital part of his program because he considered that the Mexican Revolution had been stalled by the forces of imperialism: "Its limitations and its defeats are the features of a people that struggles in isolation to get rid of imperialism and its internal allies, under the pressure and the formidable and nearby power of their great enemy."[114] Haya argued that "our primary task is to defend our sovereignty."[115] The argument was a reaction to the U.S. foreign policy of the period, which had prompted repeated military interventions in the region.

While the five-point APRA program would be applicable to all the countries of Latin America, it needed to be applied in each according to the conditions of that country. Haya explained the interrelation between the five points: the fight against imperialism (point 1) required unity across the continent (point 2), leading to the nationalization of land and industry (point 3) and the internationalization of the Panama Canal, which "is the liberation of a means of wealth circulation, indispensable to the economic freedom of our peoples."[116] As for the fifth point (solidarity with oppressed peoples), Haya argued that it expressed much more than a lyrical or romantic sentiment— he saw Latin America (Indo-America) as the region most threatened by imperialism because of its proximity to the United States, and he therefore argued that it needed to liberate itself from this danger in order to then lead other regions of the world in the struggle against imperialism.

El antimperialismo y el APRA is also a theoretical treatise on the nature of the state in Latin America. Drawing on Marxism, Haya interpreted Latin American historical development in terms of historical stages. The Mexican Revolution, according to Haya, had dealt a definitive blow to the feudal order in Mexico.[117] In his unorthodox reading of Marxism, Haya also claimed that the resulting state was representative not of a single class but of the peasant, working, and middle classes. The spontaneous movement that began as a demand for electoral rights and devolved into a demand for social rights "remains in the history of social struggles as the first victorious effort of an Indoamerican people against the double oppression of feudalism and imperialism."[118] The Mexican Constitution of 1917, antifeudal, anti-imperialist, and democratic, enshrined the struggles of these three social classes.[119] The fact that the Mexicans were still struggling to bring this project to fruition did not diminish the magnitude of the achievement in Haya's view: "It does not matter that this historic mission of the State has not been fulfilled and absolutely fixed in Mexico.... It is important not to confuse the State with the government."[120] He included as an appendix to *El antimperialismo y el APRA* Articles 27 and 123 of the 1917 Mexican Constitution, which referred to national ownership of land and resources and to labor legislation, respectively.

The Mexican Revolution had created the anti-imperialist state, although it had been achieved only incompletely in Mexico. Referring to Marx and Friedrich Engels's views of the 1848 Revolutions in the preface to the German edition of *The Communist Manifesto*, Haya reminded his readers that the working class could not use the structure of the old state to further its goals. Likewise, the Mexican state, which remained subservient to imperialism, had not undergone the complete transformation into an anti-imperialist state. Nonetheless, the attempt to build a new state made the Mexican experience "incomparably valuable for our peoples because it offers the foundations for the true Indoamerican Antimperialist State."[121]

Part of the power of Haya's writing lies in its theoretical implications. He offers a normative view of what the anti-imperialist state should look like and anticipates some of the tensions inherent in the very model he is proposing. It is a model with wide-ranging implications in twentieth- and twenty-first-century Latin America. The new state would have some elements of the state capitalism developed in Germany during World War I. However, under the anti-imperialist state, there would be a conflict between absolute individual economic freedom and the need to combat imperialism. He gives the example of how a miner, selling his property to a U.S. company, is not simply carrying out an economic transaction—what is being sold as well is "sovereignty."[122] Hence the anti-imperialist state is forced to limit economic freedoms.

In Mexico, Haya demonstrated his penchant not just for theory but also for action in the Leninist tradition. During this time he put in motion APRA's first attempt to start a revolution in Peru, the "Plan de Mexico." Haya had begun to write about this idea while a student at Oxford. He conveyed his plans to Pavletich, then in Mexico, and suggested seeking financial support from the Mexican government of Calles: "I wish today more strongly than ever to go to America to begin a great oratorical campaign to predispose the public spirit in favor of our cause. I guarantee success. For all this we need money. Things are tight. . . . I had thought of proposing, if you are in agreement, that Calles finance the Revolution in Peru. With just a few thousand we could start an uprising."[123] He was also hoping for the possibility of getting help from supporters in Venezuela, Colombia, and Panama. There is no evidence that any of this was more than wishful thinking on Haya's part, but it does demonstrate that he envisioned the Aprista revolution as a transnational effort.

Haya also attempted to recruit some of the men who had fought in the Mexican Revolution with Pancho Villa and Zapata. In a letter from Mexico to Heysen dated March 27, 1928, Haya wrote, "Let us hope that over there you are able to achieve what we have here: to encourage many Mexican and non-Mexicans to enroll in the ranks of the National Liberation Party and count on them as soldiers. In my last trip to the Northern states of Mexico I received the allegiance of many future soldiers of our Revolution, among them many soldiers belonging to the 'dorados' of Villa."[124] Later, in another nod to the Mexican Revolution, once he initiated his political career as the leader of APRA in Peru, Haya's bodyguards came to be known as La Guardia Dorada.[125]

The plan was to topple the Leguía government in Peru and put a new party, the Partido Nacionalista Libertador, into power with Haya as its leader. During these months, the National Liberation Party existed only on paper, a vehicle for Haya to legitimize his political project of revolution in Peru.[126] Apristas borrowed the slogan "Tierra y Libertad" (Land and freedom) from Zapata's agrarianist movement.[127] The person assigned to implement this plan was an old school friend of Haya's and ex-officer, Felipe Iparraguirre, who was now living in El Salvador. Iparraguirre landed on Peru's northern coast, but he failed to start an armed uprising and instead ended up in jail.[128]

The writings and lectures of other Apristas also highlight the centrality of the Mexican Revolution. In her 1929 lecture tour of the Caribbean, Aprista leader and founder of the Mexican APRA cell, Portal, included in her repertoire of lectures one titled "Defense of the Mexican Revolution."[129] After he returned to Peru in 1931, Haya continued to promote the Mexican Revolution as a model for the continent. In 1938, while living in hiding in Lima, he wrote an article titled "We Must Make the Mexican Revolution 'Ours,'" which was published in the Cuban journal *Patria*.[130] Other party members also continued to refer to Mexico. In 1951, more than a decade later, party leader Seoane, who was exiled in Santiago, Chile, wrote to Luis Alberto Sánchez and predicted that Peru was entering a period of crisis that would lead to a revolution—"a rev. like the Mexican one that can have a profound effect and for which it will be worthwhile to fight and to die," wrote Seoane, who also called for some nationalizations in Peru, such as of the sugar industry.[131]

From Mexico to Berlin

After the failure of the Plan de Mexico, Haya left Mexico City by train and traveled south to Central America with the goal of making his way back to

Peru. In Guatemala, where he lectured on Aprismo, *El Nuevo Diario* referred to him as "the presidential candidate opposed to Leguía's reelection."[132] After a month and a half in Guatemala, the police expelled him. He traveled to El Salvador, where he lectured at the university. He also had to flee El Salvador, where he thought his life might be in danger, and moved on to San José, Costa Rica, on September 14, 1928.

In Costa Rica, a democracy, Haya could express his ideas freely in both his lectures and his writings. He published in Joaquín García Monge's journal *Repertorio Americano*, which had a continent-wide circulation and supported the anti-imperialist cause. The Partido Aprista de Costa Rica was founded while Haya was there. A writer reporting on one of his lectures described it as follows: "At the Teatro America last night, Haya de la Torre constructed an admirable lecture whose points of view, which were new to us and we will never forget. Haya speaks of America, anti-imperialism, indigenous cultures, university reforms and other topics."[133] From Costa Rica, Haya made his way to Panama. Here he was arrested, apparently by order of the Peruvian government, and put on a ship that took him to Germany. He would spend the next two years of his life in Berlin.

While Haya was in Berlin, APRA almost reached a point of dissolution as some members left the party and Haya himself became disillusioned with the prospects of continuing to promote his cause. He found lodging with a family in the Charlottenburg neighborhood. He also used the library at the newly founded Ibero-Amerikanisches Institut, which was dedicated to collecting books and studying Latin America.

Haya's two years in Berlin completed this remarkable chapter of his international political education. He arrived at a fascinating time politically and was able to observe firsthand the rise of the Nazi Party. Haya rejected the racist ideology of Nazism but was fascinated by Nazi political rituals. He would later imitate these rituals as the leader of APRA in Peru. I was able to observe the effects of this influence personally at a gathering in Lima to celebrate the ninetieth birthday of an old Aprista leader, Armando Villanueva. As excitement mounted in anticipation of the birthday song, young Apristas began to sing some of the party songs and a young man standing next to me raised his right hand in what he thought was the Aprista salute. An older man next to him quickly grabbed the hand and lowered it, saying, "That is the Nazi salute; you need to lift your left hand." The accusation that APRA has Fascist roots is not uncommon. It contains some truth regarding not the program—for Haya abhorred Fascism and its call for racial purity—but rather the forms of political organization.

As a city with an active gay subculture, Berlin also offered Haya a degree of freedom in the development of intimate relations with men that he would not find in his own country. We can only speculate on the degree and the ways in which he exercised this freedom. However, a handful of letters, written in English, confiscated by the Peruvian police, attest to one such relationship with a man who signed his name with the nickname "Bridi." Although these letters tell us nothing of Haya's feelings for this man, they point to an intimate relationship of some kind and express Bridi's longing for Haya after his departure from Berlin in 1931.[134] Early in 1932, Bridi wrote to Haya, who had left Berlin to enter Peruvian politics, asking whether to give up a flat that they had either shared or that Haya had helped to pay for. In this letter, Bridi expresses how much he missed Haya: "I myself feel still so low down as I feelt [sic] after you left. The rememberances in the flat and the district are for me to [sic] great."[135] The imperfect English would suggest that Bridi is German. Almost two years later, Bridi laments having received no letters from Haya: "Each day without news makes my life feel very very bitter.... I am not sentimental, I am just writing as I feel."[136] Another common friend named Bruno wrote to Haya urging him to reply to Bridi's letter and emphasizing Bridi's depth of feeling toward Haya: "Bridy [sic] is very unsettled and nervous, as you have not written him yet. Last night Bridy [sic] and I sat together and he spoke of you and cried. Victor, you mean so much to him, and through your not sending him a line, you are breaking his heart. So please write, I will be very grateful."[137] It is likely that Haya never received these letters, as they were intercepted by the Peruvian police.

While Haya was in Berlin, back in Peru the mestizo Colonel Luís Sánchez Cerro staged a coup that brought down the Leguía government. Apristas quickly took advantage of the political opening. On September 20, 1930, Haya's followers, many of whom had returned from exile, founded the Partido Aprista Peruano in Lima. The following year, Haya decided to take advantage of the new democratic opening by launching his candidacy for the presidency in the upcoming October 1931 elections. His candidacy generated resistance among some sectors of the party that were committed to armed revolution. Haya ultimately overcame these protestations and returned to Peru. A photograph of him on the deck of the ship that brought him back to Peru shows him posing by the side of an unnamed young woman. He is elegantly outfitted in white pants and a white shirt, holding a dark jacket casually in one hand and smiling with the relaxed air of a traveler free of the pressures of life on dry land. Things were about to change dramatically for him. When he disembarked in the port of Talara in northern Peru on July 12, 1931, he stepped into the messy world of Peruvian politics. The genteel-looking young man from the boat now mounted one political podium after another as he led massive campaign rallies to support his candidacy for president. He relied on the party that already showed a remarkable organizational capacity to launch campaign events throughout Peru.

Internationalism as a Handicap in Peruvian Politics

On August 23, 1931, the young Aprista presidential candidate spoke to a huge crowd in Lima's colonial bullring, the Plaza de Acho. His vision for a new Peru was one that blended APRA's nationalist and internationalist visions: "Our continental concept does not exclude our national concept.... We must first contemplate the national problem, we must be total nationalists in order to be truly continental, and, thus together, be able to incorporate ourselves to the march of world civilization."[138] He would even label the political programs for Peru and for Latin America as APRA's *programa mínimo* (national) and *programa máximo* (Latin America). The vision was true to his insight that the struggle against imperialism could not be restricted to the national scene and required the countries of Latin America to join forces.

Despite the fervor for APRA, the student activist turned politician lost the election to the military officer. Colonel Sánchez Cerro, a mestizo to whom ordinary people could relate, rode his prestige as the military man who had ended the Leguía regime. More importantly, he won the support of Peru's oligarchy, who saw him as a less radical alternative to APRA. Nonetheless, Haya's young party secured twenty-three seats in the Congress charged with writing a new constitution. Yet armed violence soon overshadowed congressional participation. Following the election, many Apristas accused the new government of electoral fraud and turned to violence in an effort to destabilize a regime they considered illegitimate.

The violence began with bombs set off at Sánchez Cerro's inauguration. In subsequent months, the violence escalated. On Christmas Eve of that year, government forces broke into the APRA party headquarters in Trujillo. The confrontation left a few Apristas dead and many injured. Soon thereafter, the Sánchez Cerro government obtained extraordinary powers from Congress, which passed the Emergency Law on January 9, 1932. The law allowed the government to intervene in public gatherings and to confiscate even legally obtained weapons. On February 29, Sánchez Cerro relieved the twenty-three APRA congressmen of their duties. Many went into exile.

During the next year and half, a cycle of violence gripped Peru—historian Jorge Basadre refers to the years 1932 and 1933 as a period of civil war.[139] In May of that year, a few months after Haya went into hiding, the government finally captured him and threw him in jail. On July 7, Apristas staged an uprising and took over the city of Trujillo, leading to a massive retaliation by the government. The violence continued to escalate and ended on April 30, 1933, when an Aprista assassinated President Sánchez Cerro at a public ceremony in Lima's hippodrome. After the new president, Oscar Benavides, granted APRA a brief period of amnesty, he changed course and once again declared the party illegal. Peru's jails filled up with Aprista political prisoners, and many of the party's leaders left the country to begin lengthy periods of exile in various Latin American cities.

The party's international identity became increasingly problematic over the course of the next twelve years. The Sánchez Cerro government had outlawed APRA in 1932 on the grounds that it was an international party with connections to international Communism and to Moscow. The Emergency Law created an entirely new scenario for Apristas. According to Melgar Bao, "The dream of international aprismo had not disappeared—it simply needed to be kept quiet: they had to remain 'silent' about the Antidictatorial International being created. . . . The Aprista project continued to dream of the formation of an Indoamerican International."[140] The international political scene became further complicated for APRA with the outbreak of the Spanish Civil War in 1936, as the notion that international forces could fight national conflicts took on a new dimension. In fact, the government of Benavides (1934–39) attempted to link APRA to the Spanish Civil War. This may help explain Haya's silence about this conflict.

Haya and other leaders chose to downplay the party's international ambitions. In 1942, the name of the party was changed to the Partido del Pueblo (People's Party) to remove the international reference implicit in the original name—American Popular Revolutionary Alliance. Furthermore, Haya now dedicated his efforts during the next decade primarily to legitimizing his outlawed party within the Peruvian political system. This left him very little energy to implement the international portion of the program. As the Argentine student leader and APRA sympathizer Gabriel del Mazo observed in 1940 about Haya, "His continentalist view seems diminished, after he promoted it strongly during his youth."[141]

However, Apristas did not entirely abandon their international aspirations. In his book *El antimperialismo y el APRA*, Haya affirmed APRA's internationalism, claiming that "the Anti-imperialist Party and united front promoted by APRA created a vast national indoamerican movement to realistically confront the task of our emancipation from imperialism."[142] Internationalism is a key part of the argument of his book, as he points to the problems the Mexican Revolution had in defeating imperialism and the need for Latin American countries to join together on this front. In a letter to Sánchez, exiled in Chile, Haya affirmed APRA's internationalism.[143] Haya also made the argument in his articles written for various journals.

The correspondence between Haya and party leader Portal, who was exiled in Santiago from 1939 to 1945, reflects the persistence of internationalism as part of APRA's identity. In one letter, Haya scolded Portal for not pushing ahead full steam with a second congress of democratic and popular parties of Indo-America, to be held in Mexico to follow the first such congress, held in Chile. He reproached her, sometimes harshly, for not defending APRA's continentalist program more forcefully, suggesting that she should have tried to hold a similar congress in Mexico: "You the ex-delegates of that Congress should have protested against the postponement of the second congress. You should have said that no national issue is worth as much as the continental issue that the Congress would confront. Say something to indicate that exiled apristas are not only involved in routine, personal and light tasks, but that they are preoccupied with maintaining the continental meaning of our work."[144] Portal, on the other hand, urged Haya to leave Peru, where she felt the party had already gained strength, and to dedicate himself once again to the task of forging a continental party: "I am convinced that you are the only person who can promote a New Indoamerican Policy, effectively moving toward the union of the 20 republics."[145] She also observed that Haya must be exhausted from a life of hiding and would benefit from leaving Peru to be in contact with different peoples and points of view. Haya held firm, arguing that his enemies wanted him to leave Peru and claiming that President Manuel Prado Ugarteche had offered him up to one million (he doesn't specify the currency) to do so, but Haya felt that this would weaken the party.

Aprista communities of exiles throughout Latin America continued to promote the party and to reflect its transnational identity over the course of the 1930s, 1940s, and 1950s.[146] During the 1930s, Santiago had become an important location for exiles, as well as a locus for the printing of political propaganda. Chile had begun since 1932 to enjoy a stable democratic system that would last until 1973 and that offered safe haven to exiles from dictatorial regimes. The correspondence between Haya and Sánchez, one of the leaders of the APRA exile community in Chile, reveals the centrality of Santiago, and particularly of the publishing house Ercilla, to Aprista activities in Peru. The long-delayed publication of Haya's book *El antimperialismo y el APRA* was the subject of numerous letters back and forth between Lima and Santiago. The correspondence between Haya and other exiled leaders in Santiago deals with important party issues. For example, in 1939, as elections were approaching in Peru, Haya called for exiled leaders to return to Peru to support the party. The call from the Comité de Acción del Partido Aprista Peruano is dated April 14, 1939.[147] The call went out not only to Santiago. Fernando León de Vivero, an exiled leader living in New York, wrote back to Colonel César E. Pardo, a retired military officer and APRA supporter living in Chile, saying that he had received the order but would have to wait to return to Lima for health reasons.[148]

Ironically, while Haya lived in hiding in Peru, he began to criticize the experience of exile. He accused exiles of living luxurious, undisciplined, and easy lives abroad. He contributed to creating a new party mythology that established a dichotomy between Apristas in Peru, who suffered government persecution, and exiles, who allegedly lived an easy life far from the dangers of Peru. A further ironic twist to this situation is of course the fact that Haya himself became subject to similar accusations as his critics looked back at his time in exile. In his memoir *The Yenan Way*, published in 1951, former Aprista turned Communist Ravines gave the following account of his first encounter with Haya in Paris back in 1927: "From a de luxe compartment, far beyond even the first-class coaches, alighted Víctor Raúl Haya de la Torre, surrounded by porters carrying shiny leather suitcases. He was dressed in the best English fashion and wore a trench-coat straight from Piccadilly. No one would have taken him for a penniless student from a backward South American country. One would have thought him, rather, the son of a rich Argentine cattle rancher."[149]

Yet through the late 1950s, exile remained a way of life for those Apristas able to go abroad. Following yet another Aprista armed uprising in 1948, General Manuel Odría took power in Peru and initiated a new and intense period of persecution against APRA. Fearing for his life, Haya sought political asylum in the Colombian embassy. The Odría government denied the request and surrounded the embassy with tanks to prevent Haya from escaping. The stalemate lasted for five long years, during which Haya never left the embassy in Lima. Isolated from his followers, he dedicated his time to reading and writing while he awaited the result of his political asylum case, which made it all the way to the International Court of Justice in The Hague.

During this period the party's exiled leaders relied more than ever on transnational networks to keep the party alive. Seoane and other party leaders scattered throughout Latin America corresponded intensely about party policy in what came to be known at the *congresos postales* (postal congresses). These postal congresses allowed Apristas in a number of different countries, from Ecuador to Chile to Argentina, to discuss party policy without having to physically congregate in a set geographic location. Seoane, one of the highest-ranking members of the party, and a rival of Haya, had called for the creation of these congresses while living in Santiago. In a letter to Sánchez, he wrote, "We must first elect a Coordinating Committee, then a Base, to organize a Postal Congress among exiles and establish a course of action, to put an end to personalism in the direction of the party so that each person can take on his particular responsibility."[150]

Exile communities also continued to hatch plans for revolution, plans that never came to fruition. The Apristas living in Buenos Aires contacted the Juan Domingo Perón government, seeking support for a revolution against Odría. The plan was to rescue Haya from the Colombian embassy.[151] In 1956, with the end of the Odría government, Peru transitioned back to democracy. Throwing their support behind former enemy Prado, APRA negotiated its way back to legality, although Haya still remained banned that year from running for president. With APRA now a part of the political system, attacks to discredit the party intensified. In 1959 anti-Aprista author Alfredo Moreno Mendiguren published a collection of articles from Lima's newspapers that accused APRA of being an international party.[152] Anti-APRA propaganda highlighted not only the party's alleged connection to international Communism but also its alleged antimilitarism.

Conclusion

In January 1949, Haya had arrived at the Colombian embassy in Lima seeking political asylum. For the next five years he lived in the embassy in a kind of political limbo. There he spent his days a prisoner in a single building while the Peruvian and Colombian governments fought out the legal details of his situation all the way to the International Court of Justice. While the government of Odría stationed troops and tanks around the embassy to prevent an escape, Haya could occasionally be sighted on the balcony of the embassy. His case became an international cause célèbre, and once the ordeal was over in 1954, Haya wrote an article about it for *Life* magazine. During his time in the embassy, he was removed from politics and pursued his intellectual aspirations by writing a book examining the philosophy of history of British historian Arnold Toynbee, whose book *A Study of History* had become a hugely popular. In *Toynbee frente a los panoramas de la historia*, Haya applied Toynbee's ideas about the origins of civilizations to understand what he saw as the emergence of a new civilization in Latin America.

He was finally able to leave in 1954 and fly to Guatemala, then Mexico, and then on to Europe, where he began a new period of self-imposed exile. His prolonged stay in the Colombian embassy had enhanced his international stature as a symbol of the struggle against dictators in Latin America. After APRA gained full legal status in 1956 (although Haya would not be allowed to run for president until 1962), the party's international ambitions became ever more diluted as efforts were directed to achieving full-fledged participation within the Peruvian political system.

In the years after his departure, his connection to Peruvian politics became more tenuous. It was not clear that he would ever return to Peru, and rumors circulated within the party that he wanted to remain in Europe. In a letter to Sánchez, written from Geneva, he acknowledged that some of these rumors might be true, that he might remain in Europe, and he expressed his disillusionment with Peruvian politics: "I remain because I was surrounded by hunger and indifference, persecution and insensitivity."[153] He commented on his precarious finances, claiming, "I now have no fixed income besides the forty dollars that El Tiempo pays me per article."[154] During his brief visits to Peru, the disconnection sometimes became evident— at one point the newsmagazine *Caretas* reveled in pointing out errors made by Haya in speeches regarding daily life in Peru.[155] Certainly his articles during this period reflect a greater familiarity with the general trends of world events than with the specifics of Peruvian politics. Nonetheless, he did continue to write numerous letters offering his opinions on how the party should proceed.

He did eventually return to Peru to run for president in 1962, only to have this election annulled. When he ran again in 1963, he lost to a young architect who had taken up the mantle of reform, Fernando Belaúnde Terry. In subsequent years, he returned to Peru periodically as a symbolic leader to be celebrated at rallies, before his definitive return in 1969.

For fifteen years, Haya spent most of his time living in Paris, Rome, and some of the Scandinavian countries. He primarily lived the life of a public intellectual, publishing numerous articles on world politics. Many of these articles once again promoted his vision of a united Latin America. He wrote articles on efforts to create a common market in Latin America. He also wrote more broadly on European politics. In an article on Lenin, written in Rome in 1960, he expressed his commitment to social democracy as a political system. He became more closely connected to social democratic politics, writing about Scandinavia and about social democracy in Germany.

Haya did eventually return to Peru for good in 1969 after the military government of General Juán Velasco Alvarado that had come to power in 1968 began to implement a series of reforms that were part of the original Aprista program, such as the nationalization of land and industry. During the final decade of his life, Haya held court daily at the Casa del Pueblo, the party headquarters in downtown Lima, sharing his vast knowledge and experience with party youths. He had become a kind of wise man and teacher. In 1978, he finally obtained his first and last elected position as head of the Constituent Assembly that wrote the Constitution of 1979, which Haya signed very shortly before his death.

When APRA finally won the presidency with Alan García (1985–90), Haya was no longer alive to witness his disciple's victory. Yet the international aspirations Haya had forged over decades for the party lived on. At the time of García's election, Latin America was in the midst of a financial crisis prompted by skyrocketing foreign debts that had become unpayable. García soon made a name for himself at his inauguration when he called for regional unity on a proposal to linked debt repayment to export earnings and announced that Peru would pay only 10 percent of its export earnings to service its foreign debt. His proposal did not gain traction in Latin America. García participated in other international efforts, such as hosting the Seventeenth Socialist International Congress in Lima in 1986. After his term as president ended, and after his successor, President Alberto Fujimori, closed down Congress in 1992, García faced political persecution and obtained political asylum in Colombia, thus joining in the long tradition of Aprista exile. By the time García became president again (2006–11) and embarked on a much more conservative path in his economic policy, the mantle of internationalism had been usurped by another Latin American populist, Venezuela's Hugo Chávez, who invoked Bolívar's visions of unity to attempt to create a Latin American front. Chávez sounded remarkably like the young Haya of the 1920s with his warnings of the dangers of U.S. imperialism and his efforts to promote continental unity.

CHAPTER TWO

Bullets and Ballots

Revolutionaries, Elections, and the Military

> When the doors of legality close, the doors of violence open.
>
> —NICOLÁS DE PIÉROLA

> The APRA party apparatus in the making was simultaneously
> built up for elections and revolution.
>
> —MARGARITA GIESECKE

> In succeeding years, anti-Aprismo became entrenched within the
> armed services. Instruction in the evils of APRA became part of
> the curriculum for cadets at the military academies.
>
> —DAVID WERLICH

> As an alternative to the popular movement which does not interest
> the Apra leader and rather causes him fear, Haya proposes a new
> scheme for taking power: to propitiate a military coup that, once
> triumphant, calls elections and gives power to the winner, which
> at that time could not be other than the APRA party.
>
> —THOMAS DAVIES JR. AND VÍCTOR VILLANUEVA

> The political rivalry between Apra and the army absorbs the
> politics of the last forty years.
>
> —VÍCTOR VILLANUEVA

When Víctor Raúl Haya de la Torre stepped off the boat in Talara on July 12, 1931, after almost eight years of exile, thronging crowds greeted him as the presidential candidate for his party in the upcoming elections. Over the course of the following months, Haya was the protagonist of similar scenes in other Peruvian cities as he drew thousands to his political rallies. Yet not all of his followers shared this sense of excitement with mass politics; some expressed dismay that Haya had betrayed the cause of armed revolution, the path to power originally outlined by the party. In fact, the Partido Aprista Peruano (PAP) had not officially approved his candidacy when he arrived in Peru. He only became the official candidate after his arrival. By running in 1931, Haya the pragmatist had followed his political instincts and taken the electoral opening when he the opportunity arose. Following his defeat, some American Popular Revolutionary Alliance (APRA) leaders cried fraud and continued over the course of the next few decades to pursue the path of armed revolution to bring their party to power.[1]

Another sector of Peruvian society had their eyes keenly trained on Haya when he returned to Peru preaching the need for social change: the Peruvian military. It, like the military throughout Latin America and unlike its counterpart in the United States, saw itself as an arbiter rather than as a neutral player in the political process. This perception can be attributed partly to the influence of the French who were invited in 1896 by the Peruvian government to professionalize the military. The French military brought a tradition of military involvement in society based on its experiences in the colonial setting. By the 1930s, the Aprista program appealed to individual members of the military seeking to bring about change in Peru. The military in many other parts of Latin America shared similar concerns with social issues. For example, Brazilian army officer Luis Carlos Prestes in 1924 briefly took over the city of São Paulo in an effort to stage a coup intended to break the landowning elites' hold on power in the country. In Cuba, members of the military participated in the 1933 revolution that ended the dictatorship of President Gerardo Machado y Morales.

Over the course of the next decades, Haya and his party attempted to gain power by various means: armed insurgencies, elections, and military coups. Whenever possible after 1931, Haya and his party participated in elections. However, as members of a party proscribed for most of the next twenty-five years, many Apristas continued to attempt at various times to start a revolution. Haya's views on the revolutionary path remain unclear, as either he was cautious enough to not write much about the issue or his writings have been kept hidden or most likely destroyed. In his writings, he does not outline a particular blueprint for getting to power, as Harry Kantor rightly points out in his sympathetic study of Aprista ideology.[2] Haya may also not have been fully in control of those Apristas committed to starting a revolution.

This chapter examines two separate but interrelated themes: Haya's changing views on the path of armed violence that some members of APRA continued to pursue, and his relationship with the Peruvian military, which he increasingly saw as a vehicle for APRA to gain power. Despite the presence of numerous military men sympathetic to the Aprista cause, the possibilities of an APRA-military popular insurgency became greatly complicated following the failed July 1932 Trujillo insurrection, which left lasting scars on APRA-military relations. A fervent strain of anti-Aprismo developed within the Peruvian military. Given this atmosphere, Haya increasingly sought out individual high-ranking officers whom he hoped would be willing to stage a military coup that would bring APRA to power.

Haya's apparent unwillingness to pursue the path of armed revolution and his constant flirtation with military officers in an attempt to bring APRA to power have led his critics to accuse him of having betrayed his followers. Nelson Manrique claims that "Haya cultivated the radical passion among the rank and file and permanently fostered a climate of preparation for insurrection that reinforced among the workers the conviction that the party planned to take power following the revolutionary path."[3] Major Víctor Villanueva, a participant in the failed Callao insurrection of 1948, directly blamed Haya for not having thrown the full support of the party behind the officers who took over military installations and navy ships in the port of Callao on October 3. He even attributed Haya's seeming ambivalence about going forward with the insurgency to a decision-making process that Villanueva characterized as depending on Haya's "state of mind, on whoever he was addressing at the time and maybe, even, to the workings of his gut, or even the daily constellations."[4] Yet Villanueva's sense of having been personally betrayed taints his interpretation of Haya's motivations.

Shedding light on a historical actor's motivations is no easy task. One must necessarily speculate and fill in the blanks as Haya moves from one approach to another. To begin with, he may have had less control over the armed insurgencies than might be expected. When the Trujillo insurrection broke out, Haya was being held in solitary confinement in Lima's penitentiary. It is highly unlikely that he could have personally coordinated an uprising with party leaders who were also being persecuted by the Luís Sánchez Cerro government. It is also unlikely that Haya approved the political assassinations carried out over the years, most likely by rogue elements, as they only contributed to smearing the party's image. In March 1932, an Aprista, José Melgar, attempted to assassinate President Sánchez Cerro while he was attending mass at a church in the Lima suburb of Miraflores. A year later, on April 30, 1933, after Sánchez Cerro had finished reviewing troops at the Santa Beatriz Hippodrome, another Aprista, Abelardo Mendoza Leiva, shot Sánchez Cerro through the heart and killed him. In the coming years, two more high-profile political assassinations by Apristas damaged the image of the party. In 1935, Carlos Steer, a member of the Aprista youth group Federación Aprista Juvenil, assassinated the editor of *El Comercio* (Lima's main newspaper), Antonio Miró Quesada, and his wife while they were strolling in one of Lima's main plazas, the Plaza San Martín. Finally, in 1947 two Apristas were accused of assassinating Francisco Graña Garland, the editor of the newspaper *La Prensa*. As for the 1948 uprising, which followed a chaotic three years in which APRA participated in a coalition government, Haya's fingerprints are nowhere to be found in existing sources.

Rather than accuse Haya of flip-flopping or of betraying his followers, I suggest that there was an evolution in Haya's thinking. A deeply pragmatic individual, he demonstrated that he was immediately willing to abandon his Leninist vision of APRA as a military organization when he decided to participate in the 1931 election. Watching insurgency after insurgency fail between 1932 and 1934, Haya may easily have lost faith in this approach to gaining power. Whenever possible, he turned to elections, knowing the strength of his own party. In 1936, he attempted to participate in an election, despite the fact that his party remained proscribed. Increasingly, however, he turned to the military in the hopes that a military coup would open the way for APRA to gain power. His strategy following the failed Trujillo insurrection seems to have been to convince the military to stage a coup, leading to elections that would in turn, according to the party's projections, put APRA in power.

However, the armed wing of his party remained active, and Aprista attempts to stage a popular insurgency continued. Critics have correctly pointed out that Haya did not discourage such attempts, although it is not clear why he would take such a step. Villanueva and Thomas Davies Jr. have accused Haya of remaining lukewarm about a planned armed insurgency and criticized him for not having discouraged those in his party from dedicating their efforts to an armed revolution. They claim that "Haya de la Torre was not interested in the least in the 'Aprista revolution' that the party militants were talking about."[5] Following the many failures of such armed insurgencies, Haya developed a preference for bringing APRA to power through the workings of a military coup rather than a popular uprising: "Apparently at that time Haya became disillusioned with the popular movements and decides to conspire only with the generals. In fact, from now on he will only deal with them, provided he has them on hand; in the worst case scenarios he deals with lower-ranking officers, but never with the people."[6] His critics are certainly correct on one front: the fact that he did not make a firm pronouncement for or against a popular insurgency resulted in the loss of lives, as occurred in 1948. In this sense, Haya bears some responsibility for the death of many of his followers in this uprising.

In retrospect, it is easy to conclude that political violence did not directly help APRA in its goal of gaining power. None of the Aprista insurrections succeeded, and the numerous failed attempts at insurgency ultimately hurt the party and probably contributed to delaying its rise to power for half a century. Yet leaving the door of armed revolution permanently open also may have strengthened Haya's hand. Analyst of Latin American politics Charles Anderson points out that in the absence of a democratic polity, Latin American political actors (he calls them power contenders) must establish a "power capability" to be taken seriously.[7] In the case of APRA, the threat of armed violence strengthened the party's "power capability." By this logic, Haya's acceptance of the armed wing of his party may have actually strengthened him politically. In one of his few public statements on the topic—published outside Peru in the Chilean newspaper *La Opinión*—Haya left the door open for a violent takeover of power, arguing for the legitimacy of such a move when governments—in this case he was accusing the democratically elected Manuel Prado (1939–45)—crossed the line into tyranny. Haya ended his article by claiming that Apristas would heed the saying of the nineteenth-century caudillo and president Nicolás de Piérola: "When the doors of lawfulness close, those of violence open."[8]

The alternation between insurgent and democratic politics has historically been a common pattern in Latin American politics. The lack of a durable democratic polity—and the shift between democratic and dictatorial politics over time throughout the region—offers the conditions for democratic actors to turn to violence. Numerous examples can be cited. Juan Domingo Perón in Argentina, following the coup against him and during his time in exile, called on his followers to engage in armed violence in the face of the legal obstacles placed on his party. The Revolutionary Armed Forces of Colombia, following the continent's longest guerrilla war, are currently engaged in a transition process from armed struggle to peaceful political participation. The Farabundo Martí National Liberation Front in El Salvador has likewise transitioned from a guerrilla group to a legitimate political party. In Nicaragua, Daniel Ortega, the leader of the Sandinista revolution, has since been able to return to power by democratic means. In some cases, individuals who once belonged to small revolutionary parties have risen to the presidencies of their countries—for example, Dilma Rousseff, former president of Brazil, and José Mujica, former president of Uruguay. Looking beyond Latin America, there are a number of parallels between APRA and the Lebanese political party Hezbollah—which in 1992, after years of armed violence, decided to participate in elections—and the Palestinian party Hamas after 2006.

The First APRA Insurgency: The 1928 Plan de Mexico

In his early writings, Haya leaves no doubt that he conceived of APRA in Leninist terms as a political and military organization. Vladimir Lenin had seen violence as a transformative force. As Ryan James writes, "For Lenin, 'revolutionary' violence was an instrument with which to realize his vision of a socialist, ultimately communist world. . . . He considered it an essential means to topple the Russian autocracy, and after 1917 considered it an essential component of proletarian dictatorship."[9] This view of violence was common on both the European left and the right at the time. The notion that violence could be a creative force goes back to a European romantic tradition that nourished fascists like Gabriele D'Annunzio in Italy who saw violence as a purifying force in history.[10] Proponents of both Communism and Fascism saw violence as a necessary instrument of social transformation. Haya does not show the same level of commitment to violence that we find in Lenin and D'Annunzio. During his years in Europe, he befriended the pacifist Romain Rolland, whom he met while living in Switzerland.

In a letter from London in 1926 to Esteban Pavletich, an APRA supporter, Haya referred to his party as a "red army": "The main thing now is to organize the national sections of A.P.R.A and to organize them militarily. A.P.R.A. will not be a party of tumults but rather a military organization, the true red army of anti-imperialism. Discipline, unity . . . and the absolute and exclusive dedication of its members will be essential conditions."[11] When Haya returned from Europe to Mexico in 1928, he and the members of the Mexican APRA cell attempted to put this military vision into practice by starting an uprising, which they called Plan de Mexico, against the dictatorship of Augusto B. Leguía. As part of this plan, Haya and his followers invented a party on paper, the Partido Nacionalista Libertador, and printed flyers declaring Haya a presidential candidate. Haya then contacted his old school friend, the ex-officer Felipe Iparraguirre, who was exiled and living in El Salvador, and asked him to lead the insurgency against Leguía. Iparraguirre landed on Peru's northern coast and was able to recruit people to support his effort, but he ultimately failed to start an armed uprising and instead ended up in jail.[12]

Haya conceived of the Plan de Mexico as a transnational effort. He attempted to recruit fighters in Mexico who had fought during the revolution with both Pancho Villa and Emiliano Zapata. He urged Aprista Luis Heysen to also recruit people in Argentina and claimed that in Mexico former soldiers of Pancho Villa had pledged their support.[13] The Plan de Mexico was to have a continental scope. Haya intended to send Aprista fighters to join the guerrilla army of Augusto Sandino, who was fighting the U.S. Marines in Nicaragua. At least one Aprista, Pavletich, made contact with Sandino in Nicaragua. The name Plan de Mexico drew on Mexico's own long insurgent tradition, which had most recently manifested itself in Francisco Madero's "Plan San Luis de Potosí," which started the Mexican Revolution, and Zapata's "Plan de Ayala," with its call for agrarian reform. Haya's Plan de Mexico called for nationalizing property, affirmed the need for agrarian reform in Peru, and even ended with the Zapatista slogan "Land and Freedom."[14]

APRA's strength lay not in the military realm but in the effectiveness of its propaganda. For this purpose, Haya made his way south through Central America, where he lectured on anti-imperialism and founded APRA cells. The governments of El Salvador and Guatemala expelled him. He was not the only one to go on such lecture tours—Aprista Magda Portal embarked on a tour of the Caribbean in 1929 to broadcast APRA's ideas. Haya's tour would be cut short when he arrived in Panama and was not allowed to disembark. Forced to remain on the German ship *Phoenicia*, he found himself headed back to Europe. For the next two years, he lived in Berlin.

The Firebrand Revolutionary Becomes a Candidate: The 1931 Elections

Haya's deportation to Germany represented a major setback for APRA and seemed to place the party further than ever from gaining power in Peru. APRA cells dissolved, and many Apristas, such as Eudocio Ravines and Pavletich, switched their allegiance to Communist parties. Numerous ruptures within the APRA organization accompanied the public break between Haya and José Carlos Mariátegui. The Parisian group dissolved the original APRA cell to form a cell of Mariátegui's Socialist Party.[15] Discouraged by these events, Haya announced his resignation as *jefe máximo* in a letter written from Berlin to the Paris APRA cell, dated February 18, 1930. Faced with criticism, Haya reaffirmed his decision in a March letter in which he informed Ravines of his total withdrawal from politics.[16] In Berlin, Haya studied at the library of the recently founded Ibero-Amerikanisches Institut. Heysen traveled from Paris to Berlin to convince Haya not to abandon APRA. Haya did not require much convincing, and by July 1929 he had converted the house where he was lodged in Charlottenburg into the headquarters of APRA. Together with Heysen and Fernando Apaza, the latter of whom was studying chemistry in Berlin, he wrote a manifesto, "Memorandum from the General Secretariat of APRA to the Buenos Aires, Mexico, La Paz and Paris Sections," with instructions on how to keep the party alive.[17]

When Haya announced that he would run for president in the 1931 election, he surprised many of his followers who had been committed to the path of revolution. In a letter from Berlin, the pragmatist Haya attributed his decision to changing political circumstances in Peru as the fall of the Leguía dictatorship had created a new democratic opening: "To face the elections, now we are not in the favorable conditions that existed in 1928 when repression excused our absence of propaganda methods. At that time, the candidacy was an act of rebelliousness. Now it must have the character of a formal candidacy, in conflict with others. This means relying on the large-scale media, the press, money and propaganda elements."[18] Haya could now embark on a full-fledged propaganda campaign. Putting an end to eight years of exile, he arrived in Peru on July 12, 1931, and immediately began campaigning against his rival, Colonel Sánchez Cerro, who was running as the hero whose military coup had ended Legúia's eleven-year dictatorship.

The campaign and election marked historic changes in Peruvian politics. The use of the secret ballot for the first time protected voters from the direct intimidation that accompanied elections. The campaign signaled the advent of mass politics in Peru. Both candidates held political rallies much larger than any Peruvians had previously seen. Peter Klaren describes the 1931 campaign as "one of the bitterest of the century."[19] Apristas accused Sánchez Cerro of being the oligarchy's lapdog, while Sánchezcerristas attempted to equate Aprismo with Communism and accused Haya of being anti-Catholic. Sánchez Cerro made the argument that Peruvians ought to grant him the presidency as a gesture of thanks for having deposed the dictator Leguía. Both candidates displayed a remarkable capacity to draw large crowds. On August 22, thousands of Sánchezcerristas marched through the streets of Lima waving Peruvian flags and shouting support for their candidate. They marched from the Alameda de los Descalzos to the Plaza San Martín, where they heard Sánchez Cerro give a short speech—his speeches were notoriously short, and he put less emphasis on his political program than on his role as a hero who had saved the country from Leguía.[20] The following day, Haya gathered thousands in the Plaza de Acho, Lima's bullring. He spoke longer than Sánchez Cerro, often with a professorial style, as he unveiled the details of the party's *programa mínimo*—the political program for Peru, which contrasted with APRA's Latin American program (*programa máximo*). Other Apristas, including Portal, also spoke to the crowds. Both candidates traveled outside Lima to rally support in the provinces.

These displays of strength relied on complex organizational networks. Sánchez Cerro relied on a network of local political clubs that organized his followers in support of the mass events held by the party, the Unión Revolucionaria. Relying on his early connections to the labor movement, Haya counted on the support of unions: "Labor leaders were invited to frequent face-to-face meetings with Haya, who was always quick to recall with affection specific instances of his past contacts with these individuals."[21] A few labor leaders, including Arturo Sabroso of the Textile Federation, even ran as congressional candidates for APRA. Despite the fact that women still could not vote in the election, Portal organized women throughout the country to support the APRA platform. APRA also drew on the support of a small but growing middle class.[22]

As he was running against a military man, Haya made specific efforts to ingratiate his party with the Peruvian military. The Aprista ideology, with its call for a social revolution, appealed to the many enlisted men of indigenous descent who daily experienced in the flesh the discrimination of a society with pronounced social-racial hierarchies. Haya deliberately portrayed the army as a democratic institution constituted by the very social classes that APRA represented—the working and middle classes: "Furthermore, we reaffirm our democratic point of view by noting that the great majority of the members of the Armed Forces are constituted by men who come from the middle and working classes. Therefore, from a social point of view we belong to the same levels, to the same classes or strata on behalf of whose welfare and justice our Party is fighting for."[23] Aprismo's appeal also threatened to create divisions within the army, where soldiers were often of peasant and indigenous background, while officers came from the upper and middle classes.[24] The economic crisis of the early 1930s kept salaries low, further fueling discontent: "So Aprista ideas found fertile ground in this period, and infiltration of the army was widespread. . . . Disaffection among the soldiers was not uncommon, and many joined the PAP."[25] The following testimony by a soldier reveals the appeal of Aprismo in the mili-

Haya with workers at the popular university in Vitarte, December 1921. *First row:*
Teófilo Faydel, Jesús Portocarrero, Julio Portocarrero, Haya, Alberto Benítes,
Felipe Osterling, Urbano Ugaz, Juan Grados, Paulino Montoya, unidentified, and
Eustaquio Portocarrero (Armando Villanueva Papers, courtesy of Lucía Villanueva).

tary: "Because it is the only party that defends the people: I became familiar with Apra together with Luis Negreiros Vega, and we learned of the
advantages Apra offered to the people; as military men we joined a special
cell."[26] The friend to whom this soldier refers, Negreiros Vega, had been
involved in a failed insurrectionary attempt in Lima on December 1.

Fearful of APRA's influence in the armed forces, Haya's political enemies attempted to paint the party as antimilitary. Peru's conservative
newspaper, *El Comercio*, spearheaded the propaganda against Haya and his
party.[27] Founded in 1839, *El Comercio* was Peru's oldest continuously running
newspaper. The newspaper represented the interests of some of Peru's
wealthiest families, which had been connected to the now weakened Partido
Civil. On August 20, 1931, in a speech to the first APRA party congress, he
argued against *El Comercio*'s attempts to discredit APRA as being opposed to
the military: "And suddenly, because the other presidential candidate, my
opponent in this electoral context, is a military man, Aprismo is considered

to be 'anti-military.' ... In other words, if in an election campaign a professional military man and a civilian run against each other, the latter must always be labeled as an 'enemy of the army.' ... The argument cannot be more nonsensical nor antidemocratic. ... I need to say here, once again, as Leader of the Aprista Party, that our position toward the army is frankly and cordially friendly."[28] *El Comercio* would maintain its opposition to APRA for decades to come.

Despite the stepped-up rhetoric, Election Day, October 11, transpired without violence. In the final count, Sánchez Cerro won 50.7 percent of the vote (152,062 votes) to Haya's 35.4 percent (106,007). Apristas immediately cried fraud and claimed the election had been stolen from them, although this remains a mere allegation.[29] They engaged in acts of violence as the party prepared to spark a mass uprising. Shortly before Sánchez Cerro's inauguration, Apristas interfered with the electrical network and left Lima without electricity.[30] On the day of the inauguration, Haya spoke to his followers in Trujillo, making a statement that either foreshadowed or perhaps incited further violence: "More Aprista blood will run. The immortal list of our martyrdom will grow, the terror will begin again its hateful task."[31] In Lima, Apristas set off bombs during Sánchez Cerro's inauguration. In the coming months, violence between the government and Apristas began to spiral out of control.

The Revolution That Was Not: Trujillo, 1932

The revolutionary cycle began as soon as Haya lost the election. In addition to the acts of violence in Lima, in November and December Apristas staged a number of smaller insurrections in the provinces. They took over the city of Cerro de Pasco for a day. Just days before Sánchez Cerro was to take office on December 8, 1931, coordinated insurrections occurred in Lima and two surrounding towns—Chosica and Yanacoto—which were intended to interrupt the political transition. This plan involved members of the police. Leaked information allowed the uprisings to be put down.[32] Insurrections with varying degrees of success occurred in Cajamarca, La Oroya, Paiján, Huacho, and Chiclayo. Some lasted only a few hours; La Oroya was occupied for two days.[33] Meanwhile, in Trujillo, a bastion of APRA support, Haya addressed his followers, urging them to continue the struggle and to never give up.[34]

To the dismay of its enemies, APRA would continue to draw members of the military to its ranks. Interrogated about an Aprista uprising in Lima,

Second Sergeant Victor Alvarado Romero of the Third Infantry Regiment revealed the degree of APRA's infiltration of the armed forces. He claimed that two friends of his who were in the civil guard "would talk about the political situation and persuaded him and others to belong to the Aprista party, and to find out whether there were Apristas in the barracks and whether the troops enjoyed advantages with their leaders." The friends in the civil guard said "that when the party reached the government the situation of the troops would be very different from the current one and that shortly there would be some action on the part of the party, referring to a future movement that would seek cooperation among the members of the corps."[35]

For a few brief months, the party simultaneously pursued two opposite directions: its twenty-seven elected congressmen took their seats in the Constituent Assembly that would write a new constitution, while other Apristas prepared for revolution. In at least one case, a seated congressional representative supported the violent wing of the party. Manuel Arévalo, an Aprista labor leader elected as representative for La Libertad, engaged in conspiratorial activities in northern Peru.[36] After the expulsion of the Aprista congressmen in January 1932, Arévalo would later be captured and assassinated by the Sánchez Cerro government and would become one of the party's most revered martyrs. Rumor has it that Haya kept Arévalo's bones under his bed.

The next two years saw violence between APRA and the government escalate into a full-fledged civil war. Events in Peru followed a broader, continent-wide pattern of revolutionary violence. In 1932 in El Salvador, Farabundo Martí led a peasant uprising that ended in a massacre, La Matanza. In 1933, Cuban students, workers, and members of sectors of the military staged a revolution that overthrew the dictator Machado. Cuba continued to experience political violence during the 1930s and 1940s. In Brazil political violence by both the Communists and the Integralists challenged the regime until Getulio Vargas claimed dictatorial powers in 1937.

Despite attempts by his followers to impose the discipline so cherished by Haya, Aprista insurrections proved for the most part to be amateurish affairs. During the brief takeover of Paiján, the insurgents "marched down the street three by three in a very disciplined way. . . . They were accompanied by a band, playing marches. Many of them carried flags, sometimes red, sometimes white."[37] In Huacho, the revolutionaries briefly decreed revolutionary measures such as reducing the prices of certain goods and services for the general population—for example, the price of a light bulb was to go down to two soles.[38] In other cases, the improvisational nature of their actions shone through. As Margarita Giesecke points out, "For all its violence and its casualties, some at least of the revolutionaries were unsophisticated, gullible and naïve, perhaps romantic! In Paiján, for example, when a revolutionary was sent to control the telephone office, he negotiated with the employee in charge, who was not a PAP sympathizer, and they reached an agreement whereby she allowed him to listen to the conversations but only from outside the building, through a window left open for the purpose."[39] Many of these armed uprisings involved some coordination between civilians and military.

Sánchez Cerro responded forcefully to these uprisings and a spiral of violence began. On Christmas Eve 1931, government troops attacked the party's headquarters in Trujillo and attempted to capture Haya, who was attending a Christmas celebration to share the traditional hot chocolate with his followers. In February 1932, the government removed APRA's congressional delegation of twenty-seven and sent its members to jail or into exile. The government passed the Emergency Law declaring APRA illegal because it was an international party. On March 6, a young Aprista unsuccessfully attempted to assassinate President Sánchez Cerro while he was attending Mass. In May, a group of sailors who sympathized with APRA staged a failed coup that ended with their executions.

Haya and party leaders had begun preparations for a revolution that would bring APRA to power in Peru.[40] Aprista historian Percy Murillo Garaycochea writes that by December 1931 it was "clear that in Trujillo Haya de la Torre was plotting."[41] Apristas reached out to sympathetic members of the Peruvian military in an effort to implement this plan.[42] Haya contacted Colonel Aurelio García Godos.[43] A few Apristas traveled from Trujillo to Chile to meet with Lieutenant Colonel Gustavo "Zorro" Jimenez, who was living in exile in Chile. Others met with Remigio Esquivel Diestra, the labor organizer of workers on the hacienda Laredo (one of the sugar plantations near Trujillo), who recruited among the sugarcane workers to create an armed group that came to be known as the Tigers of Laredo. The planned revolution even had a preestablished political leader, Haya's brother, Agustín "Cucho" Haya de la Torre, secretary general of the Departmental Committee of the PAP in Trujillo.[44]

In a letter to Lieutenant Colonel Jimenez, with whom Apristas were coordinating to start a revolution, Luis Alberto Sánchez revealed the party's conception of the coming revolution as a joint civilian-military uprising. The party had a plan, he claimed, "to provoke the civil-military-police uprising at any place in the country or at various places at the same time, which we are already trying to do, and that Lima be taken over as a result of the arrival of coordinated forces. We are also working on this, and so far with very good results." Furthermore, he presented his vision of the need for a postrevolutionary regime divorced from personalism and driven by ideas: "A movement to destroy something must also be planting the seed, the concrete seed, of what will now begin." Sánchez claimed to "see no incompatibility between the campaign on paper and through an armed attack" and argued that APRA would easily win in an election.[45] On May 7, the day before Sánchez wrote this letter, government forces caught Haya, who had been living in hiding in a house next to the Mexican embassy, and put him in jail. In fact, his capture led to the breaking of diplomatic ties between Peru and Mexico when it was revealed that Haya had been using the Mexican diplomatic pouch to receive correspondence. For the remainder of the Sánchez Cerro regime, Haya remained in jail, often in solitary confinement. It is therefore highly unlikely that he could have had much of a say in the events that would follow.

On July 7, 1932, the revolution the Apristas had been planning broke out unexpectedly and took the party leadership by complete surprise. Tired of repeated postponements, a group of Apristas ignored party orders regarding the timing of the events and took matters into their own hands. In the darkness of the early-morning hours on that day, an automobile mechanic and Aprista labor leader named Manuel "Búfalo" Barreto led a group of men that included the Tigers of Laredo and broke through the gates of the O'Donovan military barracks on the outskirts of Trujillo. The heavyset Barreto—who got his nickname from his apparent resemblance to Buffalo Bill—was shot and killed just outside the gates of the barracks. Yet the siege continued. The Apristas eventually overpowered the military garrison at the barracks. In the process, sixteen more Apristas lost their lives and fourteen government soldiers were killed.[46] By morning the Apristas had taken the building, captured weapons and ammunition, and marched triumphantly into Trujillo with captured soldiers, officers, and Krupp cannons. They occupied strategic positions and built barricades to defend the city. A revolutionary government was quickly improvised with both civilian and military leadership as APRA national leaders were forced to back an insurrection they had not planned. The party named Agustín Haya de la Torre prefect, the main authority in the city. He in turn named Captain Leoncio Rodríguez Manffaurt as the military authority in charge of the revolutionary troops (*jefe militar de la plaza y director de las tropas revolucionarias*). The rebels built barricades to defend the city and at some points during the fighting were able to defend their positions and rout military attackers. However, the barricades proved to be a flawed strategy, as they eventually trapped the revolutionaries when the military forces attacked the city. A number of smaller insurrections simultaneously erupted in towns throughout the region, including in the larger towns of Huaraz and Cajamarca.

President Sánchez Cerro responded quickly and with overwhelming force, sending the army, the navy, and the air force to recapture the city. Trujillo's residents witnessed one of the first aerial bombings of civilians in history, predating the more famous Guernica bombing in Spain.[47] A total of 746 troops were sent to Trujillo, some from Lima, others from cities in northern Peru, as well as the warship *Almirante Grau* and two submarines. On July 8, a squadron of seven airplanes and hydroplanes began to bomb the city, using the nearby port of Chimbote as a base. The newspaper *El Comercio* described the bombing in the following terms: "The bombing intensified by air and land and the bombs would accelerate and descend, turning in a closed curve, indicating the falling of a bomb or of a round of machine gun fire. A number of airborne bombs fell on the Trieste Hotel, located on Progreso Street. Another bomb fell on the Colón Theater."[48] The Belén Hospital was bombed, even though its roof had the Red Cross flag.[49] While the aerial bombing continued, army forces were able to retake the port of Salaverry on July 9 and began to attack Trujillo by land. On July 10, the warship *Mantaro* brought 140 troops from the Seventh Regiment. That same day the government forces surrounded the city and attacked the remaining Aprista barricades. Simultaneously, airplanes and hydroplanes dropped bombs on a series of targets outside the city. The warship *Almirante Grau*, located offshore, fired its guns at Trujillo. By nightfall, the government forces, led by General Manuel Ruiz Bravo, had taken back most of the city.

Just four days after the insurrection began, the last Apristas had been captured or had fled from the city. Now in control of the city, government forces rounded up anybody suspected of having participated in the uprising. Often a bruised shoulder, evidence of having fired a rifle, was enough to be thrown in jail. Military tribunals hastily condemned ninety-seven rebels to death. An undetermined number of rebels who received no trial were marched out to the ruins of the massive pre-Columbian city of Chan Chan that lie on the outskirts of Trujillo. Here, under cover of darkness, the military shot them. The government forces also quickly subdued the uprisings that had broken out in other cities in northern Peru. Government persecution of Apristas now intensified. Jails filled up with hundreds or perhaps thousands of Apristas, while others fled abroad.

One particular incident fueled a lasting hatred of APRA in the Peruvian military and cast a long shadow over APRA-military relations.[50] Upon retaking the city, the military discovered the bodies of thirty-five army soldiers and officers in the city jail. They had been held as prisoners during the uprising, then brutally murdered. The perpetrators of the crime had disfigured some of the bodies beyond recognition; in one case they ripped out a heart, in another they removed genitals. The crime was never investigated. While Apristas blamed people outside the party for carrying out the executions after APRA authorities had relinquished control of the city, the military squarely blamed APRA for the murders.[51] The incident helped to fuel anti-APRA sentiment in the military for decades to come. This sentiment became institutionalized as the military singled out APRA as a threat to the nation.

The government attempted to accuse Víctor Raúl Haya de la Torre of being the "intellectual author" of the uprising. Haya had been in jail since May. Convinced at this point that he would be executed, he allegedly wrote a farewell letter on pieces of cigarette paper. The Colegio de Abogados wrote a letter that questioned the evidence presented by the Peruvian government in its accusation of Haya for the crime of "rebellion." Lacking any evidence that linked Haya to recent conspiratorial activity, the government based its case on three letters Haya had written from Europe some years earlier. One of them discussed the Plan de Mexico. The indictment alleged that these documents contained Communist principles and sought to subject the country to an "International Committee."[52] The government also accused three other Apristas connected to these letters, César Mendoza, Rómulo Meneses, and Juan de Dios Merel. One of Haya's lawyers, Biélich Flores, argued that "there was no crime in the writings of Haya de la Torre, since these were opinions expressed in private correspondence. The crime . . . should refer to a physical fact that alters the normal order and not to ways of thinking about social problems."[53]

Haya's questioning had begun on May 16 (thus violating the law that required a prisoner's interrogation to begin no more than twenty-four hours after arrest) and continued until May 31. The government's questions attempted to link Haya to Communism. Most of the questions addressed issues of political doctrine. Asked whether he believed in the struggle between capitalism and the proletariat in Peru, Haya replied that capitalism was a necessary stage in Peru's development and that his party sought simply to make capitalism more humane. He also alluded to the fact that even Civilista authors referred to historical materialism and class conflict without it being considered a crime to do so.[54] The Civilistas were the political party that represented Peru's elites.

When asked to clarify specific passages in the various letters, Haya persistently explained the clear difference between Aprismo and Communism. In defense of the term *revolution*, he pointed to the fact that Sánchez Cerro's party, the Unión Revolucionaria, used the same term. He also stated that the letters had been written in opposition to the Leguía regime, which had already fallen.[55] In his defense, Haya claimed that these explanations of political doctrine had taken place before the founding of the PAP, had not become part of its political program, and were not part of the party's archive. When confronted with phrases such as the "dictatorship of the proletariat," found in one of the letters, Haya claimed in his defense that "none of the documents has been public or propaganda ... but ... simply controversial and reserved."[56]

His interrogators also attempted to link him to the recent attempt to assassinate President Sánchez Cerro in a church in the neighborhood of Miraflores. Haya responded, "After February 15, I, personally, have not had any participation in the leadership of the Party as since then I, like all its leaders, have been persecuted."[57] He also stated that APRA did not sanction violence and made his case by pointing out that the party had officially stated its opposition to the custom of settling disputes by duel. He also defended himself against the accusation that APRA's slogan "Only Aprismo Will Save Peru" pointed to sectarianism and fanaticism by claiming that it was a fraternal call for others to help with the party's program. Aprista exiles in Ecuador published the proceedings the following year with the title *El process Haya de la Torre: Documentos para la historia del ajusticiamiento de un Pueblo* (1933). The book includes the *instructiva* (pretrial interrogation) documents, the letters on behalf of Haya, an introductory essay by Alcides Spelucín on modern Peruvian history, and copies of letters that would arrive from abroad calling for Haya's release. Haya remained in jail for the remainder of Sánchez Cerro's presidency.

A Tenuous Alliance: The 1933 Insurgency of Lieutenant Colonel Gustavo Jimenez

When, the following year, Lieutenant Colonel Jimenez attempted to stage a coup against Sánchez Cerro, the difficulties of post-Trujillo APRA-military coordination became evident. On March 11, 1933, Jimenez led a military uprising of the Eleventh Infantry Battalion.[58] He coordinated with APRA and received support from sectors of APRA's grass roots. Yet while seeking the party's support, he always remained uneasy about the joint military-civilian nature of the uprising. Giesecke attributes the difficulty of APRA-military alliances to APRA's damaged image following the Trujillo events: "From this time on, neither the military in general nor officers individually could form an effective alliance with Apristas. The failed attempt by Gustavo Jimenez in 1933 is suggestive: he shrank from being identified with PAP and the PAP were reluctant to collaborate with him."[59]

This was not Jimenez's first incursion into violent politics. In 1921, he had led a failed coup against Leguía. He had later been the minister of war during the Junta Nacional de Gobierno that briefly ruled Peru while the country prepared for the 1931 elections. The following year he was expelled from the country at the same time that the Aprista representatives were removed from the Constituent Assembly. He had gone into exile in Chile, where he was in contact with Aprista exiles Manuel Seoane, Sabroso, Juan Arce Arnao, Víctor Colina, Carlos Boado, and Enrique Cornejo Koster in Arica, Chile.[60] They agreed that the military part of the operation would be entirely in the hands of Jimenez, with Aprista militants acting in a supporting role. He was supposed to take command of the APRA revolution that began prematurely in Trujillo in 1932.[61] Jimenez also expected to gain support within military sectors unhappy about the nondemocratic direction of the Sánchez Cerro regime. However, this support did not materialize.

In February 1933, disguised as a mechanic, Jimenez disembarked at the port of Chimbote, near Trujillo, where he received the support of Aprista networks. Following the failure of a plan to begin the uprising in Trujillo, Jimenez headed to Cajamarca. The uprising began as scheduled at dawn on March 11, 1933, with the support of the Eleventh Infantry Regiment stationed there. After issuing a proclamation declaring the 1931 elections fraudulent and calling for a return to democracy, Jimenez took over the city of Cajamarca. He proclaimed himself "supreme political and military commander of the Republic and delegate of the revolutionary organizations" in opposition to the Sánchez Cerro government.[62] Jimenez published a manifesto to legitimate his action in which he condemned Sánchez Cerro for putting himself "outside of human laws." He claimed to have no intention of staying in power. In another statement directed to the military, he framed his actions in patriotic terms, claiming that he was defending the law: "I do not come to make a political revolution or a social revolution. I come to make an almost biological Revolution, to restore the very life of the Nation blinded in all its sources; the very honor of Peru."[63] In Cajamarca, Jimenez relied on APRA networks. A participant in the events, Aprista schoolteacher Manuel Chávez Vargas, recalls having trained a group of men for military action and prepared to support Jimenez's effort.[64]

When Jimenez marched toward Trujillo, he found that government forces had destroyed a railroad bridge and interrupted the movement of troops by train to Trujillo. Before he could get to Trujillo, he was stopped by government troops that had been ordered to put down the uprising. Reinforcements had also arrived from Lima. On March 14, he was defeated in the town of Pacasmayo before he even reached Trujillo. Although there are different versions of the details of the events, the records show that after surrendering, Jimenez committed suicide. He was buried unceremoniously in Trujillo. Jorge Basadre assesses him in a very positive light: "Jiménez will go down in history for his tenacious rebelliousness against Leguía, a sign of his civic courage and moral honesty, for his effort to give Peru the first clean Electoral statute in more than a hundred years of independent life, for his spirit of sacrifice, for his honesty."[65]

Despite his connections to APRA, Jimenez regarded himself as an independent military officer fighting for the national interests. His supporters were by no means all Apristas. For example, the person that he left in charge of Cajamarca once the city had been taken, Captain Daniel Villafuerte, had fought against the Apristas in Trujillo in 1932. Jimenez believed that the revolution in Peru needed to be the work of various groups and not only of APRA: "The revolution or transformation that we pursue must be the work of all of them and . . . Aprismo alone, with all the resources you mention[,] is not enough for this."[66] Apristas were understandably concerned about the role the party would play following the uprising. Writing from Panama to Jimenez in Chile, Sánchez had asked about what would happen after an armed uprising: "We do need to know the plans and projects for after the victory, and to discuss them quickly and sincerely. In this order, we need to know your ideas, those of the group that you integrate."[67] When Sánchez proposed a plan to put APRA in power, Jimenez responded that APRA needed to participate together with other political groups.

After the revolution occurred, Jimenez proposed dissolving the existing congress and returning to democracy. Emphasizing the need for APRA to work with other political groups, Jimenez wrote to Sánchez saying that: "Following the revolution resulting from the combined effort of all groups, each will have equal participation in the constructive work, and each will be subordinated only and in direct relation with the effectiveness of its action, that to be pure and clean—as you advise—must be characterized by abnegation and detachment."[68] In the use of such terms as "pure" and "clean," Jimenez demonstrated a highly idealistic conception of a politics that needed to be driven by sacrifice rather than self-interest. He called for a strong leader who would not "defraud" the revolution and could lead the country back to democracy. In the back and forth with Sánchez, Jimenez suggested that under the present critical circumstances, the needed leader ought not be tied to a particular political party—reading between the lines, he was pointing to himself rather than Haya as the appropriate individual.[69] Jimenez also complained about the difficulties of financing a revolution and about how little money was available for his purposes.

While sympathetic to APRA, Jimenez was also highly critical of its exclusivist tendencies. He accused it of "sectarianism" and of promoting the belief that only Apristas could "save Perú"—a popular slogan within the party. He wrote to Sánchez and told him, "You attributed to yourselves exclusivity regarding the methods and people who would save the country. And believe me, this has done you much damage and has created resistance that today has backfired and almost unconsciously served the dictatorship."[70] He recommended that Apristas reframe their discourse and become more open to the possibility of working with other political groups in the national interests. He pointed to the tension between APRA's program that promoted larger ideals and the exclusivism of the party's methods. He proposed that Apristas themselves close this gap: "Now it is necessary to explain to the country . . . that within that motto, apparently I repeat, strictly exclusivist, there is the spiritual amplitude that the rest of its declaration implies."[71] The motto he refers to is probably "Only APRA Will Save Peru."

Jimenez expressed uncertainty about the exact roles to be played by civilians and the military. He wondered whether it was best to begin the revolution with a traditional military coup or with a civil insurgency to be backed by the military.[72] He was not shy about criticizing the members of his own institution. Following the failed Trujillo uprising, he expressed great disillusionment with and "indignation" regarding the military men he had called on to second the effort. At that point, he advocated for a civil insurgency to "destroy, do away with, in a nutshell, this immoral Army, without ideals and without concept of his mission."[73] However, he was careful to exempt from this sweeping criticism "a respectable group of chiefs and officers who still have patriotic sentiments in the heart and an ideal in the brain but who cannot act for reasons of rank or because they constitute a small proportion within the respective organisms."[74]

Sánchez Cerro's government ended suddenly, not with an Aprista revolution or a military coup but with the president's assassination. On April 30, 1933, after Sánchez Cerro had finished reviewing troops at the Santa Beatriz Hippodrome, a young Aprista named Abelardo Mendoza Leiva shot the president as he departed in an open car. Members of the presidential guard and police officers standing guard killed Mendoza Leiva, firing on him and ramming his body with bayonets. Following Sánchez Cerro's death, persecution against Aprista briefly ended as his successor, Oscar Benavides, declared a period of amnesty. The new government released Haya and other Apristas from prison. Although the amnesty period did not last long, it allowed Apristas to briefly operate as a legal party once again.

Between Insurgency and Democracy, 1934–1945

Over the course of the next decade, Haya displayed great versatility in his continued attempts to reach the presidency while leading a proscribed party. Armed factions of the party continued to stage small-scale insurrections, although none succeeded. Apristas hatched at least one revolutionary plan in which they turned to a foreign government for support. Haya did not discourage these efforts. When he finally published his book *El antimperialismo y el APRA* in 1936, eight years after writing it in Mexico, he had not removed its calls for revolution: "As in Nicaragua, as in Haiti, as in Santo Domingo, etc., imperialism will attack. Apra, in that case, will lead, perhaps, the national single front towards the fields of war.... The front in such case would be political and military, would become national. The fight would take on a more violent dimension, but it would be another aspect of the same struggle against the same enemy."[75] Yet the anti-imperialist language of the 1920s no longer reflected the thinking of an older and more mature Haya—he was now forty-one years old. Confident of the power of his party, Haya increasingly attempted to break into the political system by convincing high-ranking military officers to stage a coup on APRA's behalf. He also knew that every time Peru held an election, he could play the role of kingmaker by directing his followers to vote for the candidate of his choice.

In his persistent attempts to reach power, Haya now had to contend with the virulent opposition from the pages of the newspaper *El Comercio*. In addition to its long-standing connection to Peru's most powerful families, who felt threatened by APRA's revolutionary rhetoric, the newspaper's editor, Antonio Miró Quesada, had a brother, Luis, who served as minister of foreign relations in Sánchez Cerro's first cabinet.[76] Sánchez Cerro's assassination fueled *El Comercio*'s opposition to APRA. The confrontation took a violent turn when an Aprista assassinated Antonio Miró Quesada and his wife in 1935. The brother, Luis, took over the newspaper and continued the campaign against Haya and his party.

While Apristas still rose up in arms, the frequency of these insurrections diminished over the course of the next decade. In 1934, uprisings occurred in Lima, Ayacucho, and Huancayo. There was just one in 1935, in Cajamarca; one in 1939, in Lima; and one in 1945, in Ancón, a small town just north of Lima.[77] None ever matched the scale of the 1932 Trujillo insurrection. Apristas staged some of these uprisings; others were APRA inspired. The government discovered some of the plots and foiled them before they started. Others went forward, but none ultimately succeeded in bringing APRA to power. No available documents connect Haya directly to any of these uprisings. In the unlikely event that such documents ever existed, his followers most likely destroyed them or kept them secret. Some of these insurrections seem destined to fail from the outset: longtime Aprista leader Armando Villanueva, who would much later be the party's presidential candidate in 1980, tells how he met up with a group of three hundred other Apristas on the night of November 25, 1934, on the slopes of the El Agustino hill overlooking Lima to stage an armed uprising. When he asked about the weapons, his coconspirators informed him that they first needed to capture the military barracks to get access to the weapons inside. Villanueva says he did not even know how to operate a Mauser rifle. Needless to say, the insurgency failed and Villanueva and many of his fellow conspirators ended up in jail.[78]

After Benavides declared the party illegal again in 1934, Apristas attempted to start a revolution in the Central Andes in Huancavelica, Ayacucho, and Huancayo. The Huancayo insurrection of November 26 was the least successful of the three: led by a shoemaker, Abraham León Gamboa, the insurgents encountered resistance and failed to take over the town's police station. That same day, in the early-morning hours, revolutionaries in Ayacucho succeeded in taking over the city for four days. A lawyer, Arístides Guillen Valdivia, led this movement, and a number of young students at a school, Colegio Nacional de San Ramon, backed him. These students also belonged to the Federación Aprista Juvenil. Following the Trujillo model, the Aprista insurgents in Ayacucho stormed an army barracks and subsequently took over the city, naming Guillen the *prefecto revolucionario*. After three days, the rebels lost control of the city and fled into the mountains, because they knew they had little chance of defeating the superior forces of the Third Infantry Regiment that had arrived from Lima to recapture the city. The third insurrection occurred on November 27 in Huancavelica, when a group made up of Aprista civilians and members of the civil guard were able to take over the police station and the prefecture. At this point, they contacted the Aprista rebels in Ayacucho to coordinate a march on Huancayo, the most important city in the Central Andes. Using the railroad, the Huancavelica contingent attempted to take over a critical communication point that joined railroad and highway, only to find that it was heavily fortified. During the morning hours of November 29, they engaged in a four-hour combat on the banks of the Ichu River, a couple of kilometers outside the city, with members of the Third Infantry division. Yet they lacked the manpower and the weaponry to win. They eventually retreated to the city, where they met defeat. An incident with echoes of the Trujillo massacre occurred when the rebels of the hostages being held by the Apristas in the city were murdered. This incident fueled anti-APRA propaganda, particularly since one of the prisoners was a priest.[79] Aprista historian Murillo Garaycochea speculates that if the insurgents had been able to achieve a better degree of coordination, they would have been in a good position to take over the strategic cities of Huancayo and La Oroya (a mining town) and thus take over the central part of the country.[80]

In some of these uprisings, Apristas sought support within the ranks of the military. Under interrogation, First Sergeant Cárlos Polo Osorio offered a detailed account of those involved in a foiled uprising that was to have been led by Colonel César E. Pardo, who belonged to the APRA party. The witness claimed that he had intended to inform about this and

> that today he went to the Barracks of his Corps at 11 A.M., intending
> to inform Captain Orion Zuñiga that Sergeants Victor Añvarado [*sic*],
> Elias Morales, Osacar [*sic*] García, had spoken to him to agree on a
> movement they were planning to start in the following days with
> Aprista elements headed by Colonel Pardo, and that he [Polo Osorio]
> had had meetings with them in the house of Sergeant Garcia, who
> was in agreement with several non-commissioned officers of Regiments
> No. 5 and No. 7 and of the No. 2 Artillery Regiment, and with
> ex-Sergeant Jave of the same Regiment. And a certain Minaya whom
> he [Polo Osorio] does not know, and that all of the orders for the

movement were in the hands of Sergeant Garcia. They had not fixed a date but it had to be before the 20th of the month.[81]

The conspiracy, according to this witness, also included at least one former member of the military.

Another witness tells of how Apristas attempted to recruit him at a movie theater. Second Sergeant Benjamín Guaremino Lara of the Fifth Infantry Regiment claimed that he and another sergeant, Arcado Romero Colchao, had gone to the movies at Cine Buenos Aires when an individual approached them and encouraged them to join APRA: "A gentleman arrived and began to talk with sergeant Romero and pointed to the movements that had existed in Cuba and those in Peru, and then they entered the cinema he and his companion. . . . On another occasion he found the same gentleman on Buena Muerte street and he talked to him about the same issue, inciting him to participate in an uprising and to adopt the same measures taken by the Cuban sergeants."[82] The comment shows that members of the Peruvian military were aware of the recent Cuban Revolution of 1933, in which the noncommissioned officers, most famously Sergeant Fulgencio Batista, had participated.

The party also continued to offer military training to some of its own members. In the 1930s, Apristas joined rifle clubs (*clubs de tiro*) to gain greater access to weapons.[83] The Federación Aprista Juvenil (APRA Youth Federation), founded in 1934 and modeled on Communist youth groups, trained its members in both propaganda and military tactics. Many decades later, Aprista Alfonso Aguilar recalled how he received such training in the late 1940s and early 1950s: "Then I was given the mission of breaking the La Mochica Bridge, the railroad bridge. I did comply with breaking something made of iron and that is to be something of a terrorist; I had to take dynamite, bombs to break the rails because that was the order that the union gave me."[84] In this interview, conducted in 2008, decades after Peru experienced the rise of the Shining Path and terrorism had become an everyday word, Aguilar acknowledged that his activities could be seen in that light. At the time, the government had categorized Apristas as terrorists. An undated pamphlet titled *La verdad sobre el APRA* (The truth about APRA) accused APRA of being a Communist, international, and anti–United States party. The pamphlet used quotes from APRA's own texts to demonstrate the violent nature of the party. For example, it cited Haya's own words in *El proceso de Haya de la Torre* to claim that "Aprismo primarily means a revolutionary force capable of reaching the most extreme actions."[85]

One of the photographs inside the pamphlet showed an Aprista prisoner, Jorge Wong Chávez, standing in front of the APRA flag—which featured a map of the entire continent (proof of APRA's international nature)—next to an arsenal of weapons.[86]

During the 1930s and 1940s, APRA was not alone in its violent approach to politics. Sánchez Cerro's party, the Unión Revolucionaria, had taken an increasingly Fascist direction under its new leader, Luis A. Flores, and developed a political-military structure. At a public ceremony on December 30, 1934, the party's militia organization, called the Black Shirts, received its black shirts.[87] In Cuba, political violence became common during the 1930s and 1940s.[88] In Brazil, both the Communist Party and the Integralists (Fascists) engaged in acts of violence during the 1930s.

Yet despite his party's violent actions, Haya remained hopeful that he would be able to reach power through elections. In 1936, Benavides decided to hold an election. Despite the fact that APRA remain proscribed, Haya attempted to run and to register his party with himself as the presidential candidate and Colonel Pardo as the vice presidential candidate. According to Víctor Villanueva, Haya named Pardo a candidate as a gesture of peace toward the military.[89] Haya had met Pardo in London in 1925 after Pardo had conspired against Leguía and been deported. Pardo had earlier been a loyal supporter of President Piérola. He eventually became one of APRA's staunchest military supporters. Over the course of his career, he had held both military and elected positions such as director of the Escuela de Tiro (Target Shooting School), division general, military attaché to Japan, elected congressman for the province of Yauyos in 1919, and congressman for APRA in 1931 and 1945. He participated in Aprista insurrections as early as 1931, when he was allegedly planning an uprising on December 5, 1931, in Lima.[90] He would eventually leave the party, following the failed October 3, 1948, uprising.[91]

The Apristas announced their presidential slate on clandestine radio. Yet the National Election Board rejected the candidacy on the usual grounds that APRA was an international party, outlawed under Article 53 of the Constitution. Haya saw this as a confirmation of his party's strength: in a letter to a Colonel Pardo in Bolivia, Haya complained, "Here, they denied us our rights for being 'international,' but the public has seen this as the government's confession that Aprismo would have won with or without fraud."[92] Denied the right to participate, Haya gave APRA's support to Luis Antonio Eguiguren, head of the Social Democratic Party. When Eguiguren appeared poised to win, Benavides canceled the election and remained in power for another three years. The event certainly reminded Haya of his own power as a kingmaker in Peruvian politics. Faced with defeat, Haya seemed undaunted in his propaganda efforts as he instructed a group of Apristas in Bolivia to print thousands of leaflets accusing Benavides not only of electoral fraud but also of having ceded Peruvian territory to Colombia in 1934, following a territorial dispute that had led the two countries briefly to war.[93]

Also in 1936, Colonel Pardo and exiled Apristas living in Chile turned to the government of Bolivia, seeking support for an Aprista revolution. The planned uprising would begin in the south of Peru. Pardo wrote to Haya from Santiago and informed him that he would be traveling to La Paz to contact members of the Bolivian military government.[94] The delegation met with President Colonel David Toro, a Socialist, who claimed to have met Haya. The Apristas solicited money and weapons from the Bolivian government and promised to pay for them by using bonds issued by the Aprista party. Toro could not offer financial support, but he did promise to provide weapons, including bombs and machine guns. One obstacle that prevented the plan from going forward was the issue of money—Pardo made a plea for money to be sent from Santiago and from Arequipa.[95] Haya wrote from Lima and approved the plan for revolution. He also expressed his concern about letters being intercepted by the Peruvian government and asked that there be no further detailed communications on this plan.[96] By all indications, the plan was something he went along with and was not his brainchild. Either way, it never came to fruition.

Three years later, Haya made a much more deliberate effort to bring his party to power. He did so by linking his fortunes to a military coup to be led by General Antonio Rodríguez, President Benavides's minister of government (*ministro de gobierno*) and third vice president. Haya recognized that at this particular point in time, APRA did not have sufficient support within the military to stage an uprising.[97] Rodríguez had risen through the ranks by demonstrating loyalty to the governments of Leguía, Sánchez Cerro, and Benavides. He had never shown any overt sympathy for APRA and did not fully trust the party. Yet he calculated that it would be best to have APRA, Peru's major political force, on his side rather than against him. Historian David Werlich describes Rodríguez as "a rank opportunist" who obtained the backing of both APRA and the Unión Revolucionaria.[98]

Haya knew Rodríguez through the members of a Masonic lodge.[99] Both men also belonged to the Centro Esotérico Nacional (National Esoteric Center), which was directed by Augusto Benavides Diez Canseco, a relative of the president and a good friend of Haya's. A number of powerful men belonged to the center: "Many high ranking leaders of the army, business-men, people with high political positions and the head of Apra himself all participated in the activities of the Center."[100] Roy Soto Rivera describes a clandestine interview between Haya and Rodríguez on September 18, 1938, at which they agreed on the need to reestablish democracy in Peru.[101] Ro-dríguez may also have been motivated by the medium at the center, who "pretended to put Rodriguez in touch with the spirit of Ramón Castilla" and convinced Rodríguez that he was somehow destined to take the reins of power.[102] General Ramón Castilla (1845–51, 1855–60) had been one of Peru's most respected nineteenth-century presidents.

On February 19, 1939, General Rodríguez attacked and took over the na-tional palace while Benavides was away on a navy excursion. He relied minimally on APRA to stage this coup: most of his followers were officers loyal to the deceased Sánchez Cerro and the police connected to the min-istry he directed.[103] Of the fourteen officers who supported Rodríguez, only one, Lieutenant Colonel Gerardo Gamarra Huerta, was an Aprista sympa-thizer.[104] Like his predecessor Jimenez six years earlier, Rodríguez legiti-mated the coup by claiming to restore democracy and to be independent of any political group: "This military movement lacks a political dimension. It is merely a movement of constitutional restoration, to return . . . the State's juridical norms to the country from which they had been taken."[105] The ill-fated coup attempt ended when a member of the president's guard killed Rodríguez. After the failed coup, Haya would claim that Rodríguez had sup-ported APRA, because a proclamation had allegedly been found on Rodrí-guez's dead body declaring APRA legal once again and authorizing Aprista exiles to return to Peru.[106]

That eventful year, Benavides ended his term, elections were held (with-out APRA participation), and Peruvians elected Manuel Prado Ugarteche as president. During Prado's presidency (1939–45), APRA's violent activi-ties greatly diminished. Nonetheless, persecution continued and most Apristas regarded Prado as their bitter enemy. Committed to reestablish-ing his party as a legitimate political actor, Haya and party leaders eventu-ally succeeded in returning to legality in 1945. That year, APRA joined the Frente Democrático, a coalition that brought the moderate lawyer José Luís Bustamante y Rivero to power. Still, the law barred APRA from running a presidential candidate—a direct attempt to keep Haya from the presidency.

Haya apparently continued to maneuver to reach the presidency via a military coup. Víctor Villanueva—later Haya's political enemy—claims that in retaliation for not being allowed to run for office, Haya had attempted to stage a coup on March 18, 1945, to prevent Bustamante from becoming an electoral candidate. According to Villanueva, Haya ordered an uprising by a parachute unit based in the town of Ancón, north of Lima, with which he had contact. The uprising failed. Villanueva portrays Haya as somewhat delusional about the military support for bringing APRA to power: "The units that only existed in Haya's feverish imagination did not respond."[107] Another coup attempt apparently involved a tank battalion, yet this attempt also failed.[108]

Democratic Interlude: The Frente Democrático, 1945–1948

In 1945, APRA finally achieved legal status once again after eleven years of clandestine existence. The party was allowed limited participation in a democratic election: it could present candidates for Congress, albeit not for president. APRA joined a coalition of parties, the Frente Democrático, to support the presidential candidacy of Bustamante. Under Bustamante, APRA enjoyed a majority in the Senate (28 out of 46 seats) and held close to a majority in the Congress (46 out of 101 seats). Party discipline made APRA a formidable force against the independent and politically inexperienced president, who lacked a strong political base. Haya, disappointed by the fact that he had not received the expected position of prime minister (the term for the head of the cabinet), took an adversarial position toward Bustamante. Using its congressional majority to block Bustamante's austerity policy of lower spending and higher taxes, APRA managed to leverage its power to gain three cabinet positions in the government. Haya clearly had more political skill than Bustamante.

The three years of the Bustamante government were a time of political stalemate.[109] A popular saying at the time—"With Bustamante we neither go backward nor forward"—conveys the feeling of this period.[110] Apristas contributed to this stalemate by wielding their power in Congress. And Peru's traditional political elite—an oligarchy—remained a powerful player, unwilling to yield its political influence: "The political liberalization was premature and unsustainable, primarily because traditional political elites were unwilling to concede power to a popular mandate, and the representatives of the popular political power—APRA especially—were unable to seize political control or negotiate a stable, long-term political opening."[111] Peru followed the broader pattern in Latin America in the years following World War II, when democratic governments rose and quickly fell throughout the region. There, the short experiment with democracy ended with a return to de facto governments.

With a hold on Congress, APRA promoted policies of state expansion for redistribution of wealth, including salary increases for workers, food subsidies in urban areas, and public works such as the building of schools and hospitals.[112] In his continued quest for political legitimacy, Haya had backed away from APRA's more radical agenda: "After a decade and a half of Aprista promises to attack vigorously the nation's fundamental problems, the efforts of its congressional bloc disappointed many Peruvians. APRA did not sponsor comprehensive programs for agrarian reform, labor, or the country's Indians."[113] The party that had claimed to stand for anti-imperialism also faced much criticism for supporting a contract granting oil exploration rights to the International Petroleum Company. APRA responded to accusations by arguing that the concessions were consistent with its program of promoting foreign investment under the supervision of a strong national state.

APRA extended its influence during this period by controlling the union movement through the Confederación de Trabajadores del Perú. Unionization increased dramatically as the government recognized 264 new unions between 1945 and 1947. Throughout the public sector, APRA also attempted to exert its influence by forming cells of loyalists. In this way, "APRA penetrated the unions, secondary schools, and universities, which then came under partisan party control."[114] According to Aprista Alfonso Velasquez, "In the year 1945, on January 2 of 1945, as it was the last semester of the government of Manuel Prado, I began to work at the Ministry of Agriculture in the area of supplies; so I worked there and in the month of April I founded the first Aprista employee cell of the Ministry of Agriculture in April of 1945."[115] If Velasquez's recollection of the dates is correct, this infiltration activity may even have begun during the last months of the Prado government, before Bustamante came to power in July 1945.

Over the course of the Bustamante government, conflict between the legislative and executive branches worsened, as did relations between APRA and President Bustamante. By mid-1947, a coalition of conservative and leftist legislators opposing APRA closed down the Senate by walking out. This move temporarily shut down the entire congressional system and allowed the president to legislate by decree. In August, APRA wielded its power over the labor movement to call a general strike. Subsequent street demonstrations led to violence. In February 1948, fears of a military coup increased as Bustamante claimed that an Aprista plot had been discovered. By this time, the president had removed and replaced APRA's three cabinet secretaries. He named an anti-APRA general, Manuel Odría, as minister of government and police.

Meanwhile, violent activities perpetrated by Apristas continued. On January 7, 1947, an Aprista (some accounts claim two) assassinated Francisco Graña Garland, editor of the conservative daily newspaper *La Prensa*. APRA denied any link to the assassination. Other, less publicized incidents linked Apristas with political violence. In June 1947, an Aprista employee apparently connected to the APRA youth organization was arrested at Lima's Jockey Club for having explosives.[116]

Although Haya took it upon himself to speak out against violence, he could not erase the fact that he had previously failed to put a stop to the armed commandos within the party. In a speech on June 18, 1947, to the National Assembly of Aprista Labor Unions, Haya warned labor leaders not to "permit the opposition to force them to violence."[117] Yet only a few years earlier, Haya had published an article in a Chilean newspaper, *La Opinión*, that left the door open to violence. In the article, he denounced the link between conservative Civilistas and the military in Peru, accused them of keeping APRA from participating in an open democratic process, and ended the article by citing President Piérola: "When the doors of legality close, the doors of violence open."[118] Yet a report from the U.S. embassy in Santiago filed at the time the article appeared downplayed the seriousness of Haya's words. It mentioned the fact that Aprista leaders in Chile rejected Haya's call to violence, and it added that the Peruvian embassy in Chile "did not attach great importance to the possibility of Haya de la Torre's resorting to violence because he was too interested in saving his own skin."[119]

The deteriorating conditions under Bustamante prompted both Aprista and conservative members of the military to prepare to stage an armed uprising or a coup. Víctor Villanueva describes the period as that of a brief honeymoon between APRA and the military, claiming that Haya met with members of the military at the Casa del Pueblo during the Bustamante government: "Who would have thought that Haya de la Torre had so many generals who had studied with him at the Trujillo Seminary, or the number of colonels who were his friends in Europe, or the number of other officers who 'always sympathized with aprismo.'"[120] Many may have anticipated the prospect of an APRA victory in the next election. Villanueva portrays Haya as naïve regarding the organization of a revolution and as envisioning support for APRA where it did not in fact exist. He mocks Haya for becoming enthusiastic and believing in a 1944 offer of five hundred machine guns to be sent from Argentina to support an APRA uprising. The Peruvian liaison for the alleged shipment, Lieutenant Colonel Alfonso Llosa, the military attaché at the Peruvian embassy in Bolivia, was in fact a fervent anti-Aprista.[121]

The Callao Insurrection of 1948

At two o'clock in the morning on October 3, 1948, a group of navy officers and soldiers, many sympathetic to APRA, staged a mutiny in the port of Callao. They seized a number of ships in the navy fleet, as well as installations on shore, including the Real Felipe Fortress, whose massive stone walls had been built during the late colonial period as part of the system of strengthening the Spanish Empire's defenses. The success of the revolt depended on APRA's armed units to go into the streets to block the army units from arriving too quickly and thus allowing the navy to secure the locations they intended to take. Yet after the revolt began with the firing of guns by the *Almirante Grau* at two o'clock that morning, the navy rebels were left on their own. Some Aprista forces did join the uprising—apparently, Apristas took over the central telephone exchange in Lima.[122] Some military failures also occurred in the taking of some of the strategic locations. By two forty-five that afternoon, government troops had taken back the Real Felipe Fortress from the rebels. The Naval Academy at La Punta was also retaken. By October 4 the revolt had been put down. The death toll was sixty men on both government and rebel sides, and 175 civilians.[123] President Bustamante outlawed APRA following the revolt. Haya maintained his contacts in the military and selected Major Luis Contero to reorganize APRA support within the military. The continued conspiratorial activities further weakened Bustamante and paved the way for General Odría's successful coup of October 27. Due to the failed uprising, the party was forced to endure another eight years of formal exclusion from politics.

The role of Haya in APRA's last major insurgency remains difficult to pinpoint based on existing sources. Major Villanueva wrote the most extensive analysis of the events. He was a participant who felt personally betrayed by Haya and later severed his connection to the party. Villanueva attributes the failure of the insurrection to Haya's reluctance and indecisiveness and accuses him of having withdrawn the party's support at the last moment.[124] Villanueva portrays Haya as somebody whose decisions were driven by emotions. He claims that Haya withheld the party's support at this particular juncture because he believed success could only be guaranteed by securing the support of army generals. In a public defense of his position at the third national party congress, almost ten years later, Haya accused those who launched the uprising of impatience: "I want to remind you here that if things had followed another path, the patient path, which implies not having succumbed to the sin of impatience, we would now in 1957 be finishing the Aprista period started in 1951."[125] Haya was of course referring to his expectations of an easy APRA victory had Bustamante been able to finish his term and had the next elections been held on schedule.

Villanueva had first met Haya in 1939, shortly after the failed coup that ended with the death of General Rodríguez. At the time, Haya had asked to see Villanueva, who recalls being taken to the house where Haya was hiding, located between the districts of Barranco and Chorrillos, near the fields used for practice at the military school. Villanueva was seduced by Haya's charming personality:

> Haya is a formidable conversationalist. At performances or popular demonstrations, he dialogues with the crowd; in private, he gives speeches. He shuffles all subjects with great versatility and avoids indiscreet questions in an impeccable manner. He is sometimes profound, superficial when he wishes to be, but is always charming. He is a great teller of anecdotes, has a prodigious memory for names and dates, is tireless when speaking and almost always manages to catch the attention of his listeners. He has a magnetic personality and, when presenting topics that he believes will please an interlocutor, it was never difficult for him to convince that person and draw him into the fight. . . . During the five hours that our interview lasted, he laid out for me the synthesis of the Aprista doctrine, gave the apology for his party, narrated his struggles, expressed his yearnings, told me about his ideals.[126]

Their talk lasted from ten o'clock at night until three in the morning. Villanueva claims that Haya had a split personality: one a very human and idealistic Haya, the private one; the other, the public Haya, who played to an audience and always sought adulation. This meant that Haya was always changing his decisions according to circumstance and according to "his moods, to the person whom he is addressing, whom he is listening to, and, perhaps, even the workings of his stomach, if not the stellar conjunctions of that day."[127] He accuses Haya of wavering on the issue of violence, sometimes opposing it and other times at least paying lip service to the need for bloodshed. He describes an occasion when Haya gave the green light for an armed insurrection with Aprista civilians, then changed his mind.

The events leading up to the 1948 insurrection, as described by Villanueva, suggest that Haya was under a great deal of pressure to control the military wing of the party at a time when APRA had achieved legal participation. In November 1947, the party assigned Villanueva to lead APRA's Comité de Defensa, an armed unit that included both civilian and military personnel. Villanueva claims that Haya had recently attempted to dissolve this unit because it had been involved in incidents of violence that gave the party a bad name, and that Haya viewed them as a kind of mafia.[128] Villanueva claims that he convinced Haya that this unit needed to be reconstituted if APRA was to promote a revolution. Haya allegedly remained indecisive about reconstituting the party's defense forces because he believed that a military coup would bring the party to power.[129] In Villanueva's judgment, General Juan de Dios Cuadros, commander general of the Second Light Division, and other generals were misleading Haya about the extent of his support in the army.[130]

The party's military faction was clearly alive and well at this point. Villanueva describes how he reorganized units and obtained weaponry. He was often forced to be resourceful, as when he turned to some chemistry students to help fabricate homemade bombs. The party had its own intelligence-gathering network that included "electricians and telephone workers [who] came to inaccessible places, providing valuable reports. Fruit vendors, newspaper vendors, shoeshine boys, and nocturnal drunkards did the same thing during the night; the mobile surveillances were in charge of the organization of drivers and the efficient Dipa [an intelligence unit within the party]."[131] Villanueva thanked the party's supporters for their cooperative spirit. He identified a number of APRA cells nationwide that could be counted on for support, as well as organizations of officers in the army, the police, the air force, and the navy. Regarding the party's support in the military, Villanueva even engages in some sociological analysis in his writing. He claims that support for APRA was highly correlated to higher levels of education within the military: "There are certain units such as the Military School, armored units and others that employ technical personnel for which Creoles with a certain degree of culture are chosen. It is precisely here that the Apra was able to capture people and organize revolutionary cells."[132]

In January 1948, before traveling to the United States on a lecture tour, Haya allegedly gave the green light for an armed uprising against the Bustamante government with military support. The leaders included Major Villanueva, General Cuadros (secretary of war), and air force colonel José Extremadoyro Navarro. The APRA Action Committee was led by Ramiro Prialé, Carlos Manuel Cox, and Jorge Idiaquez. Infighting within APRA contributed to stalling the uprising. Party leaders Manuel Seoane and Luis Alberto Sánchez, who objected to the timing, put a halt to ongoing preparations. On February 6, Villanueva and his followers challenged the party leadership and decided to go ahead with the revolt on their own. Aware of Villanueva's plans, the party leaders managed to immobilize many of the units involved.[133] While the conspiracy was not made public, President Bustamante was probably aware of these events. Soon thereafter, pro-APRA general Cuadros was replaced as secretary of war by anti-APRA general Armando Artola. According to Daniel Masterson, "The transfer of General Cuadros from the command of the strategically important Second Light Division in Lima to the Superior Council of the Army in late February deprived APRA of its most prominent potential ally in the army."[134] However, Apristas were not the only ones dissatisfied with the government. President Bustamante also had detractors among the anti-APRA factions in the army. That year Lieutenant Colonel Llosa staged a conspiracy in the town of Juliaca, an important transportation hub in the southern Andes on the shores of Lake Titicaca, the highest navigable lake in the world. The conspiracy, intended to put General Odría in power, failed to gain support, and Llosa and his coconspirators fled across the border to Bolivia.

Haya remained committed to the strategy of using a military coup to bring APRA to power. He hoped that General José del Carmen Marín, who represented a middle ground within the army, would lead such a coup. Haya "was clearly attracted by Del Carmen Marín's proposal as it seemed to him to represent a less risky path to national power than a broad-based revolutionary movement."[135] Yet Major Villanueva remained suspicious of the general. When no coup took place during the following month, Villanueva and other APRA militants decided to act on their own, contrary to the strategy devised by Haya.

Villanueva and Haya had a major falling-out after the failed revolt. Villanueva even accused Haya of having tried to assassinate him. Following the 1948 uprising, Haya briefly reconstituted the Comando Revolucionario (a group of retired military officers sympathetic to APRA) until it was disbanded following General Odría's coup. Villanueva claims that the members of the dissolved Comando Revolucionario all left the party, some joining the Communist Party, some joining the new centrist party Acción

Popular, and some eventually joining the numerous leftist revolutionary movements that emerged in the 1960s.[136]

The failed 1948 insurrection struck a final blow at any attempt by Haya to seek support with the military. The events leading up to 1948 had severely undermined discipline in the army. The new government of General Odría now sought to purge the armed forces of Aprista influence. Immediately following the rebellion, more than 800 navy officers (out of 4,800) faced arrest and interrogation.[137] A number of officers were forced to retire early. The search for Aprista cells in the army and air force also intensified. Within the armed forces, the "main concern was the re-establishment of discipline and morale within the officer corps after the massive breach of discipline inspired by Apristas during the three years of the Bustamante government."[138] The military trials that began in 1950 led to the convictions of both military and civilians. Out of the 248 military men who were tried, 238 received convictions. However, the sentences were not very severe, and this "apparently reflected a desire on the part of the tribunal to avoid exacerbating naval morale problems resulting from the Callao mutiny."[139] Masterson credits Odría with having healed the divisions within the armed forces, and he contrasts him with Perón, who left badly divided armed forces in Argentina.[140]

The memory of the 1948 insurrection now became another means of reinforcing the military's anti-APRA identity. At an evening ceremony the following year in the municipality of Lima, civilian and military authorities gathered to honor the fallen members of the military. In his speech, Colonel Alberto León Díaz referred to APRA as a "sect" that sought to undermine national integrity: "The Homeland expects of its professional soldiers not only days of Glory but that they surrender their life when it demands the defense of their sacred interests and when some sect, as the one that unfortunately has existed until the 3 of October, tries to undermine the integrity of the nation."[141] By this point, APRA's ideological influence in the armed forces had waned as a result of the disarray within the party and its diminished prestige as a revolutionary force.

Under Odría APRA seemed to have less leverage than ever in Peruvian politics. Political persecution of Apristas became fierce. Haya, who had attempted to leave the country by seeking political asylum, remained isolated for five years in the Colombian embassy in Lima as the Odría government labeled him a terrorist and refused to let him leave the country. Party leaders scattered in different parts of Latin America were left trying to formulate policy by corresponding with one another across the continent.

Meanwhile, Odría developed close ties with the United States, which looked favorably on the general for his anti-Communist stance. Peru received military aid from the United States, and Peruvian officers developed stronger ties to the country, often traveling to tour U.S. military bases. A couple of high positions within the navy were even filled by U.S. naval officers, part of a U.S. naval mission. After the government finally granted Haya permission to leave Peru in 1954, he initiated a fifteen-year sojourn in Europe, returning to Peru only for brief periods. Although his role as leader of APRA remained unquestioned and he continued to attempt to reach the presidency, he had ceased to enjoy the kind of influence that he had during the 1930s and 1940s.

The Ultimate Betrayal? Coalition Politics, the *Convivencia*, and APRA's Alliance with Its Former Enemies, 1956–1968

An anecdote tells of jailed leader Prialé being hidden in the trunk of a car and shuttled back and forth from prison to the government palace to negotiate APRA's return to legality with the Odría government. Haya was living in Europe at the time. When the return to legality finally occurred in 1956, the political waters had shifted considerably. APRA now faced competition on its own turf with the emergence of a new reformist politician, Fernando Belaúnde Terry, of the Acción Popular. According to Sinesio López Jiménez,

> APRA ceased to be a majority party . . . and became part of a polarized extreme pluralism. This situation redefined the political conflict and the rules of the game that became more complex and competitive. For the APRA leadership the political game was more difficult: it had to join the institutional game in the best conditions and take care of its own political space threatened by new competitors, especially by Belaunde and Acción Popular. All this led the APRA, when faced with a choice between representatives of the oligarchic order ([Hernando de] Lavalle and Prado), to select the one that offered better conditions for its incorporation into the institutionalized political life and to combat Belaunde, who posed a threat to the APRA leadership, but was regarded sympathetically by the Aprista rank and file.[142]

As the country moved once again to democratic rule in 1956, Aprista leaders chose to forge an alliance with their former enemy Prado, who won the presidency once again in 1956. This period is known in Aprista history as the *convivencia*. By this point, APRA's conspiratorial activity had come to an almost complete standstill. Under Prado there were only two attempted conspiracies: a military-civil conspiracy in February 1958 and a police uprising in July 1959.[143] Neither received APRA support, proof of "the strength of the APRA's adherence to the conditions of the *convivencia* with the Prado government."[144]

Meanwhile, developments within the military were also undermining APRA's status as the country's main reformist force. The Centro de Altos Estudios del Ejercito (whose name was soon changed to Centro de Altos Estudios Militares [CAEM]), founded in July 1950, promoted a much greater role for the military in the country's modernization and economic development: "National development and national defense were thus considered closely interwoven concepts. The instruction offered at the CAEM for senior armed officers was aimed at defining the military's relationship to Peru's basic problems of underdevelopment."[145] The CAEM was modeled on the National War College (Washington, D.C., founded in 1947) and a similar center for military studies founded in France in the 1920s. Brazil and Argentina established similar centers.[146] Odría initially attempted to marginalize the CAEM. However, the center soon gained prestige because its "reformist doctrine was a far more acceptable alternative than the autocratic paternalism of the Odría regime."[147] However, as Masterson points out, the CAEM was not the only place where this kind of thinking was taking place. Officers outside the center were also seeking a more expanded role for the armed forces in the process of national development. For example, General Edgardo Mercado Jarrín "insisted that the army was one of the key agents for change as it best understood the strategy of modernization and most acutely appreciated Peru's array of social and economic problems."[148] It is important to point out that this kind of thinking was well in line with the French tradition imparted decades earlier by the French military mission.

The election of 1962 brought the issue of APRA-military relations once again to the forefront of Peruvian politics. APRA's strategy of negotiation had apparently paid off: after thirty-one years, the party was once again allowed to run in a presidential election. Haya seemingly had the opportunity to become president. Yet as the election approached, it became clear that the military would not tolerate Haya as president. In a conversation with U.S. ambassador James L. Loeb, the navy minister Vice Admiral Tirado Lamb warned that the United States should refrain from supporting APRA given the military's continued resistance to the party. There were a number of charges against APRA—one being that despite its statements to the contrary, it remained at heart a Communist party. Another factor playing against Haya was the persistent anti-APRA indoctrination within the military.

Haya's alleged homosexuality now also became a political issue. In a statement to the U.S. ambassador, another military leader, General Aléjandro Cuadra Ravines, "claimed that an important factor motivating the military's antipathy to APRA was the belief of many officers that Haya de la Torre was a homosexual."[149] Aprista leaders attempted to smooth over these accusations by claiming that Haya remained in contact with military leaders, some of whom had approached him with the hope of cabinet positions in a future APRA government.

In the months before the election, high-ranking officers in the Peruvian military expressed their concern to U.S. officials that if Haya were to win, he would attempt to severely weaken the armed forces. Vice Admiral Lamb claimed that Haya would "destroy the armed forces within three months."[150] The final tally gave Haya a slight lead, but not a high enough proportion of the votes to win outright. The election would have to be decided in Congress. On July 4, in a speech at the Casa del Pueblo, Haya referred to rumors in the U.S. press and announced to his followers "that the military had vetoed his candidacy."[151] The military warned Prado that Haya would be unacceptable as president, then proceeded to claim that there had been electoral fraud, thus paving the way for a coup against Prado.

By the time the coup occurred on July 18, Haya had also bowed out and reached an agreement whereby Odría would take the presidency with Seoane as vice president. Speaking to his supporters, Haya highlighted the theme of sacrifice that had always helped to frame the party's history. This time, he told his disappointed followers, he was sacrificing himself for Peruvian democracy.[152] When the military junta headed by General Ricardo Pérez Godoy organized new elections the following year, Haya ran again, but he lost to Belaúnde, the leader of Acción Popular, the new center-left party that had managed to steal the mantle of reform from APRA.

A wave of insurrections during the 1960s now pitted the armed forces against newly emerged Communist parties, some made up of ex-Apristas disillusioned by the party's shift to the right. Luis de la Puente Uceda, founder of the Movimiento de Izquierda Revolucionaria, had been a member of APRA. His organization's attempt to mimic a Cuban-style uprising with *focos* in the Andean region stood no chance of success against the Peruvian military. A new kind of insurgency had emerged. The kind of joint civilian-military uprisings that had brought APRA and military men to-gether during the 1930s and 1940s now seemed inconceivable. However, APRA's military capabilities had not completely disappeared. Following a military coup in 1968 that prevented Belaúnde from completing his term as president, APRA leader Armando Villanueva called for a "counterrevo-lution."[153] Although it consistently had been neutralized both on the bat-tlefield and in the electoral arena, APRA seemed to have remarkable staying power; it "remained Peru's only coherent and disciplined political party . . . [and] still retained significant populist appeal."[154]

The political crises that beset the Belaúnde government (1963-69) were to some degree exacerbated by APRA's congressional opposition to Be-laúnde's reforms. The situation paved the way for the direct intervention of the military under General Juán Velasco Alvarado, who initiated a wide-ranging set of reforms that had now been talked about for almost four decades. When Belaúnde took initial steps toward agrarian reform, APRA found itself in the ironic position of opposing the very reform that had once been part of the party's original platform. The Aprista program of 1931 based on the Mexican Constitution of 1917, put in place during the revolution, had included nationalization of foreign companies and agrarian reform. The party had progressively backed away from this program as it saw itself in-creasingly hampered in its ability to gain power in Peru. Now events had come full circle as the armed forces implemented the reforms that Haya and APRA had introduced into Peruvian politics four decades earlier. In an in-terview with Masterson, Haya insisted that "the Velasco government has simply stolen our program."[155] Masterson sees the Velasco regime "as the cul-mination of the armed forces' search for a meaningful national mission."[156]

Conclusion

Now living the last years of his life permanently in Peru, and probably con-vinced that he would never hold an official position of power, Haya wit-nessed what decades earlier would have seemed impossible: an end to the enmity between his party and the military. The process was initiated by General Francisco Morales Bermúdez, who had ended the Velasco govern-ment with a military coup in 1975. While visiting Trujillo, Haya's home-town, in May 1976, Morales Bermúdez, as the new president, made a public speech calling for the need to put behind the legacy of the 1932 Trujillo massacres. The military had continued to commemorate the Trujillo events with yearly tributes to the dead soldiers and officers at Lima's main cemetery. The military high brass attended these ceremonies. That year the commemoration of the Trujillo massacre took place as scheduled on July 7. Yet Morales Bermúdez eventually prevailed and the ceremonies ceased altogether after this. His gesture paved the way for APRA's definitive incorporation into Peruvian politics.

When Peruvians elected the Constituent Assembly in 1978 to write a new constitution and return the country to democracy, APRA obtained the highest proportion of votes. Haya became the president of the assembly. The new relationship to the military had not gone unquestioned. In the high-level discussions among the military that preceded Haya's taking office, a general had apparently objected to the naming of military officers as Haya's aides-de-camp (*edecanes*), claiming that he did not need them. The political leader who had lived in hiding for a quarter of a century and had been the object of hatred of generations of men within the military was now entitled to a military guard. According to his own account, in a gesture intended to honor Haya as a kind of elder statesman of Peruvian politics, President Morales Bermúdez went ahead and chose colonels as Haya's *edecanes*, a higher rank than that held by the president's own guard of honor.[157] Much water had passed under the bridge to arrive at this moment.

On the afternoon of July 28, 1978, Peruvian Independence Day, Haya arrived at the building of the Peruvian Congress as president of the Constituent Assembly. A member of the reception committee, Aprista leader Andrés Townsend Ezcurra, captured the irony of this historic moment, in which Haya was greeted by a military detachment: "I was by his side at that spectacular moment, at the doors of Congress, when a military detail honored him, while the band played the march of the flags."[158] Another Aprista, Haya's then-secretary Luis Alva Castro, described a teary Haya, now finally stepping into the halls of power, almost half a century after he first ventured into Peruvian politics.[159]

And what of the party's inclinations to violence? In July 1974, APRA had participated in a series of violent riots that sought to undermine and depose the Velasco regime. Militarized groups within the party continued to operate at least until the 1970s. More recently, in 2005, army officer Ollanta Humala (later president from 2011 to 2016) met with APRA's oldest leader, Armando Villanueva. According to Humala, Villanueva incited him to stage a coup against then-president Alejandro Toledo (2001–6).[160] To this day, APRA's armed wing lives on in popular memory, dubbed *bufalos* in commemoration of Manuel "Búfalo" Barreto, the leader of the Trujillo insurrection.

Haya receiving military honors as he arrives at the Congress as president of the Constituent Assembly, 1978 (Caretas).

CHAPTER THREE

Marinera with the Yankees
Haya de la Torre and the United States

Am of the opinion that Haya deserves our moral support in
appropriate fight against Communism and I understand at least
one American university is contemplating conferring an honorary
degree upon Haya which in my opinion would be fortunate at
this time.

—Secret telegram to U.S. secretary of state, December 2, 1947

While the U.S. embassy in Lima was notably sympathetic to the
party and urged President Prado to relax the campaign against the
organization, several Aprista leaders enjoyed red-carpet treatment
during visits to the United States under State Department auspices.

—DAVID WERLICH

On January 11, 1929, the U.S. chargé d'affaires in Venezuela, C. Van H.
Engert, informed the State Department that the Peruvian "agitator" Víctor
Raúl Haya de la Torre "does not, as yet, appear to have visited Venezuela,
and it is not likely that he will be permitted to do so if the Venezuelan
Government knows anything about his identity. The Legation will therefore informally and discreetly advise the authorities of his past activities.
There is no local branch or organization of the 'Alianza Popular Revolucionaria Americana' (APRA) in existence." The United States could rely on
President Juan Vicente Gomez to clamp down on organizations of this
nature, Van H. Engert informed. Nonetheless, Haya needed to be carefully
watched. Van H. Engert assured his superiors that "should Haya de la Torre
arrive in this country the Legation will endeavor to follow his movements
and will report further."[1] The U.S. concern about a man seeking to start
a continent-wide revolution and whose party defined its first objective as
"action of the countries of Latin America against Yankee Imperialism" is
understandable. Already Haya had demonstrated that he meant to implement his ideas. After founding APRA in Paris 1926, he had traveled to Mexico
the following year and developed a plan to start a revolution in Peru and

overthrow the dictator Augusto B. Leguía. Between July and December 1928, he visited Guatemala, El Salvador, and Costa Rica, denouncing U.S. imperialism before receptive audiences. He had allegedly established contact with the Nicaraguan revolutionary Augusto Sandino, and at least one Aprista, Esteban Pavletich, had joined Sandino's forces in fighting a guerrilla war in Nicaragua against the U.S. Marines.[2] Alerted of Haya's arrival in Panama in 1929, U.S. authorities in charge of the Panama Canal prevented him from disembarking. Forced to remain on the German ship *Phoenicia*, Haya found himself sailing to the ship's next destination, the port of Bremen, Germany. For the next two years, Haya remained in exile in Berlin, Germany, where he continued to organize his young political movement.

Two and a half years later, when Haya had returned to Peru as presidential candidate for his party, U.S. ambassador to Peru Fred Dearing seemed to be describing an entirely different man from the one who had caused concern in Venezuela. Dearing informed his superiors in Washington that "from what I know up to this point . . . I should think that if he should become president of Peru, we should have nothing to fear and on the contrary might expect an excellent and beneficent administration of strongly liberal tendencies in which justice in the main would be done, and a period of confidence and wellbeing be initiated."[3] After the meeting, Dearing reported that Haya's warmth had impressed him.

What provoked such dramatically different reports by U.S. diplomats on Haya in the course of two short years between 1929 and 1931? What had changed? Had Ambassador Dearing merely succumbed to the charm of Haya's charismatic personality? Had Haya told Dearing what any U.S. ambassador would want to hear? A pragmatist, Haya clearly understood that he had stepped out of the role of student rebel and into that of a political leader who needed to work with the United States if he was ever to reach the presidency of Peru. Haya's critics have accused him of abandoning his anti-imperialist rhetoric and cozying up to the United States. They have interpreted the change as further evidence of the many ways Haya abandoned his youthful revolutionary ideals and courted his former enemies in his quest for power in Peru. Yet the story is not so simple. As Nelson Manrique acknowledges in a critical history, "APRA's doctrine was never as radical as people have been led to believe."[4]

Over the course of the next decades, Haya and U.S. officials remained wary and cautious in their dealings with one another. The United States never fully supported APRA's quest for power in Peru. Haya continued his public criticism of the U.S. support for dictatorships in Latin America.

As Steven Schwartzberg points out, "Throughout his long career he showed himself capable of bitterly criticizing the United States and American policy whenever he thought such criticism was warranted."[5]

This chapter traces the changing relationship between APRA and the United States. It examines Haya's writings, the contact he and other Aprista leaders had with U.S. government officials both at the embassy in Lima and in the United States, and his relationship with independent U.S. citizens interested in supporting various political causes in Latin America. The chapter's title refers to an elaborately choreographed Peruvian dance in which the man and woman circle one another with handkerchiefs in their hands, drawing close at times, then moving far away from each other. It serves as a metaphor that captures the caution on both sides as Haya sought the support of the country he had early labeled as "Yankee imperialist" and as the U.S. government assessed whether to back an opposition politician in Peru who promised to support successive U.S. policy objectives of combatting first Fascism and then Communism in Latin America.

Haya's relationship with the U.S. government and with North Americans went through a series of stages. Throughout his political career, he attempted to rally the United States to support APRA. His connection to the country began early when, as a young student in Lima, he met the North American writer and teacher Anna Melissa Graves, who contacted him with a network of international Protestant organizations interested in promoting pacifism. After he left Peru in 1923, Haya began to cultivate ties on his own with U.S. intellectuals eager to support leftist causes in Latin America. The Good Neighbor Policy opened up doors for Haya to establish more direct contact with U.S. government officials charged with fostering a better relationship with Latin America. With the advent of the Cold War, Haya played the anti-Communist card as he attempted to position his party as an ally of the U.S. fight against Communism in Latin America. Yet throughout his career Haya also remained a critic of what he saw as the United States' double standard when it came to democracy in Latin America. As Schwartzberg points out, "Haya's support for the United States was never uncritical. He was particularly opposed to its efforts to group together both dictators and democrats. It was only for the oppressed peoples of the Old World, he protested, that Washington had eyes and ears; only for them that it offered anti-totalitarian condemnations. In its dealings with Indoamerica, it had treated the brutal tyrannies of Guatemala and Peru as though they were equal to the effective democracies of Colombia, Costa Rica, and Chile."[6]

Haya the ideologue cannot be understood separately from Haya the prag-matic politician—they must be studied together. His views on the role of international capitalism in Latin America can be traced back to the Aprista program he laid out in his book *El antimperialismo y el APRA*, written in 1928 and published in 1936. Here Haya proposed a mixed system of capitalism and redistributive government for Latin America, modeled on the ideals of the Mexican Revolution. This program would become central to popu-list governments throughout the twentieth century. In his assessment of the need for national governments to put limits on foreign capital, Haya cre-ated a model that can be seen as a precursor of dependency theory, which arose decades later in Latin America to analyze the issue of economic de-velopment from a global perspective. Proponents of dependency theory (*de-pendentistas*) would attribute Latin America's disadvantageous position in the global economy to structural factors that kept the region in the role of producer of raw materials, a continuation of its colonial legacy. During the 1960s and 1970s, *dependentistas* also struggled with the issue of how to pro-mote the transformation of Latin America into an industrial economy. Whereas *dependentistas* called for a strong state to develop national indus-tries as opposed to multinational corporations, Haya saw foreign capital as the path for Latin America to industrialize: "Foreign capital in our coun-try represents technology, because foreign capital is the one that brings ma-chines. We are not an industrial people because we have not created the machine; we only use the machine that comes from abroad. Therefore, for-eign capitalism that is inevitable in countries such as ours, fulfills its stage; the important thing is that it do so under the control of a State that truly represents the majority of the nation that is interested in not being ab-sorbed."[7] Haya thus lays out important concepts for a theory of the mod-ern state in Latin America that serve as a basis for analyzing Latin America's classic populist regimes of the twentieth century, as well as the radical pop-ulist regimes of the twenty-first century.

Haya's views on the relationship between Latin America and the United States changed in response to changing political events. When he launched APRA in 1926 as a party opposed to "Yankee imperialism," the United States was pursuing the foreign policy colloquially known as gunboat diplomacy in Latin America. During the 1930s, Haya witnessed a dramatic change in U.S. policy toward Latin America. He pointed out in his writings that even before Franklin D. Roosevelt came to power, Herbert Hoover had already begun to withdraw the U.S. Marines from Nicaragua. In 1934, Roosevelt repealed the Platt Amendment that had allowed the United States to legally intervene in Cuban domestic affairs. When Mexico nationalized the oil fields in 1938, the United States had abstained from intervening militarily. These concrete changes in U.S foreign policy led Haya to conclude that Roosevelt could be trusted to uphold his new Good Neighbor Policy. Haya even regarded these changes as a victory of APRA's anti-imperialist propaganda during the 1920s: "Faced with this promising change in Pan Americanism—that in many ways represents a victory of the Indoamerican anti-imperialist crusade—Aprismo faced the new reality without exaggerated illusions but free of intolerant prejudices."[8] Schwartzberg concludes that Haya was unique in this sense as "the first anti-imperialist in Latin American history who believed that Yankee imperialism—if met with sufficient Latin American resistance and cooperation—was ultimately destined to do more good than harm."[9]

While living in hiding from 1934 to 1945, Haya remained in contact with U.S. embassy officials. He met with numerous U.S. citizens who visited Peru, some directly connected to the Roosevelt administration's efforts at cultural diplomacy in Latin America. Haya pledged APRA's support in the global fight against Fascism. The United States sought to combat Nazi propaganda and remained wary of Latin America's small but influential communities of citizens with German and Japanese heritage. Haya also remained critical of the U.S. support for dictatorships in Latin America.

As the party regained its legal status during the three years of José Luís Bustamante y Rivero's democratic government (1945–48) following the end of World War II, U.S. concerns in Latin America centered on Communism as the Cold War began. Haya aligned himself and his party with the United States in the global fight against Communism. Contact between Haya and Aprista leaders and the United States intensified. Aprista leaders traveled to the United States, where U.S. government officials often gave them red-carpet treatment. Political ties to the United States also increased after APRA took control of the Confederación de Trabajadores del Perú (CTP)—the non-Communist labor organization affiliated with the American Federation of Labor and Congress of Industrial Organizations (AFL-CIO).

The call in the 1926 article "What Is the APRA?" for "action of the countries of Latin America against Yankee imperialism" can be misleading when it comes to understanding Haya's view of the economic role of the United States in Latin America. Just two years later he had developed his ideas further when he wrote *El antimperialismo y el APRA*. Haya inverted Vladimir Lenin's dictum about imperialism as the last phase of capitalism and claimed that in Latin America, imperialism represented the initial phase of capitalism, necessary for economic development. In *El antimperialismo y el APRA*, Haya argued that Latin America needed to build strong anti-imperialist nationalist states that would be able to channel the benefits of foreign capitalist investment toward the middle, working, and peasant classes of Latin America. In his response to a public letter from Víctor Guardia Quiros, the Costa Rican lawyer and writer, that had been published in *Repertorio Americano* and *La Tribuna*, Haya made a distinction between Aprismo's fight against economic imperialism and its desire to avoid national and racial rivalries: "In our struggle against modern imperialism—capitalist, industrial, from the United States, the imperialism that most strongly subjugates us—there does not and cannot exist a national or racial rivalry."[10] The statement reflects a Marxist internationalist thinking that ignores nationalism and concentrates on the economic mode of production as a driving force of history.

The evolution of Haya's ideas over the next decade reflects his hopes of improved relations between North and South. In his 1941 *La defensa continental*, a collection of articles written over the course of the previous few years, Haya argued that the Good Neighbor Policy offered an opportunity for better relations with the United States: "We Apristas have always maintained that our movement is not one of aggressive jingoism against the people of the United States. . . . We know and we cannot forget that North America and Indoamerica are and will be neighbors so long as they exist as populated continents. Our attitude of alertness and of protest against the tendency towards the hegemony of the strongest has had as its constructive inspiration the search for new and more just forms of intercontinental harmony."[11] The first part of this statement clearly defies the facts. Understanding the power of language and propaganda, Haya ceased to denounce "Yankee imperialism" and coined the phrase *continentalismo sin Imperio*—hemispheric unity without an empire. To confirm the seriousness of his intentions, the following year Haya eliminated the term "Yankee imperialism" from the party platform.

Haya both understood the nuances within U.S. politics and acknowledged his indebtedness to anti-imperialists in the United States. He pointed out that "until now the best books against North American imperialism—we say it frankly—have appeared in North America."[12] Haya cited Scott Nearing and Joseph Freeman's book *Dollar Diplomacy* as proof of the fact that North Americans themselves acknowledged the existence of imperialism. He also cited an article in *Current History* by Senator Henrik Shipstead that recognized the role of U.S. imperialism in Latin America.[13]

Later in his life, Haya acknowledged more fully the role of the United States in the development of anti-imperialist thought. In a 1953 letter to Luis Alberto Sánchez, he wrote, "Anti-imperialism—as a movement and as a term—was born in the United States between 1890 and 1900. The first anti-imperialists that were called such—that were under that banner, using the word and concept—were Bryan's Democrats in their struggle against Theodore Roosevelt and Henry Cabot Lodge."[14] The Democratic Nebraska congressional representative (1891–95) William Jennings Bryan ran for president three times and served for two years as secretary of state under President Woodrow Wilson (1913–15).

Haya the Student Revolutionary, 1918–1931

One of the first accounts of Haya in the United States appeared in the *New Leader*, a liberal weekly newspaper dedicated to labor issues. The articles praised his role as a student leader in Peru.[15] It was penned by his friend Graves, the writer, teacher, pacifist, and internationalist. This friendship proved to be one of the most influential in his life, as he would become Graves's protégé in later years when he was exiled from Peru. She would connect him to important personalities and providing funding for his studies abroad. The two met as teachers at the Colegio Anglo-Peruano in Lima—today called the Colegio Sán Andrés—which was founded in 1917 by John Mackay, a Scottish missionary, with the support of the Scottish Presbyterian mission. Graves would soon become one of Haya's staunchest supporters. She was a member of the Women's International League for Peace and Freedom, and her "personal wealth helped support numerous peace and social justice efforts. In fact, Graves' generosity would enable Haya to study in England and to devote himself full time to building his APRA movement."[16] During these years, Haya also received the support of the school's director, Mackay. Mackay offered Haya encouragement and financial support for a 1922 trip by invitation to attend a YMCA summer camp in Uruguay and Argentina. At the event, Haya met important student leaders of the University Reform movement in Argentina.

Both Graves and Mackay connected Haya to a network of transnational Protestant organizations and pacifist organizations. For Graves and others, Haya became a symbol of pacifism and of resistance to despotism. They acted as his mentors and also used him to promote their own religious agendas.[17] The Colegio Anglo-Peruano was a center for Protestant social thought: "MacKay's perspective was to prepare Christians and citizens committed to the Kingdom of God, on the basis of Protestant ideas of liberty, equality and social justice."[18] After he was exiled from Peru by the Leguía regime in 1923, Haya found these networks useful for distributing propaganda for his newly founded political movement in 1926. Through Graves and the Protestant networks, Haya had access to a number of important personalities while he was abroad.

After 1923, when the Leguía government deported Haya, accusing him of having participated in a Communist plot, Haya remained connected to these networks. In Panama in 1923, on his way to Mexico, he gave a series of lectures for the Iglesia Evangélica Metodista del Malecón.[19] Once in Mexico, he began to form new contacts of his own. He met various members of the community of expatriate U.S. intellectuals and political figures, admirers of the Mexican Revolution and leftist causes in Latin America. Among them was the writer and journalist Carleton Beals, who would later be critical of Haya for trying to incorporate too many social groups into his political platform. Haya also met Bertram Wolfe, a founding member of the Communist Party of America. Wolfe lived in Mexico for two years, joined the Mexican Communist Party, and was involved in labor organizing that ultimately led the Mexican government to deport him back to the United States. In 1924, Haya traveled with Wolfe to New York and both attended the Fifth Comintern (Communist International) Congress in Moscow later that year.[20] Haya spent the next three years in Europe, where he founded APRA as an anti-imperialist party. In 1927, he returned to Mexico in the hopes of implementing his political ideas.

On his way back to Mexico, Haya visited the United States. As he traveled through the country, he spoke first at Harvard and then at Columbia University. At Harvard, he participated in a debate organized by the Debating Union, where he defended the position that the United States ought to give up the Monroe Doctrine.[21] Graves helped to get him an interview with Senator William Borah in Washington, D.C.[22] Borah was known for his pro-Soviet position. He also spoke at the Institute of Politics in Williamstown, and at the convention of the Fellowship of Reconciliation. He describes a heated moment at the debate at Williamstown in which Horace Knowles (who had been a diplomat in Nicaragua and Bolivia) accused his own country of having assassinated thousands in Haiti, Nicaragua, Santo Domingo, and Mexico. A representative of the navy, whom Haya does not name, lost his temper in response to this accusation. Demonstrating his people skills, Haya intervened to ask "whether he had lost his Anglo-Saxon equanimity and whether it was necessary for a Latino to remind him of it." Upon which, by Haya's own account, the admiral smiled and sat down.[23] Haya also lectured for the League for Industrial Democracy, an organization connected to the Socialist Party.[24] From early on, Haya had understood that Latin Americans could find allies for their cause among liberal, middle-class intellectuals in the United States.[25]

The U.S. government remained wary of the young activist as he traveled south through Mexico and Central America, lecturing and publishing articles about U.S. imperialism in the region. At the time of his travels, the United States was engaged in prolonged guerrilla warfare in Nicaragua, where the rebel Augusto Sandino evaded capture by the U.S. Marines occupying the country. Meanwhile, Haya—an obsessive propagandist—made sure that his ideas circulated widely throughout the region. An activist promoting the idea of continental unity of the countries of Latin America against the United States posed a potential danger to U.S. hegemony in the region. A letter directed to "the Diplomatic and Consular Officers in Latin America and Mexico" began as follows: "The Department has been informed that Señor Víctor Raúl Haya de la Torre, a Peruvian citizen, contemplates a tour of certain Latin American states, presumably for the purpose of disseminating anti-American propaganda."[26]

His articles appeared in journals and newspapers from Costa Rica to Argentina. He visited Mexico, El Salvador, Guatemala, and Costa Rica, preaching ideas of anti-imperialism. He also sent his followers to lecture on Aprismo and founded Aprista cells in a number of Latin American countries, from Cuba to Mexico to Argentina. Other Apristas helped him in his tasks. The State Department kept tabs on Aprista Magda Portal, who in 1929 embarked on a propaganda tour of the Caribbean and lectured on anti-imperialism to audiences in Havana; San Juán, Puerto Rico; Santo Domingo, Dominican Republic; Barranquilla, Colombia; and San José, Costa Rica. She called for the unity of Latin American nations against U.S. imperialism and for an alliance between workers and middle-class intellectuals in the revolutionary process.[27] A Peruvian poet and political activist, Portal would soon become the most powerful woman in the APRA party.

Upon the request of the Department of State, U.S. embassies in Central America tracked Haya's movements through the region and wrote dispatches on his activities for Washington. A dispatch of February 2, 1929, from El Salvador claimed that "the only branch of the organization in this country is the one that was inaugurated by Raúl Haya de la Torre in Santa Ana during his stay here months ago," but the dispatch stated that this branch remained inactive. Haya had intended to found a branch in San Salvador but had had to leave the country before he was able to do so.[28]

The embassy also reported on fund-raising activities, including the printing in Mexico of ten thousand buttons with the portraits of Haya and Sandino, to be sold to raise funds for the party.[29] Haya attributed his expulsion from Guatemala and El Salvador to U.S. influence on these governments: "I was expelled from Guatemala and El Salvador as a result of insinuations made by the North American Legation, in other words, as a result of orders by the government of those countries whose only liberty is that of abusing their own peoples."[30] On February 15, 1929, the U.S. embassy in Costa Rica reported that Haya, whom it called an "agitator," had sailed from Puntarenas to Panama on the German steamer *Phoenicia*, had subsequently been arrested on board that ship when it stopped at Cristobal, and then had continued to sail to Bremen, Germany—this brought the beginning of Haya's German exile, which lasted until his return to Peru in 1931.[31] Haya blamed his expulsion from Panama on the influence of the United Fruit Company on the U.S. government, although he stated that he did not yet have the documents he needed to prove his allegations.

From Student Rebel to Persecuted Political Leader, 1931–1945

After his two years of exile in Berlin, Haya returned to Peru in 1931 as presidential candidate for the party he had founded. By the time he met with Ambassador Dearing in 1931, Haya had clearly understood the need to relinquish his old role as student rebel and adopt a new one as presidential candidate. As he stepped into the fray of Peruvian politics, Haya transformed himself from the young student activist who had denounced "Yankee imperialism" into the presidential candidate who would need the support of the hemisphere's most powerful country to succeed. Haya was keenly aware of the difference between operating in the virtual setting of international propaganda and operating in the real setting of Peruvian politics. A U.S. embassy report dated April 22, 1931, before Haya's return to Peru, accurately anticipates the direction Haya would take: "Although I do not want to underestimate what the Apristas might do in the way of making trouble in view of their ultra-nationalistic tenets and their violent anti-imperialist campaign, I still think that authority and the desire to keep it would sober them and make them try to get down to realities."[32] Haya understood politics as the art of negotiation and compromise rather than absolutes. That he eventually may have gone too far for many of his supporters in the compromises he made is undoubtedly part of the story of Haya. His pragmatic political instincts help to explain his longevity as Peru's most important twentieth-century politician.

The transition from student rebel to pragmatic politician was a gradual one. When he arrived in Talara, the newspaper *El Tiempo* reported that he delivered an address at the Peruvian Club denouncing the United States and claiming that APRA "proposed, above all to end once and for all the 'reign of Yankee imperialism' which has been dominating the country for many years, under the protection of the last Peruvian Presidents."[33] By the time he arrived in Lima the following month, Haya, a brilliant public orator, was presenting a more nuanced position on imperialism to the thousands who gathered to hear him at Lima's bullring on August 23, 1931. Yet while he changed his emphasis, his ideas were not new—he was drawing on a more comprehensive explanation of the phenomenon of imperialism, one that he had already written about in *El antimperialismo y el APRA*. In an almost professorial style, he explained that imperialism represented a necessary economic stage in Peruvian development: "Imperialism is not, therefore, a dangerous and frightening word; imperialism is an economic concept.... Imperialism means the expansion of those people who are more advanced in technical production toward the less developed peoples."[34]

The night before, in a speech at APRA's first party congress, Haya explained that the Aprista program recognized "the need and the benefits of foreign capital that arrives and brings advances, but [conditions] and demands measures to control its possible excesses."[35] Continental unity would help the countries of Latin America to combat the dangers of imperialism. Latin America depended on foreign capital in order to industrialize. The APRA program even proposed that foreign capitalists be represented at what Haya called an "Economic Congress," an institution that would promote what he referred to as functional democracy with decision-making power granted to the representatives of each of the economic agents in the country, from labor to capital.

After Haya lost the 1931 election to Colonel Luís Sánchez Cerro, his life changed dramatically. He went from being a presidential candidate in the spotlight to being a persecuted individual. Increasing violence between APRA and the Sánchez Cerro government resulted in the Emergency Law of 1932, which declared APRA illegal on the grounds that it was an international party. Haya hid for a number of months, until he was finally arrested and imprisoned. He spent over a year in Lima's penitentiary, often in soli-

APRA leaders. *Left to right:* Carlos Manuel Cox, Haya, and Manuel Seaone
(Armando Villanueva Papers, courtesy of Lucía Villanueva).

tary confinement. Letters and cables arrived from all over the world plead-
ing for his release and his security—among them many from his supporters
in the United States. He was finally released in 1933 as part of an amnesty
granted by Peru's president Oscar Benavides following the assassination of
Sánchez Cerro.

The brief period of legality at the outset of the Benavides government
in 1933 soon ended, and another long period of proscription began in 1934.
For the next eleven years, Haya lived in hiding, moving from one safe house
to another in the city of Lima. Apristas refer to this period as "the cata-
combs," a reference to the persecution suffered by Christians under the
Romans. His safe house came to be known as Incahuasi—the house of the
Inca—a reference to Peru's ancient rulers and a sign of the party's *indigenista* sympathies. His articles during these years indicate Incahuasi as the location. Abundant lore exists around Haya's hiding places. Some stories tell
of him dressing as a woman to move from one hiding place to another and
avoid detection. Other accounts tell of how he narrowly escaped death when

government agents arrived to arrest him only moments after he had been alerted and fled. Aprista Alfonso Velasquez claims that Apristas became assiduously punctual, in a country known for its unpunctuality, in order to coordinate secret meetings that could at any point be disrupted by the police. Referring to the month of March 1937, Haya wrote, "This has been a terrible month for me. I hop from one house to another, from one danger to another, these two years have been my most dangerous days."[36]

Yet in contrast with the fate suffered by other Apristas, many of whom were persecuted, jailed, and even killed during this period, Haya's situation remained a relatively privileged one. Even his location appears to have been at many points something of an open secret, both for the Peruvian government and the U.S. embassy. Anecdotally, Pilar Chocano, the daughter of a high-level employee at the Ministerio de Hacienda, stated that her father had once returned from having had lunch with Haya, who was in hiding, only to be gently admonished by President Benavides, who said to him, "You had lunch with the *compañero*, didn't you?"[37] At one point, Haya's "hiding" place was the home of Augusto Benavides Diez Canseco, whose sister Francisca Benavides Diez Canseco was the wife of President Benavides, the leader who was persecuting Haya and APRA.[38]

During this underground period, the U.S. embassy also knew his whereabouts, as Haya assiduously cultivated relations with North Americans. He urged his followers to do likewise and draw on the network of sympathetic U.S. intellectuals to denounce the government that had outlawed his party. In a letter to Sánchez in March 1937, Haya urged him to draw on the support of friendly intellectuals in the United States to denounce the persecution under Benavides: "It would also be advisable to write to the United States to see if now that P is here, intellectuals who are our friend would write a well published letter asking that the horrors cease in Peru."[39] Haya also had greater ambitions and widened his web of contacts in the hopes that the United States might eventually support an APRA government. A 1943 twelve-page report on APRA sent by J. Edgar Hoover, director of the Federal Bureau of Investigation, to the assistant secretary of state claimed, "As of possible interest, it has been noted that Haya de la Torre has probably contacted more Americans and representatives of other governments than the official government of Peru."[40]

The U.S. embassy used Haya and other Apristas to find out more about events in Peru, particularly those concerning the activities of Communist and Fascist groups within the country. Haya attempted to use his relationship with the United States to strengthen his political position within Peru.

There seems to be no evidence, so far, of any kind of coordinated action between Apristas and the United States—rather, the documentation reveals a developing relationship that could be characterized as both friendly and cautious on both sides.

The U.S. embassy remained concerned about Aprista revolutionary activities. In 1934, the embassy reported on a set of letters that had been recently published in a clandestine Aprista newspaper, *Acción Aprista*, proudly linking Haya to the recently slain Nicaraguan revolutionary Sandino, who had defied the U.S. Marines occupying Nicaragua and become a Latin American popular hero. In the 1929 letters, Sandino thanked Haya for his public support and Haya wrote from Berlin that it was both an honor and an obligation to support him.[41] Tabs on APRA's revolutionary activities continued over the next years. In 1936, the U.S. embassy reported that Aprista exiles in Chile had issued bonds for $1 million, to be paid once APRA had succeeded in coming to power through revolution.[42] Later that year, after President Benavides canceled elections for fear of an APRA victory, the embassy informed on an Aprista leaflet that called on party members to help overthrow Benavides.[43] The following year, 1937, the embassy picked up a report on the arrest of a number of Apristas, including Manuel Arévalo, in the city of Trujillo for possession of weapons and subversive propaganda.[44] After his arrest in Trujillo, Arévalo was tortured and assassinated by the Benavides government. He was allegedly favored by Haya as a possible successor. Arévalo remains the most venerated of the party's martyrs, and a huge cross commemorates the place of his death on the Pan-American Highway south of Trujillo.

During the Eighth Pan-American Conference, held in Lima in 1938, Apristas took advantage of the occasion to launch propaganda against the Benavides dictatorship. Pan-Americanism dated back to 1889, when U.S. secretary of state James Blaine organized the First Pan-American Conference in Washington, D.C., to develop greater cooperation on matters of trade and issues of arbitration. Latin American critics saw this and subsequent conferences simply as efforts by the United States to assert its hegemony throughout the region.

In anticipation of the conference, the clandestine APRA publication *Cuaderno Aprista* published an article claiming that President Roosevelt's planned absence from the Lima conference was meant as a protest against General Benavides's dictatorial regime. The mimeographed publication claimed, "It is well known that President Roosevelt has always condemned usurpers and tyrants. No one is ignorant of the fact that the great Yankee democrat, freely elected and re-elected by millions of his fellow-citizens, abominates all those who seize the power of government by artifice and by force."[45] It argued that although Roosevelt had offered an excuse for not attending, the real reason was his rejection of Benavides. The U.S. embassy dismissed the article as "a tissue of half-truth and unwarranted deductions" but forwarded it to the State Department, as it might be of interest "as indicating the unrestrained nature of the APRA publicity campaign."[46]

The party rallied its followers to engage in propaganda during the conference. In a written directive to Apristas nationwide, the party's National Action Committee called on party members to help with the propaganda efforts. A priority was the call for amnesty for Aprista prisoners. Another was to demonstrate the strength of the party, in light of the fact that the Benavides government was interested in proving that the party was weak.[47] The embassy commented on what it stated to be false Aprista propaganda claiming that Roosevelt intended to pressure Benavides to grant amnesty to Apristas. The cause of amnesty was also being pursued in New York by exiled Aprista Alberto Grieve, who on October 21, 1938, met with Frank Tannenbaum, professor of Latin American history and economics at Columbia University; Samuel Guy Inman, professor of international relations at the University of Pennsylvania; and journalists from *Current History* and *Fortune* magazine.[48]

While Haya apparently managed to meet with some of the delegates who arrived in Lima for the conference, he remained critical of Pan-Americanism, which he associated with U.S. dominance in the region. He wrote extensively about the need to replace it with what he called "Inter Americanism without an Empire." He offered an idealized view in which the two Americas retained their separate identities and interacted with each other as equals: "This is not the 'Pan Americanism,' which infers tutelage and patronage, that is to say, disequilibrium, the disdain of the strong and the resentment of the weak. If we abandon the enveloping and absorbing tendency of the old Pan Americanism—under the auspices of which have flourished the imperialist and dictatorial tendencies of so many governments—we shall enter into a new Inter Americanist stage without empire."[49] To guarantee strength, the countries of Latin America needed to unify. He wrote of an incident in which "a little Panamanian negro" had approached him after he gave a lecture in Panama critical of the Pan-American Union. Using a play on words—the word *pan* meaning "bread" in Spanish—the man said, "I think that Pan Americanism is a *pan* [bread] which is going to be eaten by the Americans."[50]

Haya called on the United States to support Latin American economies rather than solely the economic interests of the United States in the region.

Other Apristas were also writing about this issue. Haya cited fellow Aprista Manuel Seoane, who in his book *Nuestra América y la guerra* (published in Chile in 1940) argued that the United States also needed to help strengthen Latin America's economies. Haya stated, "The United States, if it lends the support of its banking resources cannot have the disagreeable role of zealous tutor of these investments, limiting their function only to what is convenient for that country."[51] He argued that the United States must recognize Latin American economic independence and consult the needs of Latin American countries. The money invested by the United States in the region "remains useless, if it doesn't strengthen an Inter-American system of just and bilaterally advantageous economic relations."[52]

While Haya proposed changes in the political relationship between the United States and Latin America, he did not question the division between an industrial North and raw-material-producing South. He referred to "the two great economic camps into which the Americas are divided; that one, in which industrialism predominates, and this one, in which agriculture and raw materials prevail."[53] He described them as "two rhythms, two ways of being and working, of producing and consuming. Two economic levels and two commercial, financial, and in the end political attitudes."[54] His writings do not include a theory of economic development that would move Latin America toward an industrial economy. He cited Wisconsin senator Alexander Wiley's support of the idea of an economic and political union of Latin America. This inter-American union "presupposes what Senator Wiley has just formulated, the coexistence of the 'countryside and raw material' America and the 'industry and capital' America, each structured in separate state groups, capable of equilibrating relations in an effective and durable good neighborliness."[55]

While in hiding, Haya managed to pursue his ties with liberal intellectuals in the United States who were sympathetic to his cause and meet with those who traveled to Lima. The U.S. embassy arranged many of these meetings. On September 8, 1938, the embassy reported on a meeting between Haya and Tannenbaum, whom Frederick Pike describes as "one of the most distinguished Latin Americanists the United States has known." Pike writes that "by 1938 . . . Haya believed he had at least a partial convert in Frank Tannenbaum."[56] Tannenbaum had begun his career as a criminologist and a leader of the International Workers of the World who supported radical causes in Latin America. In Lima, the two men had dinner in Haya's hiding place and conversed until the early hours of the morning.[57] Haya told Tannenbaum that if elections were to be held, APRA would win by a large margin. In the event of a coup against Benavides, the army would turn to Haya, who claimed to enjoy support in the military, particularly among young officers. Haya predicted that even Benavides might still seek his support. The embassy concluded, "Therefore, Haya is convinced he will play an important role in any political change that may occur."[58] Haya reiterated to Tannenbaum "his repugnance with the shedding of blood and declared that he would not try to seek power by force."[59] While Haya told Tannenbaum that he had no plans to attack foreign companies in Peru, Tannenbaum pointed to the inconsistency in Haya's position of seeking to redistribute land used for sugar cultivation but claiming that he would not expropriate the lands of Grace and Company. Regarding the location of the meeting, the author of the embassy report states, "Prudently, he did not say where Haya was and I did not insist in knowing it."[60]

In 1940, Haya received a visit from Inman. Originally a missionary in Latin America, Inman had published books on Latin America and held a number of important positions, such as secretary of the Committee on Cooperation in Latin America (1915–39). He contributed to the formulation of the Good Neighbor Policy, was the first cultural attaché for Latin America (1935), and advised President Roosevelt at the Inter-American Conference for the Maintenance of Peace in Buenos Aires in 1936. When he visited Haya, he was a professor at the University of Pennsylvania. In his book *Latin America, Its Place in World Life*, he observed the change in Haya from student rebel to a supporter of the United States against the Axis powers. Haya had chosen to stay in Peru, "however dark the dungeon or difficult the dodging of the authorities."[61] He had visited Haya at midnight in Lima in a suburb and a location that Inman described as "semi-hiding": "Different indeed was this fleshy, heavy-shouldered, brown-eyed, black-haired, middle-aged man from the flighty young student or the imprisoned martyr I had known in the past. Different also was his fundamental reasoning. Not the imperialism of the United States, but the fascism of the Axis was the great enemy of Latin America. From midnight to dawn, in the presence of a dozen liberal leaders from various sections of America, we discussed the war and democracy."[62] Although Inman doesn't name these leaders, his comment indicates that Haya received visits from Latin American political leaders. Inman commented on Haya's influence on these visitors: "His deep influence on the pilgrims who had journeyed to Lima to see him was evident. More, it was heartening. Especially after the loud shouting of the Axis propaganda machine in the Peruvian capital!"[63]

When Nelson Rockefeller spearheaded the creation of the Office of the Coordinator of Inter-American Affairs in 1941, which he led, efforts at cultural diplomacy intensified. The office sought to promote hemispheric solidarity, including mutual defense and the improvement of commercial and cultural relations among the American republics. It sought to counter similar efforts of Nazi propaganda in Latin America. In 1942, Haya met with Waldo Frank, who was seeking to mobilize support in Latin America for the war effort through a lecture tour sponsored by the State Department. A Hispanophile, Frank was a strong proponent of closer relations between North and South and developed ideas on the need for a spiritual synthesis between the two cultures. The meeting was arranged by the U.S. embassy. In a book published the following year, Frank reported favorably on Haya: "He is strong, solid, energetic, at forty-seven; with the natural body rhythm which one finds in all leaders whose life is strictly harmonized about a single purpose. Unlike other persecuted men, Haya has grown spiritually, and kept his humor."[64]

While pursuing ties with Haya, U.S. embassy officials also continued to display caution in their dealings with the Apristas. In a 1942 letter to Secretary of State Cordell Hull, Laurence Duggan, who had been appointed personal adviser for Latin America to the secretary of state, alluded to close ties between APRA and Roosevelt's government. Duggan informed Hull that the Aprista leader Seoane had returned to Chile from the United States and that "Seoane made a very favorable impression upon me." He also alluded to the fact that Vice President Henry Wallace "has been receiving information regarding Peruvian internal conditions from Seoane." With a note of caution, however, he suggested that the embassies in Cuba and Chile be instructed to keep an eye on Aprista activities in those countries, as well as "to make a point of cultivating Aprista leaders."[65]

The U.S. embassy remained concerned about whether APRA would pursue violence to gain political power. Considering APRA's anti-imperialist rhetoric and the significant U.S. business interests in Peru in areas such as mining and petroleum, the United States certainly must have watched the development of APRA with some concern. On January 2, 1945, the embassy in Chile reported to the State Department on an article published by Haya in the Chilean newspaper *La Opinión* that accused Manuel Prado Ugarteche's (1939–45) government of ruling undemocratically with the support of Washington, D.C. Haya ended his article by claiming that Apristas would heed the saying of the nineteenth-century caudillo and president Nicolás de Piérola: "When the doors of lawfulness close, those of violence open."[66]

The U.S. concern with the possible use of violence persisted after APRA became legal and joined the government of Bustamante. On June 23, 1947, the embassy reported on a couple of public speeches by Haya in which he specifically called on his followers to refrain from any form of violence. Yet the same report also informed that according to anti-Aprista newspapers, the APRA youth organization had been inciting violence among soldiers and that an Aprista employee at Lima's Jockey Club had been arrested for possession of explosives.[67] On January 7, 1947, the party was accused of being behind the assassination of Francisco Graña Garland, editor in chief of *La Prensa*, one of Lima's main newspapers. Graña was gunned down while in his car. His newspaper had been highly critical of APRA for supporting laws that would favor foreign petroleum companies—an ironic twist, given APRA's early anti-imperialist stance. Although the assassin was most likely a rogue member of the party, Haya was forced to distance his party from such incidents of violence. With this purpose, Haya met with *La Prensa*'s new editor in chief, Pedro Beltrán, at the French embassy to reassure him that APRA was not interested in violence "and that Pedro Beltran's life was definitely not in danger from the Apristas as Beltran seemed to think."[68] Beltrán had been ambassador to Washington in 1944; he also founded a conservative political party, the Alianza Nacional, and was very critical of Aprista violence.

Haya also tried to reassure foreign businessmen that an eventual APRA government would remain friendly toward them. According to a report from the British embassy, sometime in June or July 1940, Haya met for dinner with a Mr. Allmand, the representative of a U.S. cotton broker in Peru, Andrews and Clayton, and explained that under an Aprista government, foreign firms would have a say in Peru's affairs through representation on a municipal council. The report then dismisses Haya's gestures as mere rhetoric and even dismisses Haya himself, claiming that were APRA to come to power, the more radical elements in the party would soon take over: "In any event, . . . I do not believe that he would be allowed to retain the Presidency for more than a few months. And his followers are certainly not friendly to foreign interests."[69]

We will never know how Haya would have performed had he reached the presidency. However, he effectively used propaganda to position himself as a supporter, albeit a cautious one, of the United States in Latin America. He published numerous articles between 1938 and 1941 expressing his views on the potential for good relations with the United States under the Good Neighbor Policy. These articles were subsequently republished in his

1941 book *La defensa continental*. In his 1938 article "The Good Neighbor: Definitive Guarantee?," Haya claimed that possible threats to his life gave him a sense of urgency to disseminate his ideas: "The majority of the issues that my interrogators raise shall be developed and commented on in a book I have written on this topic. But since it is difficult to ensure that a book will actually be concluded and as a life may end prematurely and suddenly when one is persecuted in Peru today . . . I prefer to put forth here my opinion on certain points."[70]

Haya was responding to a changing international atmosphere both within the Americas and in the global context of World War II. At the 1933 Montevideo International Conference of American States, the United States announced the Good Neighbor Policy. The 1934 Reciprocal Trade Agreement Act had authorized President Roosevelt to negotiate bilateral trade agreements without prior approval from Congress. Under his Good Neighbor policy, the United States ceased to use direct military intervention in Latin America as a policy tool. A series of commercial agreements with Latin American countries allowed the United States to forge closer ties and to open up Latin America as a market for U.S. industrial and agricultural products. With the outbreak of World War II, the United States reached out even more aggressively to Latin American countries to create a continental system of mutual defense. Meetings in Lima and Panama established the Doctrina de la Solidaridad Interamericana, paving the way for the Acta de la Habana at the 1940 Pan-American Conference in Havana, an act that included the Declaration of Reciprocal Assistance and Cooperation for the Defense of the Nations of the Americas.

In *La defensa continental* Haya argued that while the Good Neighbor Policy offered an opportunity for closer ties with the United States, Latin American countries still needed to proceed cautiously with regard to their northern neighbor. The book covered a number of different topics having to do with North-South relations: Indo-American unity, inter-Americanism and Pan-Americanism, democracy and totalitarian imperialism, the internationalization of the Panama Canal, and continental defense. Yet Haya also cautioned that U.S. policy could easily change under a new administration and concluded that the Good Neighbor Policy "toward the people of Indoamerica guarantees security, but not a stable security."[71]

Latin American support of the United States need not be unconditional. Haya remained consistently critical of the United States for its support of dictatorships in Latin America. In a 1938 editorial published in Cuba, he contrasted the U.S. support of Latin American tyrants with its disapproval of European ones.[72] Some years later, in 1945, in a private interview with an unnamed American businessman, Haya continued to complain of the U.S. double standard with respect to Europe and Latin America: "It was inconsistent to send an army of millions of men to combat totalitarianism throughout the world and on the other hand apparently overlook this type of government in Latin America." Haya argued that this kind of approach was damaging to the United States, and that furthermore "this attitude of the State Department made it particularly difficult for leaders of democratic groups, such as himself, to combat a feeling of unfriendliness toward the United States among the rank and file of their members."[73] He thus positioned himself as a reluctant critic, seeking better U.S. behavior to facilitate the support of the APRA party. He also warned that the Argentine government was promoting the dissemination of published propaganda in Lima—he does not refer to the content, but the implication is that this is Fascist propaganda.

Haya believed that the threat of Fascism obliged Latin America to support the United States in this global struggle in defense of democracy. Haya took seriously the threat of Nazism in Latin America, writing that "it is obvious that Nazi fascist imperialism plans to conquer the peoples of Indoamerica."[74] He also pointed to the threat of Spanish Fascism that had made inroads throughout the continent, cloaked in the guise of Hispanism, an affirmation of the continent's Spanish cultural heritage. Haya accused the Benavides regime of alignment with "Nazi fascist imperialism" and thus likened it to other pro-Fascist groups in Latin America. Benavides had demonstrated sympathy toward Germany and Italy and had a lukewarm position toward the United States.

By aligning his party with the United States, Haya hoped to obtain that country's support in his quest for power in Peru. Following the election in 1939 of Prado, a strongly pro-U.S. ally, Haya's task of presenting APRA as a more viable alternative than the current Peruvian government became more difficult than it had been under Benavides. Prado went as far as to round up members of the Japanese community in Peru and send them to internment camps in the United States.

Nonetheless, Apristas continued with their propaganda efforts. And the rumor mill also continued to function. On March 12, 1943, a rumor was circulating in Lima that Haya had received a personal letter from President Roosevelt. In this rumored letter, Roosevelt allegedly advised Haya (still in hiding at this point) that the United States could not give him direct support but would be able to give "at least moral support . . . at some later date."

Yet the U.S. embassy report dismissed the rumor as "farfetched," arguing that had such a letter been sent, the Apristas would have immediately used it to their advantage. The report attributed the rumor to Apristas seeking to cause friction between the United States and the government of Prado, or to others unfriendly to the United States.[75]

The Return to Democracy: Haya Plays the Anti-Communist Card, 1945–1948

In 1945, Peru joined the short-lived democratic springtime that bloomed throughout Latin America following World War II. The moderate lawyer Bustamante was elected president with the backing of a coalition, the Frente Democrático, that included APRA. While Haya had remained banned from running for president, APRA regained its legal status as part of the coalition. For the first time in over a decade, Haya could now act publicly. While he held no official government position, as leader of the strongest political party in the coalition that had brought Bustamante to power, Haya enjoyed a newly gained sense of legitimacy, which extended to his party. Haya held great power and, according to one historian's assessment, "while he formally did not hold any political post, he was the most powerful man in the country."[76] Yet Bustamante refused to become a puppet of Haya. The intensified political conflict between Bustamante and the Apristas added to the instability of this brief democratic period.

APRA now had a strong presence in Congress, as well as among labor unions, universities, and municipal governments. The high-ranking Aprista leader Sánchez was elected as president of Peru's largest and oldest university, the Universidad Nacional Mayor de San Marcos. APRA had now emerged as the head of the CTP, a national union of workers affiliated with the AFL-CIO and its efforts to promote non-Communist labor unions in Latin America.[77] In 1948, the CTP hosted the founding meeting in Lima of the Confederación Interamericana de Trabajadores (Inter-American Workers' Confederation). The head of the CTP was Arturo Sabroso, a textile worker and longtime member of APRA who had been jailed during the times of political persecution. Sabroso's contact with the United States also proved personally useful to him, as he used his connections to the AFL-CIO to help his daughter to go study in the United States.[78]

Haya continued his internationalism by envisioning APRA as a party playing not only on the Peruvian stage but also on a larger, international one. Soon after the party regained its legal status, in a speech on October 9,

1945, in Lima's Teatro Municipal, Haya framed APRA's economic program in global terms. He saw World War II as a historical struggle of Hegelian dimensions between different ideologies. Russia had offered the "thesis" that human liberty needed to be temporarily put aside while a planned Socialist economy guaranteed people economic rights. Nazism presented the Fascist "antithesis" that human liberty could be done away with altogether. After having fallen into a slump, democracy had now moved away from the combination of classical liberalism and laissez-faire capitalism to emerge ideologically renewed and offer a new "synthesis": the reaffirmation of human liberty in the context of a planned economy. Hence Roosevelt's New Deal, which Haya described as follows: "[The] first attempt at economic planning in which the State asserts its role as a factor of production ... is with the 'New Deal' in which the United States announces the possibility of a planned democracy."[79]

How did Peru fit into this scheme? Haya reminded his audience that Apristas had always insisted on the uniqueness of Latin America—he referred to his own theory of "historical time-space." In simpler terms, Haya insisted on the particularities of historical development in each geographic location. In the case of Peru, the Andean region was a defining factor, with its high altitudes and the persistence of its native economies. In *indigenista* fashion, Haya praised the works of pre-Hispanic Peru. He even ended his speech with the Quechua invocation often attributed to the Incas: "Ama Sua, Ama Llulla, Ama Kella," meaning, "Do not steal, do not lie, and do not be lazy." Peru had a kind of double economy—one tied to the rhythms of international capitalism, the other a local economy, slower and poorer.[80] These "two speeds" made Peru's economy very different from European economies. Haya claimed that the country needed to be understood in four dimensions: latitude, longitude, altitude, and time. Apristas offered an approach to a planned economy for Peru: the Economic Congress (harking back to Haya's 1931 campaign), in which different sectors of Peru's diverse economy (including foreign capitalists) would decide together on economic policy and create an economy that would guarantee social justice. He pointed to the need to coordinate the two economies: "We cannot declare ourselves to be proudly insular and close our borders, and say that nothing in the external world interests us during a period of growing interdependence."[81]

Haya was well aware of the ways in which the international atmosphere was changing with the advent of the Cold War. Drawing on his party's long-standing rejection of Soviet Communism, Haya positioned himself as an ally of the United States in its fight against global Communism. Having emerged from hiding, he could now once again operate on the international stage, where he felt most comfortable. Haya remained in contact with the U.S. embassy and offered APRA's help as a bulwark against the spread of Communism in Peru.

By this point, he had begun to play the anti-Communist card quite deliberately as a way of developing better relations with the United States. His party's connection to the AFL-CIO further bolstered the party's non-Communist credentials. On October 29, 1947, an embassy official named Maurice Broderick met with Haya at the Casa del Pueblo, the APRA party headquarters. In his report to the U.S. ambassador, which was forwarded to the secretary of state, he pointed out that "Haya wanted to remind the Embassy that the principal reason for the lack of a large and powerful Communist party and of a large Communist labor group in Peru is the APRA Party."[82] In a secret telegram dated December 2, 1947, U.S. ambassador to Peru Prentice William Cooper Jr. reported that Haya had been his guest at lunch. During the luncheon, Haya spoke of who APRA's allies were among the military members of the Bustamante cabinet. He also announced, according to Cooper's report, that he wished to visit the United States, "mainly for the purpose of solidifying the fight against Communism and informing American labor of its dangers." In his telegram, Cooper conveyed his view that the United States ought to support Haya: "Am of the opinion that Haya deserves our moral support in appropriate fight against Communism."[83]

In May 1947, Haya attempted to involve the United States in Peruvian politics on his party's behalf. At the time, Apristas were planning a coup against the regime of Bustamante. Haya informed the U.S. embassy that a group of Fascist and anti-American army officers was seeking to overthrow President Bustamante. Haya suggested that the United States invite the three Peruvian army officers (Colonel Alejandro Villalobos, General Alfonso Llosa, and Lieutenant Colonel César Pando Esguzquiza) to the United States with the ostensible purpose of observing U.S. democracy and winning them over to the democratic cause. But the underlying motive was most likely, in the words of the U.S. chargé d'affairs, "a desire to rid the country, even though for a brief period, of elements considered troublesome to APRA."[84] The request was not granted.

Haya also continued his use of propaganda to undermine Bustamante. He suggested "the planting of certain information of an internal political character in New York financial circles."[85] Specifically, his hope was that this information—about political divisions in Peru—would prompt financiers to react and that their reaction would encourage greater cooperation between the different branches of the Peruvian government and the APRA party, making it more likely that U.S. capital would flow to Peru. The embassy official commented that this "appears to indicate either that Haya de la Torre does not fully comprehend the American viewpoint concerning the payment of financial obligations or American reluctance to be a cat's paw in internal politics."[86]

No longer forced to live in hiding, Haya was able to travel back and forth outside Peru. He traveled to a number of Latin American countries. He also made three visits to the United States. A number of other Apristas also traveled to the United States, many receiving red-carpet treatment. Sánchez was among the Apristas with the best contacts in the United States. On Haya's first trip there, in 1947, during the Bustamante period, he visited Princeton University, where he met Albert Einstein. The meeting was most likely arranged by Haya's old mentor Mackay, who was president of the Princeton Theological Seminary from 1936 to 1959.

Apristas have continued to exploit the meeting with Einstein for propaganda purposes. They have reproduced the photograph of the two in conversation numerous times. Einstein allegedly claimed that Haya was one of the few people in the world who understood the theory of relativity. Haya, in turn, had incorporated the concept of relativity into his writings with the publication of his book *Espacio—Tiempo Historico* (Historical space-time), which consisted of five essays and three dialogues. Haya argued against a Eurocentric view of history and claimed that Latin America needed to be understood in the context of what he called its own "historical space-time."

During his second trip to the United States, in February 1948, Haya traveled to New York, where he participated in a meeting organized by the *Herald Tribune*, together with prominent figures such as the Socialist leader Norman Thomas, former vice president Wallace, Tannenbaum, the union leader John L. Lewis, Governor Nelson Rockefeller, the human rights activist Frances R. Grant, and the actress, dancer, and singer Claire B. Luce.[87] His third trip took place in May 1948. During this trip, Haya gave a lecture at Columbia University and traveled to California.

In California, he briefly visited his old friend Gabriela Mistral, the Chilean poet, at her home in Santa Barbara. Mistral had won the Nobel Prize in Literature in 1945. She pointed to the contrast between the young student activist she had last seen decades earlier in 1924 in Switzerland and the power-hungry and overweight politician Haya had become. Mistral wrote, "I was saddened to see how these years living on the run, who knows with what other little creoles, and Power, Great Power, have erased, eliminated what Oxford, Switzerland and Europe in general gave him. He has put on a great deal of weight, and as it is not a good kind of weight, he has fatigue and a happiness that is not real. With me he was reticent and optimistic to the point of euphoria, and this was not real. He only showed mistrust toward me—this was abundantly clear. He spent ½ an hour with me. He said he would return. I do not think he will."[88] Furthermore, Mistral lamented what she saw at the fall of APRA and suggested that the party needed to be renewed. Haya recalled the encounter in a very different light, as one in which their earlier friendship had been reaffirmed.[89]

Mistral portrayed Haya as a man whose sense of his own power had gone to his head. After all, Haya had become a kingmaker in Peruvian politics. Bustamante had only been able to win the presidency with Aprista votes. Even fellow Aprista Sánchez noted a change in Haya's personality following the end of his period in hiding, describing him as the "Haya of the period of his drunkenness with power, the Haya of 1947, dry and often uncourteous."[90]

After the failed 1948 uprising in Callao, during which Aprista sympathizers in the Peruvian navy attempted to overthrow the Bustamante government, the government outlawed APRA once again. Haya went back into hiding. When General Manuel Odría staged a coup against the weakened Bustamante government and intensified persecution against Haya, the party finally decided that Haya should seek political asylum to evade capture. By Haya's own account, he wanted to remain in Peru, but he yielded to the wishes of the party after the issue was decided at a meeting.

Mr. Asylum, 1948–1954

On the night of January 3, 1949, Haya got out of the car of a woman friend of his to enter the residence of the Colombian ambassador in Lima. "I whispered my hasty goodbye," he later wrote, "stepped out of the car and through the open gates and strode swiftly across the garden. My belongings consisting only of a small suitcase and a portable typewriter, bumped against my legs as I jogged up the steps. The butler appeared slightly startled, but he took my bag and typewriter, ushered me in and showed me a seat in the hall."[91] When the Colombian ambassador returned home, he accepted Haya's request for aid in obtaining political asylum and informed the Odría government to begin the procedure. Odría refused to do so. Instead, he ordered troops to surround the embassy, install searchlights, and dig trenches around the building to prevent Haya from leaving.

The months extended into a year, then two, three, and eventually five, as Haya remained in the embassy mansion that would be his home for the next five years. The Odría government had refused to recognize his right to political asylum on the grounds that he was a "terrorist" and therefore a common criminal rather than a political refugee. The Peruvian and Colombian governments launched a legal battle over the issue that reached the International Court of Justice in The Hague and that had repercussions on the legal interpretation of political asylum—the case continues to be studied today by students of international law.

In an article he later published in *Life* magazine, Haya described in detail the routine of his days in the embassy. Fearful of going out onto the embassy grounds, he took his morning exercise on the roof of the building. After exercising, he showered, had breakfast in his room, and then spent the morning reading books from the ambassador's library and books bought for him by the embassy staff. He also dedicated his mornings to writing. He had lunch downstairs and then returned to his room, where he read newspapers and magazines, had a nap, and then played ping-pong with the embassy staff. He had dinner with Ambassador Carlos Echeverri Cortés and his wife in the main dining room and then continued with conversation late into the evening, avoiding the topic of politics given the political differences he had with the ambassador. He outlasted Echeverri and saw the arrival of new ambassadors during his stay.[92]

Cars driving past the embassy would sometimes honk their horns in a triple staccato *ta ta ta* in which each staccato stood for one of the syllables of the APRA slogan SEASAP—"Sólo el APRA salvará al Perú" (Only APRA will save Peru): *se, a, sap*. When APRA supporters engaged in bolder shows of support, such as yelling "Viva el APRA" or "Víctor Raúl," they put themselves at risk. Haya tells of how he saw a man arrested in the middle of the night: "He had just shouted my name when 20 policemen pounced on him. They mauled him unmercifully. I could only stand at my window, in the glare of the searchlight, and listen to his screams as they bore him away."[93] Haya also described lighter moments such as birthday parties for the children of the ambassador inside the embassy, and the honor he felt at being allowed to carry in the cake with lighted candles. A barber periodically sneaked into the embassy to cut Haya's hair.

Haya managed to keep up with world news through a shortwave radio and continued to pay attention to events in the United States. He listened to the speeches of Adlai Stevenson and Dwight Eisenhower during the 1952 presidential campaign. He continued to gauge the degree of support he might get from the United States. "We have many friends in the United States," he wrote to Sánchez on May 21, 1953. "Many are working for us" Haya keenly sought an opening for APRA's ideas and assessed the situation in the United States as one of confusion that could be favorable to APRA:

> The Republican Party is beginning to fail to deliver on basic promises: tax cuts, for example, and the 'I shall go to Korea' have resulted in what it was: bombastic demagogic electoral resource. Stevenson drew more votes than any defeated candidate in the US. . . . Democrats and Trumanism are regaining strength. . . . If there is no war, the U.S. will have to abandon the current conservative extremism and give liberalism a chance. . . . Precisely because of the confusion, the clear ideas of our approaches may suddenly break through. That is why we must embark on irreparable statements. Remember Scripture! "As gentle as doves, as cunning as serpents." Cold, active, objective.[94]

Haya had once again become the focus of international attention as newspapers abroad reported on the proceedings. On June 14, 1951, the United Press International article titled "World Court Backs Colombia in Sheltering Outlaw" described one of the International Court of Justice's initial rulings.[95] The Peruvian government challenged this decision, and the case dragged on undecided until a settlement was finally reached independently between the two countries. Local newspapers throughout the United States reported on Haya, who was described as "bushy haired" and "dark and heavy set." A Florida newspaper stated, "The Columbian [sic] diplomatic staff maintains a rigid reserve as to the daily life of their four year guest behind the walls of the swank establishment, surrounded by flowers and grass. But it is assumed that he continues to spend most of his time reading and writing."[96] After he finally left the embassy in 1954, Haya described the details of his five-year stay in the article that he sold to *Life* magazine.

Always the consummate propagandist, Haya urged his followers to use his legal case as a way to further the cause of his party. In the court of international public opinion, Haya had become a symbolic figure, a hero and democratic champion confronting a repressive dictatorship. Yet the U.S. government showed little interest in promoting democracy as Cold War concerns took over U.S. foreign policy in Latin America. The issue of democracy took a back seat as the United States supported the Odría regime as a procapitalist and anti-Communist regime. Besides, isolated in the embassy, Haya remained very limited in his ability to maintain his contacts with U.S. officials as he had in the past.

Rather, Haya now became the focus of a growing web of transnational organizations that sought to support human rights in Latin America. Thus began his friendship with Frances Grant, head of the Latin American Committee of the International League for the Rights of Man (after 1976, the International League for Human Rights) and founder of the Pan-American Women's Association. A native New Mexican born in Abiquiu, Grant had traveled extensively in Latin America during the 1920s to promote cultural exchange between the United States and Latin America, first in the realm of art and then in the realm of politics.[97] Grant met with the Colombian ambassador in an attempt to secure safe conduct for Haya, as she had done for Rómulo Betancourt of Venezuela. During the early 1940s, in light of the growing threat of Fascism, the Pan-American Women's Association had turned from cultural issues to defending human rights, and it continued to do so after the end of World War II. In 1949, Grant had provided a testimony to the United Nations Commission on Human Rights regarding human rights violations in Latin America during that year, at a time when many democratic governments were replaced by dictatorships. The web page for the Frances Grant Papers at Rutgers University shows a photograph of her meeting with Haya in 1965.[98]

After 1950, Grant acted mainly as a representative of the Inter-American Association for Democracy and Freedom (IADF), an organization founded at a conference held in Havana, Cuba, on May 15, 1950. In addition to Grant, the organizers of the conference included Betancourt; Roger Baldwin; Serafino Romualdi, Latin American representative of the AFL-CIO; Walter White, secretary of the NAACP; Eleanor Roosevelt; Arthur Schlesinger Jr.; Hubert Humphrey; and Congressman Richard Nixon. The organizers in Latin America included Senator Salvador Allende, Dominican writer and later president Juan Bosch, and Costa Rican president José Figueres. However, despite the membership of Latin American leaders and the fact that the organization was headquartered in Montevideo, Uruguay, the IADF was mainly operated by Grant, who was based in New York. The organization campaigned against a number of dictatorships in Latin America—particularly the Trujillo regime in the Dominican Republic.

Had he not been captive in the Colombian embassy, Haya would most certainly have been among the prominent participants at the Havana conference. He certainly must have read about the conference while captive and

experienced some feelings of regret at not being able to join the participants, many of whom he knew personally. Despite the fact that he remained
in the embassy, Haya became a member of the IADF's Executive Council
(together with Baldwin, Germán Arciniegas, Romualdi, and Senator Juan
Guichon of Uruguay). The Havana Declaration resulting from the conference "condemned the actions of the dictators and recommended conditions
for diplomatic recognition based on respecting principles of human, civil,
and political rights. It also advocated social and economic reforms which
would strengthen the democratic forces in the hemisphere."[99] These became
a central part of the mission of the IADF. With the advent of the hard-line
Cold War–era military dictatorships during the 1960s and 1970s, the IADF
became less influential in the region.

In 1953, *The Ideology and Program of the Peruvian Aprista Movement*, an academic study very favorable to APRA, was published in the United States.
Some years earlier, on April 1, 1948, in Los Angeles, Haya had met with its
author, Professor Harry Kantor, and had a series of long conversations that
led to the book's publication. The work clearly helped to further Haya's propaganda strategy. In the preface, Kantor thanked Haya for his contribution
to the book and identified him as the person "who encouraged the writer
to undertake it."[100] In highly favorable terms, the book portrayed Aprismo
as a movement that supported democracy. "The Aprista state," Kantor wrote,
"would be democratic. . . . [It] would be based on a system of democratic
political parties which, according to the Apristas, has always been missing
from Peru."[101] Originally published by the University of California Press,
Kantor's book was subsequently reprinted in 1966 and republished in 1977
by a division of the New York publisher Farrar, Straus and Giroux.

Kantor placed Aprismo in a global perspective as a "third force"—neither
Communism nor capitalism. He grouped APRA with "the Socialist parties
of France, India and the United States; the labor parties of Great Britain,
Scandinavia, Australia, and New Zealand; and the Cooperative Commonwealth Federation of Canada."[102] Kantor praised Haya's foresight in antici-
pating the need to create large, powerful states and proposing that the Latin
American countries be united: "The attempt to establish a United States of
Western Europe, the cooperation of the British Commonwealth of Nations,
and the weakness of the small countries at the present time all point to the
conclusion that the era of large and powerful states is emerging. It is to the
Apristas' credit that they forecast this need as far back as 1924 and have continued to urge the unification of Latin America ever since."[103] Kantor is

referring to the erroneous foundation date of APRA, 1924, promoted by Apristas to connect APRA to Mexico and downplay its European place of birth. Haya truly did show foresight, as becomes clear when we put his ideas into the context of the later twentieth-century creation of the European Union and the increased importance of trade blocks in the twenty-first century.

Kantor commended Haya for his proposals to forge common ties between Latin America and the United States. For example, regarding his proposal of shared ownership of the Panama Canal, Kantor states, "The Aprista proposal that all the American states share ownership of the Panama Canal is also a reflection of their desire to see the United States and Latin America cooperate for mutual benefit. The Apristas think joint ownership of the canal would knit the twenty-one republics and serve as a symbol of inter-American unity. Joint ownership, they believe, would also strengthen the defenses of the canal."[104] Kantor also pointed to the mystical nature of APRA, the strength of its followers' allegiance, which made it "more than a political party."[105] Kantor noted that Haya had distanced himself from Marxist analysis: "Few would dispute that the Apristas are correct in believing that the Marxian analysis no longer fits the contemporary world."[106] Constantly adapting to new political circumstances to benefit his party, Haya would later emphasize the party's revolutionary trajectory, as well as its fight for democracy, once a leftist military government came to power in Peru in 1968 under General Juán Velasco Alvarado.[107]

After his release from the embassy in 1954, Haya traveled to Mexico—the Peruvian government issued him a very limited passport only valid for travel to Mexico. In the account of his stay, Haya describes his emotions of sorrow at leaving what had been his home: "Now I experienced an emotion I had not expected—an almost overwhelming sadness at the prospect of leaving what had been my home for so long."[108] The limitations on his passport caused visa problems that prevented him from attending a banquet he was invited to in the United States in early June.[109] Haya then applied for a UN passport.

Turning Away from the United States: Haya's Years in Europe, 1956–1969

After his release from the embassy in 1954, Haya spent the majority of the next fifteen years living in Europe, removed from the day-to-day turbulence of Peruvian politics. He was reluctant to return to Peru and expressed disgust with the way he had been treated in Peruvian politics. His letters to Sánchez express not only this reluctance to become a presidential candidate but also his continuing fear of death. On February 4, 1955, from Geneva, Haya expressed the fear that he might be assassinated if he returned to politics in Peru: "I find that job, that mission tremendously repugnant. Not because of fear of the death that will be its epilogue with 95% probability, but because I have not healed myself of an organic disgust that filled me to the brim during the previous experience. This is something very deep inside, very much in my heart."[110] Haya expressed fear that, even if he were to stay in Europe, he would die soon: "If I go to Scandinavia I will have work, security and peace until my death, which I do not think is very far away either."[111]

His engagement with the United States diminished, but it did not disappear altogether. He wrote very little about the United States in comparison to earlier years.[112] The U.S. press in turn paid less attention to him now that he was no longer captive in the embassy. In 1956, when Haya returned to Peru for the first time following the election of Prado and a new period of legalization for APRA, *Life* magazine published a brief note titled "A Tamer Rebel Comes Home" that showed a photograph of his supporters enthusiastically waving to him as he returned to Trujillo, the city of his birth. The article reported that Haya "had lost some of his former zeal. He spoke warmly of the APRA's new policy of *convivencia*."[113] However, the United States secretly continued to keep an eye on him. A CIA report stated that Haya had written in the party newspaper calling for the internationalization of the Panama Canal and had "stated that canals such as Panama and Suez should be internationalized and that Egypt wants to do in Suez what the United States has already done in Panama."[114] A few years later, in a 1959 article written in Rome for the party newspaper *La Tribuna*, Haya referred to the fact that Eisenhower's visit to Latin America had coincided with an initiative on the part of a group of Latin American countries to establish an economic union, an effort he applauded.[115]

Despite the feelings of "disgust" he had reported to Sánchez about his experiences in Peruvian politics, Haya returned to Peru in 1962 and 1963, to run for president, and he remained a relevant player for the United States during these years. When Schlesinger, special assistant to President John F. Kennedy, was in Lima in 1962, he met with Haya. He praised Haya and APRA for their pro-U.S. position. Yet as it became increasingly clear that the military would not allow Haya to become president, the United States also had less reason to seek him out. After Haya's narrow win in 1962 led the military to call for a new election, the United Press International reported that this scenario was not a new one for "a hawk nose, burly man who for forty years has been a storm center for Peruvian politics."[116]

His view of Latin America's relationship to the United States can be summarized in Cold War terms: given the fact that Latin America would have to engage with one of the imperialist powers, it was best to engage with the democratic rather than the totalitarian one. Also using Cold War language, Haya defended Latin America's right to engage rather than disengage from the United States. If Russia could engage with the United States, why not Latin Americans?"[117]

Haya did not denounce the United States for its intervention in Guatemala in 1954, which brought down the democratically elected government of Jacobo Arbenz. In a letter to Romualdi, Haya criticized Arbenz and accused him of being an "agent" of Moscow: "Arbenz and Castillo Armas, the one an agent of Moscow and the other of Washington, were nothing but miserable military mercenaries, like all of the military dictators in our countries. I attacked the cowardice of Arbenz, who should have fought and died like a soldier struggling against the North American intervention."[118] Haya's comment on Arbenz fails to indicate that Arbenz was democratically elected.

Haya's writings also reflect a distancing from the United States and a greater interest in European and world affairs. An article he published in 1954 expressed his disappointment with the U.S. record with democracy. In the article, titled "What Would You Call an Ideal Democracy," written in Hammerfest, he voiced admiration for Uruguay and argued that Uruguay was more democratic than the United States, pointing to the latter country's poverty and racism.[119] The majority of his articles discussed European and global affairs, touching on a vast array of subjects: the beginnings of the European Economic Community, David Ben-Gurion in Israel, Patrice Lumumba in Africa, and Yugoslavia. These articles helped to pay for what, by most accounts, was a frugal life in Europe. The architect Oswaldo Nuñez, a fellow Peruvian in Europe, recalls that Haya asked him to act as a courier by bringing him a payment that a Spanish publication owed Haya for one of his articles. Nuñez also recalls a late-night meeting in Haya's small Rome apartment, where fine wine and cheeses contrasted with the frugality of the setting.[120] Anecdotally, Haya was known to have sold in Europe a fine alpaca overcoat that had been given to him as a gift by his wealthy friend and APRA supporter Carlos Raffo Dasso.

Conclusions

Haya would return one last time to the United States, in 1979. The brief visit occurred for health reasons at the end of his life, following his definitive return to Peru in 1969. During these years, with Peru under military rule, Haya had now taken on the role of elder statesman and educator, meeting every night to impart wisdom to his followers at the party headquarters La Casa del Pueblo (the People's House), on Avenida Alfonso Ugarte. He traveled there from his house, Villa Mercedes, located east of Lima in Ate, a house that belonged to his cousin Mercedes de la Torre de Ganoza. In 1978, as the military prepared to return political power to civilians, Haya had been elected to his first political position ever, that of president of the Constituent Assembly tasked with writing a new constitution for Peru.

When he took the presidency of the Constituent Assembly in 1978, the eighty-three-year-old Haya was no longer a healthy man. In March 1979, he traveled to Houston for a lung cancer treatment. A sign of how far relations with the military had improved, President Francisco Morales Bermúdez offered Haya the presidential airplane, a small Focker, to take him to the United States. Haya refused the offer, as the party had already arranged for his travel.[121] Luis Alva Castro, then acting as his secretary for the Constituent Assembly, accompanied him to Houston.[122] When the time came to sign the completed constitution, Haya was so frail that the document had to be brought to him for him to sign on his deathbed.

Haya succeeded over the course of his long life in transforming himself from a symbol of anti-imperialist revolution to a symbol of democracy in Latin America. He constantly adapted his ideas to changing times. To what degree his democratic leanings were the result only of pragmatism, and to what degree they became heartfelt beliefs, is probably impossible to know. Yet his engagement with the United States during the period of the Good Neighbor Policy transformed him into a willing fighter for the cause of democracy in Latin America. That he may have still been willing to use nondemocratic means to get to power is not surprising, as we see how at every turn he attempted to overcome the obstacles he faced to becoming president of Peru. It is in some ways fitting that he ended his life while presiding over Peru's transition from military rule to democracy and that the Constitution of 1979 bears his signature.

CHAPTER FOUR

El Jefe y el Partido
Party Discipline and the Cult of Personality

> A party without a caudillo, or names, ours must be a Party of
> principles and not of people.
>
> —HAYA DE LA TORRE, "Address to the First National Congress of
> the PAP," August 20, 1931

> The charges that Apra is fundamentally a personality cult were
> found to be bolstered by Haya's incorrigible caudillismo, but that
> the PAP [Partido Aprista Peruano] enjoys an existence separate
> from that of its founder and undisputed jefe máximo was also
> demonstrated.
>
> —RICHARD LEE CLINTON

> The innovating capacity cannot be attributed to Haya de la Torre
> alone. As we shall see, it stemmed from the combination of his
> Marxist-Leninist approach with influence from grassroots
> organizations. There were on the one hand anarcho-syndicalist,
> and on the other, the *células residenciales*, urban associations of
> migrants with common regional origins, arising from the massive
> new influx into the towns.
>
> —MARGARITA GIESECKE

> Haya was a great organizer.
>
> —NELSON MANRIQUE

A Lima taxi driver once commented to me that even in the most remote
Peruvian town one could always find a police station and an American Popular Revolutionary Alliance (APRA) party headquarters. The comment, although less true today than before, reflects the success of Apristas in
establishing a lasting institutional presence that has made APRA into Peru's
longest-lived political party. The party, built by networks of individuals
both in Peru and abroad, depended on a cult of personality of its leader
Víctor Raúl Haya de la Torre. As Julio Cotler writes, "Party integration crys-
talized around the figure as a savior of Haya who took the role of 'older

brother' who embodied all of the virtues of commitment, dedication and teaching that the insecure and disconcerted younger brothers expected of him."[1] Taking a more critical view of Haya, Aprista leader and writer Luis Alberto Sánchez recognized APRA's organization as a "mixture of human solidarity and caudillo arrogance."[2]

Haya encouraged the cult of personality that began to develop around him and reinforced his position as the all-powerful Jefe of the party—a title that only he ever held in the history of the party. Haya understood the power of such a cult of personality from his direct observations of both Fascist and Communist parties when he lived in Europe. He was also ideally suited to fit that role given his charismatic personality. Haya demonstrated an almost obsessive interest in the issue of party organization. During his lifetime, he transformed APRA from a handful of cells scattered in many countries to one of Latin America's longest-lasting political parties. The fact that APRA eventually came to power in 1985, after the death of its founder, and that it has outlived Haya by almost four decades, attests to this legacy.

In focusing so much attention on himself as leader of the party, Haya also risked raising a controversial issue: his sexuality. Rumors of his alleged homosexuality have become part of Peru's political culture. These rumors have lived on to the present day, sometimes in the form of jokes. An early admirer turned detractor, Alberto Hidalgo, wrote a pamphlet arguing that Haya's homosexuality disqualified him as a politician. Hidalgo also delved briefly into Haya's psychology by pointing to what he termed "existential duplicity." Haya may or may not have felt that he was leading a duplicitous life. Perhaps, as George Chauncey has argued in his book on gay New York, Haya was able to find ways to express his sexuality despite the prevailing prejudices against homosexuals.[3]

Haya's larger-than-life stature has understandably attracted more attention than the inner workings of a party with a well-defined organizational structure. For many decades, the party functioned both nationally and transnationally. Party leaders in Peru and in exile engaged in discussions and disagreements that would shape the direction of the party. Many of these leaders, such as Manuel Seoane, Sanchez, Ramiro Prialé, Nicanor Mujica Alvarez Calderon, Luis Heysen, Alfredo Tello Salavarría, and many others, await their biographers. Discipline was highly prized and disciplinary committees imposed punishments and sometimes expulsions. Haya's status as Jefe of the party did not make him immune from criticism. The correspondence with the exiled leaders in Chile reveals continued disagreements regarding the party's course of action. For example, in his letter to Haya

Haya on the back of a truck during the 1962 presidential campaign
(Armando Villanueva Papers, courtesy of Lucía Villanueva).

dated April 27, 1939, Seoane, long considered the second most important
leader within APRA, challenged Haya for publicly criticizing some of the
party's leaders and hence undermining their authority. The language of this
letter points to the importance of Aprismo as a doctrine not connected to
any particular personality but rather embodying a set of ideas that guided
action: "I only want to say that I will do my duty, that I will never cease to
be an Aprista because it is as if I had been told that I would sometime cease to
have a human form, or some such thing. Yet I think that the rapport between
the 'jefe' and the affiliates must obey rules of mutual consideration that
stimulate and encourage rather than mistreating and diminishing."[4]

Despite the "caudillo arrogance" of which Sánchez accused him, Haya's
actions demonstrate his concern with the continuity of the party and with
its institutionalization. He dedicated enormous energy to the process of
indoctrination, of instilling values such as discipline that would allow Apristas to carry out the numerous party tasks with total allegiance to the party.
In fact, Apristas were so successful on this front that many have compared

the party to a religious sect. The allegiance to APRA passed from one generation to another. Apristas founded a youth organization, the Federación Aprista Juvenil (FAJ). They created popular universities to educate their followers. They built a complex structure of national and regional committees that enforced party policy. The APRA organization even extended down to the level of neighborhood committees. During times of persecution, the party's cellular structure allowed it to survive.

Haya put a strong personal imprint on the party's political culture. Throughout his texts and speeches, he framed party participation in gendered terms by emphasizing the importance of brotherhood. The heavily gendered language of male brotherhood permeated party discourse. The party's main celebration became the "Día de la Fraternidad" (Day of Fraternity). Haya's letters to Aprista prisoners reinforced these values. The prison experience thus became another vehicle for articulating a new masculinity, one strongly influenced by Victorian conceptions of manliness latent in such institutions as the YMCA.[5] His obsession with the dangers of what he termed "sensualization"—of surrendering to pleasure, be it sexual or other, that would detract from the work of the party—echoes the kind of homoerotic tension that existed in the YMCA organization with its attempts to discourage sexuality and emphasize exercise and the disciplining of the body. Scholars have identified YMCAs as loci for the development of intense same-sex friendships that could open the doors to the expression of sexuality.[6] And Haya's warnings that exile created the setting for such "sensualization" also had deeply personal roots: during both his European exiles (1924–31 and 1955–69), Haya lived in cities such as London, Berlin, and Rome that allowed him a degree of personal freedom that he would have lacked in Peru, where he was constrained by the scrutiny of his own party and by a society that lacked spaces for the expression of same-sex relationships. The lack of such spaces makes the notion of "the closet" relevant for understanding the kind of dual life that those pursuing same-sex relationships would have lived. The letters that Haya's friend, nicknamed Bridi, wrote Haya after he left Berlin in 1931 suggest a degree of emotional intimacy that would have been difficult for Haya to sustain as party leader in Peru.

Haya's influence also extended to formulating a party mythology with its very own origins story. The idea that APRA was founded in Mexico in 1924 remains alive among Apristas and continues to find its way into the scholarly literature on APRA.[7] Why Mexico, and why 1924? Mexico served numerous purposes: it was the place of the Mexican Revolution, so central to Aprismo, and it helped to legitimize APRA as a Latin American party— admitting that the party had been founded in Paris could undermine this claim. The year, as Haya himself pointed out, marked the one hundredth anniversary of the Battle of Ayacucho, led by Simón Bolívar, which sealed the fate of Latin America as an independent continent. The date therefore helped to reinforce APRA's continentalist claims and Haya's Bolivarian dreams.

Haya's concern with the continuity of his ideas and his party stemmed in part from his early awareness of his own mortality, which arose from the dangers he faced during times of incarceration and persecution. The rhythms of persecution and exile that marked Haya's life required the existence of a strong organization alongside the strong leader. Haya spent most of years between 1932 and 1945 in hiding. Between 1949 and 1954, he lived in the Colombian embassy in Lima, mostly isolated from party matters, while his political asylum case made its way to the International Court of Justice in The Hague. Meanwhile, exiled leaders discussed policy by writing letters in what came to be known as the *congresos postales* (postal congresses). These allowed party leaders living scattered throughout the continent to maintain communication and a degree of party unity during the years of persecution under the dictatorship of General Manuel Odría (1948–56). After his release, Haya spent most of the next decade and half living in Europe and returning only occasionally to Peru.

Haya's hold on the party was so strong that even during his long absences his role as leader remained uncontested. No other leader in the party ever achieved Haya's popularity among the party's followers—the only one who came close during the early years was Magda Portal. The cult of personality was built on Haya's common touch, which drew adulation from his followers. With his seductive personality and oratorical skill, he captivated his audiences with his political speeches. In person, he was equally charismatic and enthralled his listeners with long conversations that reflected his charm and intelligence. Although his disciple and successor Alan García never rivaled Haya's status as a larger-than-life leader, he had similarly captivating qualities as an orator. Since 1985 if not earlier, García has dominated the party. Once again, the combination of a strong organizational structure and a magnetic personality helped to keep the party alive. García was very different from Haya. Unsullied by the exercise of power, Haya had been able to cultivate the image of grand old statesman who stood above the fray. García presented a very different image—that of a wily politician able to spring back from the political abyss and brush off constant accusations of corruption. Following García's humiliating loss in the 2016 presidential elections, the party today faces the challenge of how to survive in the absence of a charismatic figure. Many Peruvians speculate that García may run again in 2021 for what would be a historic third term as president. A charismatic leader and strong party organization have remained opposite sides of the same of the coin in the history of APRA.

From Revolutionary Cells to Mass Political Party

The young Haya modeled APRA on Vladimir Lenin's vanguard party: a hierarchical organization made up of cadres capable of instilling revolutionary consciousness among its followers. Haya's writings echo Lenin's concern with the issue of party organization and discipline. Haya saw the role of Aprismo from the historically deterministic perspective of Marxism: "Aprismo as a historical, Marxist force, has its own evolution, and it must advance and develop according to the reality of the people, for which it has been conceived."[8] Following the 1926 publication of the article "What Is the APRA?," and while living in England, Haya constantly wrote his supporters about the issue of organization. At the time, he conceived of the party as a military organization.

In a letter he wrote in Berlin in 1930 on behalf of the International Executive Committee of APRA to the APRA cell in Cusco, Peru, Haya refers constantly to Lenin. "These are words of Lenin: 'The fundamental question of all revolution is the question of power,'" Haya writes. "Apra, consequently, wants to guide the working masses toward power. But power cannot be conquered without struggle, without war."[9] In the letter, he declares open allegiance to Communist ideals yet also shows a large dose of pragmatism in realizing that these ideals could not be achieved "magically." Haya writes, "If we could today, by the touch of a magic wand, impose universal communism, suppress human pain, destroy at its very roots the exploitation of man by man, give happiness to all the settlers of the earth, we would do it. . . . The fundamental question is that there are no magic wands."[10] Rather, it would be necessary to establish "the dictatorship of the peasant and working class proletariat." Yet in the unorthodox twist that already characterized Haya's thinking, he refers specifically to his writings on the need to rely on the middle class in Latin America in order to further the revolution. To bolster the case, he cites Friedrich Engels on the important role of the middle class in European revolutions: Martin Luther's revolution in Germany, Oliver Cromwell's revolution in England, and the French Revolution.[11] He further quotes Lenin on the need to recruit the peasantry in order to start a revolution, given the similar agrarian realities of Peru and Russia, and he concludes that, "parodying Lenin[,] we can say it is necessary to begin with the Indian."[12] This directive may have been tailored very specifically to the Cusco region, with its heavily indigenous population. The fact that the letter is written in the first person plural and is signed by Haya in the name of APRA's International Executive Committee reflects the importance of the party for Haya as a source of political legitimacy.[13]

The cellular structure of a revolutionary party served Haya well in achieving his initial goal of organizing exiles scattered in a number of different countries. During its first years as a transnational organization, APRA remained fairly loosely structured. Haya founded APRA's first cell in Paris in 1926 due to the presence of many Peruvians in this city. The numbers remained small. Sánchez, referring to a famous Paris café, claimed that the members of the Paris cell "fit comfortably on the sofa at La Rotonde."[14] Meetings often took place in cafés. Apristas founded cells in Havana, Buenos Aires, and other cities, including New York. The members of emerging cells in different countries communicated through letters and were responsible for spreading propaganda. Despite Haya's claims that APRA needed to be a military organization, these cells did not function as military units. When the Mexico cell put forth a plan for armed revolution against the Augusto B. Leguía government in 1928, Haya had to go to great lengths to contact a retired army officer living in El Salvador to set the revolutionary plans in motion in Peru.

Once the Leguía regime fell in 1930 as a result of a coup and elections were called for 1931, Haya changed course. Rather than plot an armed revolution, he decided to take advantage of the political opening to launch his candidacy for president. On September 20, 1930, Apristas founded the Peruvian branch of APRA in a small carpenter's workshop in downtown Lima. With signatures in a red notebook—which has survived to this day in the archive of Armando Villanueva—those present gave birth to the Partido Aprista Peruano (PAP). Among the signatories were a number of individuals who would become prominent party leaders. Now legally established, the party began to recruit openly. Manuel Chávez Vargas, a schoolteacher, recalls that a young boy with propaganda about APRA approached him while he was crossing the Puente Piedra over Lima's Rimac River. He later registered at the workshop of a carpenter (perhaps the same one where the party was founded) whose wife took Chávez Vargas's information and gave him a small cardboard inscription card.[15]

Despite Haya's role as founder and leader, divergences between him and the party existed from the outset. There was resistance within the party to Haya's launching his candidacy for president from Berlin. Haya pressured the party in order to pursue his candidacy: "Haya's insistence forced Apra's National Executive Committee to urge him to submit to the party's authority, which considered his initiative untimely. Instead of obeying, Haya had thousands of leaflets printed in Berlin and Paris, in order to flood Peru."[16] The PAP did not want him to launch his candidacy from Berlin. Apparently, Haya could not return to Peru earlier because he had not yet been issued a visa.[17] When he finally obtained his visa, he returned from Germany via New York, where he embarked on the ship *Santa María*, which belonged to Grace Lines. The party's executive committee did not proclaim Haya its presidential candidate until after his arrival in Peru.

On July 12, 1931, Haya disembarked in the town of Talara, on Peru's northern coast, to a hero's welcome. Thousands greeted him two weeks later when he arrived in his native Trujillo. The crowd that gathered when he arrived in Lima displayed not only the Peruvian but also other Latin American flags, a sign of the party's transnational identity at the time.[18] When on August 23, 1931, Haya spoke to thousands of his supporters in Lima's bullring, the Plaza de Acho, the members of the audience had each paid thirty centavos to contribute to the party. The fund-raising work by the party committees from different Lima neighborhoods demonstrated the efficiency of party organization at this early stage.[19]

Haya embarked on a nationwide campaign that took him to towns in the Central Andes such as La Oroya, Cerro de Pasco, Tarma, and Huancayo, as well as the jungle town of Iquitos.[20] He relied on the party's incipient national organization. When he left Lima, he charged party leaders with coming up with a program for the party: "I am the man who points out the great path. You are my political engineers, who must put tie after tie, rail after rail, securing the way by which our convoy will advance."[21] Those who joined the party made small payments that helped to sustain the party.

At this early stage, Haya had not yet become an iconic figure. In fact, fellow Aprista Portal reports that during the campaign, people chanted her name and not Haya's. Apristas were not the only ones drawing large crowds.[22] Haya's political rival, Luís Sánchez Cerro, held similarly large political rallies. Having been absent from the country for seven years, Haya had difficulty matching the popularity of his rival, who had led the coup against Leguía and who eventually won the election.

After the election, many Apristas questioned the results, cried fraud, and took to violent protest. During Sánchez Cerro's inauguration, Apristas set off bombs. By December, the party was in full conflict with the government. On Christmas Eve of that year, government agents broke into the Trujillo party headquarters and a number of people were killed in the confrontation. Shortly thereafter, all twenty-seven Aprista congressmen were removed from the Constituent Congress and the party was declared illegal. To avoid being captured, Haya hid in the two-story house of Carlos Plenge, on Avenida Pardo in the suburb of Miraflores, next to the Mexican embassy. He grew a beard and pretended to be a German guest of the family by the name of Herr John. The Mexican ambassador next door, Manuel Falcón, frequently visited the house and remained discreet about Haya's presence. Thanks to a tip by a gardener who worked at the house and had recognized Haya, the police learned of his location.[23] On May 6, armed government agents surrounded the house, arrested Haya, and led him to Lima's penitentiary. He would remain imprisoned for the following year. Jail time, persecution, and exile characterized the life of the party for the next decade and a half. Clandestine printing presses published the party newspaper *La Tribuna*, which came to be known as *el pan caliente* (hot bread) because it was delivered secretly to Aprista homes together with the morning's bread. What held the party together during these difficult times? A letter that Haya wrote from jail reflects his hope that party discipline would keep his ideals alive.

In a passage worth quoting at length, Haya proudly contrasted Aprista discipline with the anarchy and hysteria that characterized Latin American politics. Claiming to cite the opinions of U.S. newspapers and magazines and authors on both the left and the right, Haya writes, "They say that it is the first time in the history of Latin American political anarchism that a great party of a modern type appears, with its own philosophy and doctrine. They add that, in the midst of the hysteria characteristic of our peoples, ready to fiercely adopt at a moment's notice any poorly assimilated European theory, our Party is a demonstration of discipline and political conscience, revealing that the Latins of these disorganized towns are preparing to give to the world a great lesson in mental maturity and an obvious sense of organization."[24] There is a certain irony in the fact that some months earlier, the Trujillo uprising had underscored the lack of discipline in the party. On July 7, 1932, Manuel "Búfalo" Barreto and his followers had disobeyed central party orders and led an armed insurrection in which Apristas briefly took over the city of Trujillo. The uprising was a challenge to party discipline, as it had taken place without the authorization of party leaders. Furthermore, another act demonstrating a lack of discipline, the massacre of officers in a city jail—perhaps committed by Apristas, perhaps not—would create a deep rift between APRA and the military for decades to come.

Haya's emphasis on the importance of individual discipline can also be traced to his early contact with Protestantism in Peru. Haya had participated in Protestant temperance leagues in Peru, a movement that encouraged ideas of individual discipline that included an emphasis on hygiene. These public campaigns sought to eradicate alcoholism. Haya also participated in the YMCA founded in Lima in 1919. He maintained his connection to this organization, which promoted spiritual well-being through physical exercise, until 1923 when he was deported. In 1922, he attended a summer camp organized by the YMCA in Piriapolis, Uruguay. When he returned to Peru, he gave lectures in Arequipa and Trujillo on the theme of "Christ and society."[25] Tomás Gutierrez Sánchez points to the influence of Protestantism on Haya at this early stage: "Although Haya de la Torre's presence in the YMCA was short (1919–1923), it allowed him to receive the influence of this Protestant institution in terms of an ethical life with Christian values; their desire for justice and solidarity with Latin American youth; and their longings for struggle and social equality."[26] Here we encounter a young and impressionable Haya, willing to "try on" different ideas—in this case Protestantism, to the point of traveling and giving lectures about Christ. The YMCA's emphasis on sports and physical activity had a lasting influence on Haya.[27] He continued to participate in sports. The cultivation of the body in connection to the making of good citizens and building of the nation is a broader theme in European history—for example, in the Czech Sokol movement.

Once they had prepared themselves physically and mentally, Apristas could embark on the task of "civilizing" others. Haya inverted the traditional use of the terms *barbarism* and *civilization*, which had been popularized by the nineteenth-century Argentine liberal Domingo Sarmiento. Sarmiento had glorified Western cultural heritage and used the term *barbarism* to denigrate Argentina's own native traditions as embodied by the popular classes and in particular the gaucho. In Peru, according to Haya, the elite was "barbarian" and Apristas were the "civilizers." He painted Peru's elite as "a caste that was ill with hatred, envy, and lack of culture that regards with disdain the rise of a force that has improved itself, that is austere, united and young."[28] Apristas needed to remember their civilizing role: "I believe that we are and must be on a superior level to that of the barbarism that attempts to victimize us; therefore, without ceasing to be energetic and firm and avoid becoming barbaric which would be to forget the Party's civilizing mission."[29]

While he was being held in Lima's penitentiary between 1932 and 1933, Haya began to tout the suffering of prison as a valuable experience that would strengthen Apristas. A prisoner could draw physical and spiritual strength from suffering. In a letter from prison to Aprista Juan Seoane, Haya wrote, "We must take advantage of our sufferings and never be bitter; we must strengthen ourselves spiritually, so much so, that we reach the cold and serene dominance of the most difficult situations. We must not forget that the Aprista must suffer to be strong." The task ahead "demands complete mental health and vigorous physical resistance."[30] After his release from prison in 1933, Haya wrote eleven letters between 1936 and 1942 to jailed Aprista prisoners highlighting Aprista discipline as one of the party's central values. In his July 7, 1938, letter addressed "to fellow prisoners of the Panopticon," Haya encouraged jailed Apristas to seek strength from their situation: "Have faith. Strengthen your bonds of brotherhood. Dominate any weakness and never weaken the cordial nexus that must exist among you. . . . Make time. Read, study, think, discipline the mind more and more."[31] He had warned his followers that it would not be easy to be an Aprista. In a letter dated January 26, 1939, Haya claimed that all great revolutions had gone through a similar stage to the one APRA was going through.[32] These letters probably reached Aprista prisoners through APRA's clandestine channels, although they were not published until 1946.[33]

Haya described the experience of hiding from the government as exhilarating and his own struggle as quixotic. In a 1939 letter to Manuel Checa, an exiled Aprista living in Chile at the time, Haya continued to criticize the experience of exile and contrast it with his own quixotic struggle in Peru. The passage is worth quoting, as it is one of the few in which Haya gives voice to his feelings:

And I feel that many young people who later will not know what it is to fight, because they lived in sweet exile, quiet, can reach the leadership of the Party. These are the most fruitful years for a fighter. That's why I do not get tired and as an old athlete I enjoy the emotion of this fight that does not cease. I have always been in love with the battle and I wanted to live it whole and in depth. Far from any kind of rage and rather peaceful . . . I feel that in the depths of conscience a warrior demon rides me that incites me not to cease as long as there is an injustice to fight or an evil to remedy. Is that demon called Don Quixote? I do not know. But I live for him. That is to say for the fight, for the danger, for the emotion of always knowing that one is in the line of combat against so much evil and so much ignorance.[34]

These feelings reinforce the Aprista heroic narrative of struggle.

Haya contrasted Apristas who had remained to suffer persecution in Peru with those abroad, whom he accused of leading a "sensual" life. In a 1936 letter he commended Pedro Muñiz and Carlos Manuel Cox, who had been jailed when they heeded the party's call for them to return to Peru from Chile in 1935. While he lamented the capture of Muñiz and Cox, "at the same time, this has proved to both *compañeros* and adversaries that the leaders are in their position for struggle and know how to fall, victims of their impatience to return to the line of fire, which is their true and only place."[35]

Haya asked exiled party members to return. He even mocked those in exile by accusing them of living an easy life while Apristas in Peru suffered. Exiled Apristas were, in Haya's words, *sensualizandose* (succumbing to sensual pleasures) that undermined their political being: "Weakness and lack of heroism are always symptoms of sensuality and spiritual flaccidity."[36] He quoted anarchist writer and politician Manuel Gonzalez Prada to warn Apristas—Aprista men—to not be driven by their sexual impulses: "These long years of struggle are showing us who among us are those who are men from the waist down—as Gonzalez Prada said—and who are those of glands, heart and brain as the party wants and needs them."[37] The true Aprista—defined as a man—must ignore the sensual impulses associated with the lower part of the body and be driven by his glands, his heart, and his brain.

The ultimate sacrifice—death—was the most highly valued by Apristas. Following the Trujillo uprising and subsequent massacre, APRA began to commemorate its martyrs as a way to further cement loyalty to the party. In a speech at Trujillo's cemetery to commemorate the fallen Apristas, Haya made deliberate use of religious language: "Our dead . . . sacrifice[d] themselves so that their stirrings would enliven our spirit. . . . Hence our party demands of us Apristas that we become giants, that we transform ourselves, purify ourselves, cleanse ourselves, bathe in our own blood, be clean and good, be great and strong because we are the fathers of a new period in History."[38] Haya deliberately drew on his understanding of the power of religious feelings to build his party: "Both his reading of the Bible and his sustained close contact with simple lower-class workers in the Popular University, had taught Haya not only that religion and social change could be compatible realities but that religious sentiment was a powerful motivating force among lower-class Peruvians steeped in traditional Roman Catholicism."[39]

This emphasis on a personal commitment and sacrifice for the party through suffering has contributed to the perception that more than a political party, APRA functioned like a religious sectarian organization.[40] The party slogan—"Sólo el APRA salvará al Perú" (Only APRA will save Peru)— helped to support this view. Some accounts attribute the popularity of the saying to Aprista Carlos Alberto Philipps, one of the leaders of an uprising in Huaraz. While facing the firing squad, he exclaimed, "May Christ save my soul; Aprismo alone will save Peru!"[41] Apristas even compared themselves to the early Christians: "Only in the age when the Roman Caesars persecuted the Christians is there a parallel to the sublimity of this struggle of a young party against an entrenched and decrepit oligarchy."[42] APRA's most famous martyr was Manuel Arévalo, a worker, labor leader, and then congressman in 1931 who was captured by the government, tortured, and then assassinated in 1937. Haya allegedly kept Arévalo's bones under his bed. Today an enormous white cross still commemorates the place where Arévalo was assassinated on the Pan-American Highway between Trujillo and Lima.

While Haya celebrated death as the ultimate act of allegiance to the party, disloyalty in turn was considered the ultimate act of treason, which led to another kind of death—death in the form of erasure from party history. Haya demanded not only discipline but also absolute loyalty from his followers. A letter that Haya wrote to Portal thanking her for a monetary contribution to the party reflects his appreciation for the sacrifice she had made for the party. The fact that he never married and never had a family allowed him to dedicate himself completely to politics. He had similar expectations of his followers. García, who would become his chosen successor much later in life and was eventually elected as the first Aprista president in 1985, claims that when he married he hid the fact from Haya for a long time because he feared Haya would see his marriage as a sign of a lack of commitment to the party.

The party punished disloyalty. Those who joined found themselves subjected to discipline. Apristas applied disciplinary procedures both in Peru and abroad: "The aprista disciplinary fever seemed to endorse, in its own way, the well-known campaigns of Stalinist Bolshevization.... On October 8, 1938, Manuel Gallardo Bolaños was officially notified that he would be subject to a disciplinary session on the 15th of the same month to provide complementary information."[43] In an incident recalled many decades later by his son, party leader Luis Felipe de las Casas, who had left the party at one point, learned the price of disloyalty when APRA thugs appeared at his house and beat him up in front of his family.[44] Luis de la Puente Uceda, an Aprista who was eventually expelled from the party and formed a new radical party, Apra Rebelde, before founding the Communist Movimiento de Izquierda Revolucionaria, claims that Haya himself disciplined him when Haya was passing through Guatemala in 1954.[45]

Over the course of the decades, those who left the party were branded as traitors. Portal, the party highest-ranking female leader, was erased from official party history when she left the party in 1948. Decades later, the Aprista Consuelo Torres Tello still referred to Portal as a *traidora* when I interviewed her in 2007.[46] Portal and many others who left also condemned the party, often in biting pamphlets. A whole genre of such pamphlets exists. In addition to Portal, other founding members, such as Luis Eduardo Enriquez and Hidalgo, left APRA with great bitterness. A common theme in many of these writings—for example, Portal's pamphlet titled *¿Quienes traicionaron al pueblo?*—was APRA's betrayal of its original ideals The accusations against Haya became very personal, as expressed, for example, in the title of Enriquez's book *Haya de la Torre: La estafa política mas grande de América* (Haya de la Torre: The greatest political fraud in America). The poet Hidalgo, who had earlier praised Haya, admits that he originally contributed to the creation of what he refers to as the "myth" of Haya and that his book was intended to debunk that myth.

Teaching Discipline: The Federación Aprista Juvenil

On January 7, 1934, Apristas founded a youth organization, the FAJ, to inculcate discipline and other Aprista values among the party's youths. The manual written to prepare them for participation in the party began with the admonition, "Youth be prepared for action and not for pleasure."[47] Haya put Ramiro Prialé and Humberto Silva Solís in charge of creating the organization. The first general secretary, Armando Villanueva, recalled that Haya had sought to model the organization on similar Communist youth organizations he believed Haya had observed in Mexico or Europe: "Haya does not create an organization, but says that the Communists have the Communist Youth Federation . . . [so] 'let's make the Aprista Youth Federation.' "[48] The FAJ began to establish a national presence. Villanueva traveled to the city of Ica to organize the FAJ while Mujica traveled to Huancayo. In Moquegua, Enrique Rivero Velez organized the FAJ. The FAJ was later renamed Juventud Aprista Peruana in an attempt by APRA to shed its transnational identity, which had led to accusations of a connection to international Communism, and to affirm its identity as a Peruvian political party.

The FAJ initially functioned both as an educational and as a military organization. In the words of Villanueva, "The FAJ . . . is born with [sic] an environment in which the revolutionary struggle, the armed struggle was very close, very close."[49] He described outings into the countryside, where they trained despite the lack of adequate equipment. "We would go on a trip to Vitarte, we would go for a walk to the ruins of Chan Chan in Trujillo, or a trip to Pachacamac, for example, to the ruins of Pachacamac. There nobody followed us, no one, no one cared about what we did." Villanueva laughed as he recalled the weaponry they used: "We did not have any weapons. . . . They had some Winchester rifles that they used to teach us triangulation to shoot, which is a trestle where you put the gun, right? And at the bottom is the target, right? And it triangulates, right? And makes a theoretical shot, right? So we did not even know how to handle the Mauser rifles, which was [sic] the example, that was the army's. We were a kind of boy scout."[50]

The military training was only part of the FAJ's broader mission to teach Aprista youths a whole ethos, a set of values by which they were expected to live. As Villanueva put it, "The FAJ was . . . a school of complete preparation for life." Discipline stood high on the list of those values. According to Villanueva, "The discipline of the Federación Aprista Juvenil was pedagogical: for the first time we created the Anglo-Saxon jury system in Peru, right? When a boy committed an error . . . above all, one that deserved a moral sanction, there was no secretariat of discipline. So if you were responsible and you belonged to the Surco sector, the young people of the Surco sector met and they voted to designate five members of the masses so that they judged you."[51] Women also participated in the FAJ. According to Villanueva, "The women in the FAJ had a very interesting role, because coeducation was implemented . . . the law of the party was coeducation, because women provided great services. Women were fully involved in action."[52] The FAJ model extended beyond Peru to Cuba, where Apristas briefly organized a Cuban FAJ.

The Popular Universities

Mae Hoyle de Armijo's main childhood recollection in Trujillo of her uncle Haya was his statement "The people must be educated."[53] The process of building the party relied in great part on a notion of education that entailed the total transformation of the individual. Describing the Aprista party in the eastern Andean department of Amazonas, David Nugent gives a good description of this conception: "a broad-ranging project of cultural transformation that had the primary political objective of undoing the existing, highly stratified social order, and of forming rational, autonomous, principled subjects out of the region's men."[54] Attending lectures and classes became a political act, one that could lead to imprisonment. When captured and interrogated in Lima, Humberto Limonchi Bajonero claimed "that all his political activities were limited in going to the Aprista Seminary, on Calle de Pobres and hear the speakers there as he is a militant of the Party."[55]

The centrality of education to Aprismo is rooted in Haya's national and international experiences. In 1919, he had been elected head of the Peruvian Student Federation (Federación de Estudiantes del Perú). In 1922, he traveled to Argentina, where he met leaders of the Argentine University Reform movement, which had had a broad impact in Latin America. He worked as an educator when he taught in the Anglo-Peruvian school in Lima. After leaving Peru in 1923, he worked with José Vasconcelos and closely observed the efforts to establish rural schools in Mexico. While in exile, he studied at Oxford University and at the London School of Economics. Haya was very conscious of the connection between student movements and revolution in global politics: "This predominant role of the intellectual and especially of the university in the great historical movements is not new in the world. The Universities of China and Russia ... were seedbeds of fruitful rebellion. Lenin and Sun-Yat-Sen ... [were] two great representatives of the historical role of so many university graduates in the service of the sacred causes of justice."[56] There are certainly some parallels to the situation in China, where student radicals with international experience (in Japan) helped to fuel Sun Yat-sen's Revolutionary Alliance.[57]

Haya's experience with the Peruvian Student Federation and the popular universities echoed and was directly related to a broader Latin America–wide context of university reform. As early as 1908, Víctor Andrés Belaúnde, later a prominent diplomat, heeded the call at the All-American Student Congress in Montevideo, Uruguay, for extension classes for workers and created the short-lived University Center in Lima.[58] Contacts across national borders were often personal, as with the visit of Argentine Socialist Alfredo Palacios to Lima at a particularly charged time of confrontation between workers and students and the Peruvian government that led to the May 27, 1919, general strike. Palacios spoke to Peruvian students about the Argentine reform experience. Some years later, between February and May 1922, Haya traveled to Uruguay and Argentina and met university reform leaders. Even at this early stage, Haya was already a somewhat larger-than-life personality. When he returned from this trip, Peruvian students greeted him with great fanfare.

While the University Reform movement undoubtedly influenced him, Haya claimed that his experience of leading the efforts to create popular universities in Peru to educate workers proved crucial to the later development of APRA. In his speech to the First Aprista Party Congress, he told followers packed into the Teatro de Lima, "Our Party comes from the great cultural movement of the Popular Universities, founded here in 1921, that were the social result of the continental University Reformation begun in 1918."[59] Haya had played a pivotal role in the formation of the popular universities. During the First National Congress of Peruvian Students, held in Cuzco in March 1920, Haya, who the year before had been elected president of the Peruvian Student Federation, was charged with "preparing the ground for setting up the Popular University."[60] The connection between students and workers would serve Haya and future Apristas well. The bulk of the students were mestizos from Lima's growing working class. These classes brought workers of mestizo origin, and in some cases even Quechua-speaking workers from nearby haciendas, into contact with middle-class intellectuals such as Haya. Jeffrey Klaiber argues that the popular universities "served as the vital testing ground for most of the ideology of the Aprista Party."[61]

The first popular university opened on January 21, 1921, in Lima's Palacio de la Exposición, a two-story neoclassical building constructed in 1872 for Lima's International Exposition. A second popular university opened soon thereafter in the working-class textile town of Vitarte, located east of Lima, where classes were taught in the movie theater and were preceded by music and theater shows.[62] Teachers traveled by train from Lima. Popular universities were founded both in Lima and in other parts of Peru, including Huaraz, Trujillo, Arequipa, Salaverry, Cuzco, Puno, Ica, Jauja, and Madre de Dios in the jungle. The universities did not grant degrees but rather functioned as a kind of extension service that depended entirely on volunteers. In his role as president, Haya "appointed the teachers, organized most of the cultural and social activities, and with his speaking abilities, drew the largest crowds."[63] He also taught geography and social studies. Literacy was an important focus of the effort, as well as practical subjects such as personal hygiene and first aid for the home, and the universities were the sites of health-oriented campaigns such as the 1922 drive for restaurant cleanliness to avoid the spread of typhoid.[64] These functioned "as a combination civic club, labor union, self-help cooperative, social and educational center for the lower classes."[65] After 1922, the popular universities took on the official name Universidades Populares Gonzalez Prada to commemorate the recently deceased anarchist intellectual and political leader.

The popular universities echoed nineteenth-century liberal moral concerns that education should play a "civilizing" role to prepare workers to become national citizens.[66] Efforts to educate the working classes can be traced back to the radical liberal priest Francisco de Paula González Vigil in Peru, who wrote the pamphlet *Importancia de la educación popular* in 1858.[67] In 1864, the mutual aid society Los Hijos del Pueblo offered evening and Sunday schools for artisans, and in the 1870s a group of intellectuals in the association named Amantes del Saber offered classes on topics that included "political economy, Spanish grammar, geography, experimental physics, English and French."[68]

Once the popular universities were founded, students and teachers interacted in other settings besides the classroom, such as outings to the countryside. One of these outings later became an annual celebration once APRA was founded: the Fiesta de la Planta (Fiesta of the Plant) in the textile town of Vitarte, intended to develop an appreciation among workers of the natural resources of the country. When Haya attended, a young girl greeted him by handing him a bouquet of red carnations as he descended from the train from Lima. The morning celebration included sports competitions (races, soccer, and so on) and the singing of revolutionary songs, followed by a commemoration of fallen workers in the "9th of January" park—the date of a workers' strike for the eight-hour workday—and the planting of trees. A worker would subsequently tend to each tree. The day concluded with a speech given by Haya.[69]

The popular universities were temporarily interrupted when Leguía, who considered them a political threat, closed most of them down after deporting Haya in 1923. José Carlos Mariátegui kept some of the popular universities alive in Lima until Leguía finally shut them down completely in 1927. While in Europe after he founded APRA, Haya promoted the concept of the popular university as a vehicle for revolution. When the party's executive committee sent written instructions to the La Plata, Argentina, cell in 1927, the popular universities stood at the heart of the newly born Aprista project: "The Popular Universities must be the instruments of revolutionary education of the APRA cells. Where they do not exist, they should be created, and bear the names of great revolutionary personalities and try to enter the masses. In the U.P. the fusion of the manual and intellectual workers must be carried out. The CE [executive committee] recommends to the Argentinian, Dominican, Mexican, Panamanian and Bolivian sections the establishment of the U.P. and to the Cuban and Guatemalan sections the recruitment of the existing U.P."[70] Back in Peru, after the fall of Leguía, Apristas reopened the popular universities. Shortly after being elected in 1931, President Sánchez Cerro once again shut them down. During the long years of political persecution from 1932 to 1945, Apristas managed to keep the universities open, operating them clandestinely in people's homes and in the jails. Filled with Aprista prisoners, the prison located on the island of San Lorenzo, off the coast of Lima, became the new location for an improvised popular university.[71]

The emphasis on morality that characterized the popular universities carried over into the Aprista doctrine. As Klaiber points out, "The Popular University's emphasis on personal hygiene, physical fitness, and honesty in dealing with others foreshadowed the Aprista's stress on moral and physical fitness as a key to national regeneration."[72] The popular universities also took up the crusade against alcoholism as "the young student-teachers gave lectures and admonitions to the workers on the ill effects of drinking, and they disseminated literature against it at every opportunity."[73]

Yet, unlike the early popular universities, which had focused on reforming and educating individuals one by one, the Aprista popular universities of the 1930s began to conceive of social reform not as "the spontaneous efforts of private individuals to improve certain aspects of the lives of the lower classes" but rather as "a total transformation of all of society itself."[74] In addition to Haya, future Aprista leaders such as Heysen, Eudocio Ravines (who would leave APRA for the Communist Party), and Seoane taught in the popular universities; future APRA labor leader Arturo Sabroso was one of the student workers who attended classes. Other teachers would eventually join the Communist Party. According to Steve Stein, "Most of the leadership of Lima's organized labor force studied at the Univ Popular at some time between 1921 and its closing by the government in 1924. Men who conducted the major unions in this period and who would direct labor in the 1930s and 1940s shared a common experience in the classrooms of Haya's school."[75]

Party Organization

The brief period of amnesty under President Oscar Benavides in 1933 and 1934 demonstrated APRA's capacity to establish an institutional presence in Peru. Party headquarters throughout the country reopened on October 12, 1933, only to close again when Benavides renewed persecution of the party toward the end of 1934. On October 30, the party newspaper *La Tribuna* was published once again, directed by Seoane, as well as, on November 12, the weekly party magazine *APRA*. The Atahualpa Publishing House published a series of Aprista books that contributed to a renewed propaganda campaign. Enrique Cornejo Koster, who had returned from exile in Buenos Aires, directed the newly founded Universidades Populares Gonzalez Prada with as many as twenty locations in Lima and a range of different courses taught in the morning and evening.[76] The party also opened *comedores populares* (popular dining rooms).[77] The first of these dining rooms was inaugurated on September 20, 1933, on the Calle de los Pobres (today Jirón Lampa). Lunch cost twenty-five centavos. These *comedores* are an example of the ways in which the PAP was able to provide the kind of services normally offered by the state and to build a following. APRA also made inroads in the labor movement—a prelude to its subsequent control of the non-Communist Confederación de Trabajadores del Perú.[78]

During its longest clandestine period, from 1934 to 1945, the party continued to disseminate propaganda. Aprista exiles published works by Haya and other Apristas and smuggled them into Peru for distribution. The party newspaper—now known as *La Tribuna Clandestina*—circulated clandestinely. Anecdotally, it is said that Haya would write "APRA" on any soles (Peru's currency) bills that passed through his hands. APRA developed an elaborate organizational structure that connected the grass roots to the party's national committees, which were connected to the leader, Haya. National committees (discipline, propaganda, and foreign relations) formulated and implemented policy. For example, the Disciplinary Committee was responsible for maintaining party discipline and punishing those who were seen as failing to perform their duties.

The connection to the grass roots guaranteed the party's strength. Aprista Alfonso Velasquez, who would later be a congressman for the party, described local neighborhood organizations around the year 1940:

> We organized in the eighth . . . sector formed by three zones . . . which was the area of Lince, Lobatón and Santa Beatriz. So in these three zones, we had appointed three zone leaders. Then when a

directive came . . . we already took it to the zone boss, the zone boss had a block chief, all the blocks formed by the four streets. Then that block chief distributed it among heads of the block. Then it was easier, because without exposing himself to being stopped . . . they went from house to house knocking on the door, one gave it to the neighbor and that neighbor passed it to the other neighbor, then all was distributed in the block and the area. So the organization as I say . . . was more practical.[79]

The organizational structure continued in subsequent decades. The Casa del Pueblo—party headquarters—in different towns throughout Peru remained centers of party activity following Haya's death in 1979. Today they continue to host events such as lectures and provide certain social services, such as inexpensive medicines, at the party drugstore.

The party retained its vertical organization. One leader, León Seminario, openly expressed his frustration with the nondemocratic tendencies within the party and the lack of consultation: "Pity that everything is in such a closed circle that all work is done in an inconsistent way with other interested parties. And as you will understand[,] more than natural discontent arises that one is not considered for anything despite having sacrificed just like everyone. It heats up a lot of feeling tossed from one barrel to another. . . . The party will not go forward until they integrate all its components."[80] The vertical structure was no guarantee against factionalism. For example, the Committee of Aprista Exiles in Mexico was divided into two factions: "the orthodox group, which rigidly followed the party line of the Aprista Party, and the other, representing the true revolutionary element of which he was a part. The latter faction included poet Gustavo Valcarcel and a group of young people who would later be expelled from APRA and join the Communist Party."[81] During the period when Haya remained confined in the Colombian embassy and isolated from the party (1949–54), Aprista exiles continued to formulate policy through what were known at the postal congresses. Organized by Seoane, these congresses allowed party leaders scattered throughout the continent to discuss policy issues by mail.

The Two Sides of the Personality Cult

The construction of the myth of Haya began early in the party's history. Even as early as the 1931 election campaign, Haya's bodyguards—the *dorados* (whose name was taken from Pancho Villa's troops during the Mexican

Revolution)—ceremonially "swore before Haya de la Torre individually."[82] When Haya was jailed by the Sánchez Cerro government, his followers began to celebrate his birthday, February 22, as the Día de la Fraternidad (Day of Fraternity), a day still celebrated by Apristas today. The rise of a mass political party with a cult of personality around its leader fits well into the pattern of totalitarian parties in Europe: "From the totalitarian parties of Europe, whose rise Haya had witnessed during his exile, APRA borrowed the heavy use of symbolism, the emotional rallies, and the cult of the leader—very effective devices for a mass-based party in a country with a low level of literacy."[83]

When, in May 1932, Haya became a political prisoner of the Sánchez Cerro government, his lengthy incarceration greatly enhanced his international image as a symbol of Latin America's struggles against dictatorship. His imprisonment also contributed to the consolidation of his image within the party as a leader who embodied the very qualities of discipline and sacrifice that he demanded of his followers. During his first ten days in prison, he remained isolated and was not allowed to leave his cell to go the bathroom.[84] During a lengthy interrogation, Haya defended his political ideas. The following year, exiled Apristas in Ecuador used the trial as propaganda and published the legal documents in which Haya defends himself. The incident foreshadowed Fidel Castro's famous prison defense that would inspire his followers in the years before the 1959 Cuban Revolution. Sánchez's hagiographic version of Haya's life, published some years later, even tells of a fellow prisoner who volunteered to try Haya's food every day to protect him from being poisoned.

The letters and telegrams that arrived in Peru from abroad also indicated his transformation into an internationally known figure. The list of individuals who wrote to the Peruvian government about Haya's case reads like a who's who of the global intelligentsia and political establishment. Some called for Haya's release; others for the protection of his life: a number of Colombian intellectuals, including Germán Arciniegas, Alberto Lleras Camargo, and Jorge Eliécer Gaitán, sent telegrams in support of Haya. A letter from Mexican intellectuals to the Peruvian Congress included the signatures of Mariano Azuela, Vicente Lombardo Toledano, Daniel Cosío Villegas, and many others. Letters and telegrams calling for his release arrived from Waldo Frank, Romain Rolland, Gabriela Mistral, and George Lansbury (the British labor leader). Spanish intellectuals José Ortega y Gasset and Miguel de Unamuno sent a joint telegram from Madrid. From Costa Rica, Haya's friend Joaquín García Monge, director of *Repertorio Americano*, stated that tyrannical government threatened the continental dimension of Haya's vision: "These are the enemy tyrannies of our America. These are the tyrannies that have ruined Bolivar's work . . . while the intelligentsia aspired to create Latin American continental citizenship."[85]

The response from institutions throughout Latin America is a measure of Haya's stature as a continental figure.[86] In Peru, the Colegio de Abogados (Lawyer's Association) protested the legality of the trial on a number of points. In Argentina, the Congress and the Senate wrote letters to the president of the Peruvian Constituent Congress calling for Haya's release. The Congress and Senate of Colombia did likewise. The letter from the Colombian Senate expressed the desire "that the life and liberty of Raúl Haya de la Torre, citizen of Peru be respected; he has announced the empire of political proposals that sustain the spiritual and administrative sovereignty of Latin America."[87] The Congress of Costa Rica pleaded on his behalf, as did the Congress of Chile, that of Mexico and the National Assembly of Panama. In addition, civil society also reacted, with letters from student associations, worker associations, and an array of other associations that included the Colombian Rotary Club, a women's association in Argentina called América Nueva, the Ateneo in the Dominican Republic (whose members included the renowned intellectual Pedro Henríquez Ureña), and the Veterans of the War of the Pacific in Chile. The response from Arica on the Peru-Chile border included a long list of workers' associations, such as the Shoemakers' Guild, the Fishermen's Guild, and the mutual aid society 26 de Mayo.

At least two prominent international human rights organizations wrote to the Peruvian government on Haya's behalf. The International League for the Rights of Man sent a letter calling for his proper treatment. The organization's members included such luminaries as Albert Einstein, Bertrand Russell, George Bernard Shaw, Mahatma Gandhi, H. G. Wells, Léon Blum (the French Socialist leader), Ortega y Gasset, Miguel de Unamuno, and Rabindranath Tagore. The International Committee for Political Prisoners sent a letter to the Peruvian ambassador in Washington, D.C., calling for Haya to be treated humanely. Although the letter focused mainly on the details of Haya's case, it also extended its call for such treatment to all political prisoners in Peru. The committee argued that Haya ought to be liberated or receive a legal trial. Among the signatories was Haya's then friend and benefactress Anna Melissa Graves. The committee had been founded in 1924 and was presided over by Roger Baldwin, also founder of the American Civil Liberties Union. It drew the attention of international public opinion to the plight of political prisoners in the Soviet Union, Italy, and Poland.

While incarceration helped magnify his personal prestige and fame, it may also have indirectly strengthened his resolve to see his party outlast him. The possibility of execution must have weighed heavily on Haya's mind during the fifteen months of his imprisonment. At one point, a rumor circulated in Lima and even reached New York that President Sánchez Cerro himself had assassinated Haya. The U.S. embassy referred to this rumor: "Some months ago, there was current a rumor that Sánchez Cerro had gone to visit Haya de la Torre in jail and the two had had a rather heated argument. According to the rumor, Sánchez Cerro became infuriated and shot Haya."[88] The report dismissed the incident as false.

The fear of death clearly exacerbated Haya's preoccupation with the fate of his ideas and his party. He expressed as much in a letter he wrote from prison, allegedly on the paper of a pack of cigarettes, to Juan Seoane, another jailed Aprista. He cautioned that the party's "old guard" might fall in battle and urged his followers to prepare the next generation of Apristas. He envisioned that the party's vanguard (whose number he estimated at half a million) would eventually lead millions of other Peruvians to become Apristas. By "bettering themselves mentally and physically from the individual point of view and making daily improvements to their contributions, giving more and more to the common cause, feeling and knowing themselves responsible and able to give more and more, is to show one will become a Good Aprista."[89] Haya also compared APRA to the German army, whose one hundred thousand men, the number set by the Treaty of Versailles, could in turn become the leaders of many more.

After his release from jail, Haya's international prestige increased his credibility among Apristas and helped to fuel a cult of personality. No other Aprista could now rival his fame. By 1936, fellow Aprista Portal openly discussed the need for such a cult of personality. In a letter to her friend Graves, Portal justified this cult of personality as something that Peruvians needed: "The adoration of Victor Raul is an almost uncontrollable phenomenon. The masses, who have always been caudillistas, can not stop putting their adoration—faith and hope—in a man, who today is Victor Raúl. . . . Does this adoration hurt? Not here, because it gives force to the Aprismo and is one of its guarantees of triumph."[90]

The letter's recipient, Graves, privately criticized the personality cult. She even suggested that Haya had become a victim of his own followers. Her criticism probably stemmed from her falling-out with Haya, whom she had fervently supported during his years as a student. It probably also stemmed from her democratic beliefs. She had developed a maternal relationship with Haya and believed that he was beginning to lie to himself. She blamed Haya's followers for showering him with praise rather than telling him the truth. She even suggested that he was being used by his followers and compared him to a child: "But I do not blame Victor. I blame the others who have always used flattery as an instrument! Poor thing! He has not received the pure truth in his whole life, except from me and after so many [*sic*] flattery he could not bear it! . . . What a life! And what a life for a man who has the character of a child!"[91] After he refused to meet with her when she traveled to Lima to see him, Graves wrote to Portal claiming that he was afraid to do so because she knew him so well, as a mother knows her son, that she would refuse to participate in the adulation.

Graves also accused Haya of having exaggerated his friendship with a number of famous people. While Haya claimed to have received a letter from Senator William Borah, Graves said that in fact they had only spoken once very briefly (during Haya's 1927 visit to the United States) and that she had arranged the meeting. When Graves later requested that Borah sign her petition to liberate Haya from jail in 1932, Borah had refused, saying he did not recall ever having met Haya. Regarding other famous personalities, Leon Trotsky had never invited Haya to Russia, and neither Ramsay Mac-Donald nor George Bernard Shaw had arranged scholarships for him at the University of London and Oxford. Graves herself claims to have paid for his studies in England. Perhaps his exaggeration of these relationships played to the personality cult or perhaps they simply reveal a desire, unsurprising for a young Latin American intellectual stepping onto the international scene, to want to be associated with famous people.

A public reference to the personality cult appears in the work of American journalist Carleton Beals. A supporter of the Mexican Revolution, Beals did not blindly accept the cause of revolution and generally took a critical approach to Latin American politics. While he recognized the importance of Aprismo, he also had critical comments about the party. In his 1934 book *Fire in the Andes*, while acknowledging that "Aprismo must be recognized as the most vital popular force in Peru," he also criticized Haya's personal control of APRA and claimed that to Haya's followers he seemed "perhaps too much of a God."[92]

However, for the most part, international publicity remained favorable and helped to fuel Haya's fame as a key figure not only in Peruvian but also in Latin American politics. Referring to an article that appeared in *Fortune* magazine in 1935, Alfredo González Prada wrote to Sánchez, "A great role is attributed to Apra in the future and Haya appears as 'the man of destiny.' It is worth taking advantage of that correctly."[93] The book by John Gunther titled *Inside Latin America* also reported favorably on Haya and APRA. This was a period when information on Latin America was scarce among the general public in the United States.

Meanwhile, back in Peru, Haya's life in hiding helped fuel his mythical aura. Between 1934 and 1945 his whereabouts were shrouded in mystery as he frequently moved from one safe house to another to escape capture. Haya perpetuated this mythology by identifying his changing location with the single designation of "Incahuasi" that appeared on his letters and articles. *Incahuasi* means "the house of the Inca" in Quechua. It reflects the *indigenista* tendencies of the period. The term also reflected Haya's deep hubris, as it implied that he represented a reincarnation of the Inca. The notion of such a reincarnation had deep roots in Peruvian popular culture. The myth of the Inkarri held that at the time of their arrival in Peru, the Spaniards had buried the different parts of the Inca's body in different parts of the land and that these would one day be joined together to mark the return. Haya had begun to acquire the larger-than-life quality that would remain his hallmark even beyond his death.

The fact that at times his whereabouts were something of an open secret (known to the government and the U.S. embassy) in no way diminishes the strength of the myth. His international prestige may have shielded him from the kind of danger faced by less prominent Apristas. The U.S. embassy clearly knew his location when it organized meetings between him and various visiting American intellectuals such as Frank Tannenbaum. At one point Haya even lived at the house of one of the president's relatives, Augusto Benavides Diez Canseco, who was both a cousin and a brother-in-law of President Benavides; the president was married to Francisca Benavides, sister of Augusto Benavides Diez Canseco. Haya may even have had his own apartment on the ample grounds of this house located in Los Condores, in the foothills of the Andes, close to Lima.

Various accounts tell of how he narrowly escaped being captured numerous times. On one occasion in 1939, while staying at a safe house in the district of Barranco, Haya escaped, gun in hand, by climbing over a wall as the police broke into the home where he was hiding. On this occasion, his bodyguard and close confidant Jorge Idiaquez was captured as he tried to defend Haya. According to Aprista historian Roy Soto Rivera, "The mystery about the whereabouts of Haya de la Torre became a legend. The Apristas were confident that any night the 'jefe' would appear unexpectedly in their homes. The police officers claimed to have seen him in the mountains or northern towns."[94] At one point, a Chilean journal, *Hoy*, published a photograph of a man who resembled Haya as part of a ploy to make the government believe he had fled Peru. The stories about Haya remain in popular memory to this day. I have heard accounts from numerous people who claim that Haya once hid in the home of one of their relatives. The accounts include details such as one claim that Haya wore women's clothes to leave a safe house and avoid capture.

The veil of secrecy around him and his whereabouts during these years created the perfect conditions to fuel stories that transformed him from man into legend. Aprista accounts claim that he singlehandedly published the clandestine newspaper *La Tribuna*, organized the party, and wrote international propaganda from his shifting hiding places. For example, Soto Rivera writes, "He personally organized the cadres of the PAP—cells and committees, trade unions and professional groups—reconstituting them as often as the circumstances made necessary, due to either incarceration, or the death of its members."[95] He did continue to publish articles abroad during this period.

This vision of the all-powerful Haya contrasts with the difficulties of his financial reality. The lack of money was a constant concern during these years. In his letters to Sánchez, Haya constantly complained about financial problems, both his own and the party's. He apparently received a stipend of two hundred soles a month.[96] The money was sent to him surreptitiously: "I told you that I received 200. This concerns something confidential: P. does not receive money but rather orders from M. I have seen one. The thing appears as a gift or something like that. I have said that it is payment of 'Ercilla.' I want to know if this is so. If it is not, discontinue it, and if it is, be smart, let money come. P. is heavily spent on other necessities. That money needs to come. I wait for May. This situation is pressing with many expenses for everything. We steal food to help P. We lack everything because of that."[97] The letter does not refer to people directly by name, as Haya was well aware of the dangers of his correspondence being intercepted.

Hagiographies of Haya

Apristas began to write hagiographies to fuel the cult of personality. The first, published by Sánchez in Chile with Editorial Ercilla in 1934 and titled *Haya de la Torre o el político: Crónica de una vida sin tregua*, had a second edition in 1936. The second, first published in Mexico in 1939 by the painter Felipe Cossío del Pomar and titled *Haya de la Torre: El indoamericano*, also had a second edition, published in Lima in 1946 during the time when APRA was no longer a proscribed party. Cossío del Pomar published another biography many years later, in 1961, titled *Víctor Raúl: Biografía de Haya de la Torre*. Portal seems also to have contemplated the idea of writing a biography of Haya, although the project never reached fruition. Graves criticized the idea: "Another book would be another method to help him to continue in this pattern of glorifying himself! Poor thing."[98] Later, once Portal became disillusioned with the party, she jotted down notes apparently for a critical biography to be titled "El mito Haya" that was never written. Instead, she wrote a highly critical fictional account of the leader of a political party, titled *La Trampa*.

These Aprista hagiographies had some echoes in U.S. academic circles. The academic journal *Revista Iberoamericana* reviewed Cossío del Pomar's book. The review, written by Antonio Rebolledo, uncritically captures the image of Haya as a leader of high moral character: "He is one of the rare examples of admirable moral austerity that rarely appears in the politico-social panorama of Iberoamerica in contrast to the venality and lack of vision of the leaders who assume the governing responsibility of our people. Flawless and with proven spiritual discipline, his analytical ability, his sagacity and intellectual preparation, his knowledge of the Indo-American reality, all designate him as the irreplaceable leader of his people."[99] There seem to have been plans to have Sánchez's book translated into English. González Prada, son of the famous Peruvian anarchist thinker and politician, had read the proofs before its publication and wrote to Sánchez saying, "It will be effective as Aprista propaganda," and he deemed it "a great thing" that a version was to appear in English.[100] The translation does not seem to have occurred.

Sánchez begins his book *Haya de la Torre o el político* by denying that it is a hagiography. He claims to set himself apart from the great hero tradition embodied by the Scottish philosopher and historian Thomas Carlyle: "Writing biography is not creating caudillos. Carlyle, perhaps, would intend it. But modern biography, on the contrary, descends from its seat of the demigods in order to speak as men."[101] He seemingly contradicts himself by later characterizing his biography of Haya as an epic, a genre associated with the deeds of a hero. He portrays Haya as an apostle: "In Haya, the apostle's adhesive joins admirably to the entrails of Politician."[102] Sánchez relates incidents for which there is no evidence and that magnify the importance of Haya. For example, he describes Haya arriving in the United States in 1927 after receiving invitations from various U.S. universities to discuss the Monroe Doctrine. Sánchez describes Haya's arrival in Boston in apotheosizing terms: "When approaching Boston, the passengers realized that Mr. Haya was 'somebody,' because there was a dense cloud of reporters and photographers that came to surround him."[103] There is no evidence for Sánchez's claim. In fact, Haya's talk at Harvard was a student event organized by the Debating Union—and Haya spoke together with three other men, two of them undergraduates, the third a history instructor in the Division of History, Government, and Economics.[104]

Cossío del Pomar's book *Haya de la Torre: El Indoamericano*, published in Mexico in 1939, is filled with anecdotes that highlight Haya's qualities as a person: his honesty, his braveness, his sense of justice, and the austerity of his life. At four hundred pages, the book, which includes lengthy quotes of often-dense passages of Haya's writings, was not designed for a mass public. Cossío del Pomar's narrative alternates between sections on Haya and sections on broader political events in Peru. This structure gives the work a somewhat scattered quality that ends up distracting from Haya to some degree. He often cities entire passages of Sánchez's book.

Cossío del Pomar's Haya was a man destined to become a revolutionary leader and recognized as such by those around him. Even his year of birth was a harbinger of his future revolutionary role: in 1895 Nicolás de Piérola had begun the revolution that brought the Partido Demócrata to power. Cossío del Pomar writes that during Haya's baptism ceremony, "seeing the chubby and cheerful boy, those in attendance anticipate that having arrived in the world to the cadence of the revolution, he might be a revolutionary."[105] People around him recognized Haya's greatness. The Peruvian poet César Vallejo, who knew Haya as a student in Trujillo, allegedly prophesied the future greatness of Haya, saying, "I, a poet, lift my cup for this condor fledgling. . . . I, a prophet, . . . proclaim that he will fly very high, and he will be great, great, great."[106] The poet Alberto Hidalgo described Haya in quasi-religious terms as "endowed with that mystery that encircles the heads of the apostles, a special magnetism to attract the masses and rule them."[107] When Haya met President Hipólito Yrigoyen in the Casa Rosada

Haya as a child with his parents. The mythologizing of Haya begins even with stories of the young child (Armando Villanueva Papers, courtesy of Lucía Villanueva).

during his visit as a student leader to Argentina, the president allegedly said to him, "I don't know where you are going, but I have a feeling that it will be far."[108] Cossío del Pomar cites the Cuban Enrique José Varona, who compares Haya to Bolívar, Karl Marx, and Lenin.[109]

Drawing on scenes from Haya's life, Cossío del Pomar presents him as an austere man, a just and honest man, a brave man of action, a great orator, a teacher, a peacemaker, and a great thinker. Despite the fact that he was descended on his mother's side from a prominent Trujillo family, Haya lived an austere life. As proof of Haya's modest lifestyle, Cossío del Pomar relates an incident in which Haya, the student leader, met with President Leguía. According to Cossío del Pomar, the elbows of Haya's jacket were so worn out that he donned an overcoat to appear properly dressed, even though it was summer.[110] The honest Haya turned down an offer by Leguía, who, seeking to get rid of the young agitator, allegedly offered to pay for his trip to Europe. Haya allegedly replied, "Tell your friends that there is not enough gold in the world to buy the conscience of an honest man. And Haya de la Torre, tell them this, is an honorable man."[111] Cossío del Pomar paints very vivid scenes, with a detailed exchange between Haya and Leguia that is clearly fictional.[112]

Haya the teacher and disciplinarian emerges in the book, steering his followers away from the dangers of sensualism. One anecdote tells of how Haya, while living in Paris, would play soccer on Sunday mornings with other Apristas. When one of the players, Edgardo Rozas, showed up tired from having stayed up too late at the city's cafés, Haya reprimanded him: "You promised me to go to bed early. I see you still have no word. And you want to be Aprista?"[113] Cossío del Pomar portrays Haya later, following the 1931 election, as a peacemaker who discouraged violence within his party. In a speech following the election, which Apristas considered to have been fraudulent, Haya spoke to followers and took the moral high ground by minimizing the importance of the electoral defeat and placing Aprismo on a higher philosophical ground: "Anyone can arrive at the palace . . . but the mission of Aprismo is to reach the people's conscience."[114]

Cossío del Pomar places Haya in the company of great men, both those whom he met personally and those who influenced his thinking. He tells of Haya's friendship with Romain Rolland in Switzerland. He makes the unlikely claim that Unamuno and Haya, who met in Paris, became "great friends."[115] Cossío del Pomar also situates Haya within a tradition of Western philosophical thought in which Haya is in dialogue with great thinkers such as Oswald Spengler and Einstein. Spengler's *Decline of the West* had a strong impact in Latin America. His pessimism regarding the course of Western civilization reaffirmed the growing tendency of Latin American intellectuals to assert the importance of their own national cultural traditions as independent from the West. Cossío del Pomar quotes Haya refuting Spengler, claiming that Spengler's view remains static, whereas Aprismo incorporates Einstein's notion of relativity, thus opening the way for new possibilities of development within the context of the "historical time-space" of different non-Western societies. Cossío del Pomar quotes Haya engaging with G. W. F. Hegel and Marx. He dedicates a number of pages to Haya's idea of historical space-time, his application of the concept of relativism to history, which allowed him to break away from a linear conception of history in which Europe and the United States represent the culmination of social development, to be followed by other countries in the world. With the notion of historical space-time, Haya gave philosophical grounding to the notion that countries can develop differently, that Latin America needs to follow its own historical path, rather than one traced by Europe and the United States. Cossío del Pomar cites Haya's own work and writes, "There is, therefore, not a single ancient history or one antiquity and one Middle and Modern age, but rather so many similar periods, how many social and cultural processes acquire development, consistency and permanence in world historical development."[116]

The Sensual Haya

By the 1950s, a number of his detractors, former Apristas who left the party, began to paint a very different portrait of Haya in a series of condemnatory pamphlets. The slew of attacks on him occurred after the party had taken a conservative direction. While ideological divisions may have prompted many of these attacks, personal enmities must also have played a role, judging by the vitriol found in the writings of those who attacked Haya. The attacks present Haya as hypocritical, as not living by the standards to which he holds his followers. An early supporter now turned enemy, Hidalgo publicly referred to Haya's alleged homosexuality. One of the earliest and most critical voices was that of Portal, whose pamphlet ¿Quienes traicionaron al pueblo? condemned not only Haya but the entire Aprista hierarchy of leaders.

In 1951, Ravines, who had left APRA very early to join the Communist Party, published a highly critical account of Haya in his book *The Yenan Way*. Ravines challenged the view of Haya as living an austere life and deliberately presented a sensual, luxury-loving Haya. Describing the young Haya when he arrived in Paris, Ravines wrote, "From a de luxe compartment, far beyond even the first-class coaches, alighted Victor Raúl Haya de la Torre, surrounded by porters carrying shiny leather suit-cases. He was dressed in the best English fashion and wore a trench-coat straight from Piccadilly. No one would have taken him for a penniless student from a backward South American country. One would have thought him, rather, the son of a rich Argentine cattle rancher."[117] While Ravines's recollection may have been accurate—at the time Haya was receiving the financial support of Graves—even Haya's critics agree that he led a fairly austere life after his return to Peru in 1931. Carlos Raffo Dasso, a businessman, Aprista sympathizer, and friend of Haya's, claims that he helped to pay some of Haya's bills: "It's not bad to say, but I have paid Victor Raul's phone because he could not communicate and he had no money. So when they say that Haya lived as a prince, wearing silks, they are being petty. He was one of the men that I knew that was most austere and disinterested in money."[118] Raffo also tells that he found out from a common friend that in the 1960s Haya had sold a vicuña overcoat that Raffo had given him as a gift: "That is, he had sold the coat I had just given him. When I asked how much, it turns out that he had sold very cheaply. That was Haya, totally detached and ignorant of the cost of money. He lived without worry."[119]

A more dramatic attack that highlights the very sensualism condemned by Haya appeared in the pamphlet of another disaffected Aprista, Hidalgo, in 1954. In *Por qué renuncié al APRA* (Why I renounced APRA), Hidalgo openly discusses Haya's alleged homosexuality in homophobic terms and claims that Haya's sexual preferences disqualified him from being a politician. Using terms such as "inversion sexual," "uranismo," "sodomita," and "pederasta," Hidalgo claims that as a young student in Lima, Haya engaged in homosexual relations with members of Lima's artistic circles, as well with aristocrats, "the literati and the gentlemen prone to the same vice."[120] He claims that when he met Haya again in Berlin, "Haya continued practicing his aberration against nature."[121] Hidalgo claimed to have a scientific basis for his conclusion. What he referred to as "pederastia," while not harmful for artists, was detrimental to politicians, who could fall prey to sexual passions to the detriment of the public good: "In the case of the sodomite politician such terms become acute, for he is forced to move within an uncomfortable existential duplicity: his public performance must appear as honorable as possible, while his lasciviousness unfolds in the ocean of physical, biological, and physiological baseness."[122] His argument reflects an acceptance of homosexuality in the case of artists.

In a further twist of the argument, Hidalgo associates strength with sexual power and claims that as a middle-aged man, Haya's waning sexual drive could have terrible consequences. In middle age, Haya now faced what Hidalgo refers to as "rectal menopause." This decrease in his sexual functions could somehow generate negative feelings that would propel Haya to act cruelly to eliminate his adversaries.[123] Claiming that his views were backed by the authority of doctors and psychologists, Hidalgo states that homosexuality "gives rise to the segregation of juices contrary to the harmonious performance of the spirit and pushes the victim through the paths of tortuosity, lack of sensitivity and irresponsibility." He finally urged that the Peruvian Congress pass a law forbidding "andróginos" from holding government positions or leading political parties.[124]

The Reluctant Leader? 1948–1969

By the time these pamphlets appeared, Haya had been isolated from his party for a few years as a result of his prolonged stay in the Colombian embassy, where he had sought political asylum following the coup of General Odría. When, as president, Odría refused to grant it, a legal case ensued between the two governments that dragged on for years at the International Court of Justice in The Hague. The new government energetically persecuted Apristas. The police surrounded the houses of well-known leaders and were able to capture a number of them, including Luis Felipe de las Casas, Prialé, and many others. Prisons were once again filled with Aprista detainees. The man in charge of political repression under Odría, Alejandro Esparza Zañartu, has been fictionalized and immortalized in Mario Vargas Llosa's novel *Conversación en la catedral*. Some Apristas managed to escape and go abroad to resume the now-familiar life of exile. One of the more spectacular cases was that of Fernando León de Vivero and Pedro Muñiz, who had both been presidents of the Chamber of Deputies in Congress. They managed to escape the police that came after them with guns in the Olivar de San Isidro, an ancient olive grove whose first trees were allegedly planted by Francisco Pizarro. The two managed to climb over the gates of the nearby Cuban embassy, which opened its doors to them. Since Cuba had not recognized Odría's de facto government, political asylum would be difficult to arrange. The Peruvian government justified its refusal to recognize the right of political asylum in this case by claiming that APRA played by rules that were not considered "chivalrous" and was a terrorist organization.[125] A few months later, in August 1950, the two fugitives escaped from the embassy and managed to go abroad.[126]

Haya was well aware that his years in the Colombian embassy contributed to his international prestige. It was the first time that a case of this nature had been submitted to the International Court of Justice for arbitration. While he still remained as far as ever from taking power in Peru, Haya's moral stature was enhanced by the years spent patiently in the embassy and by the notoriety of the case. Even before the case began, two months after his asylum started, *Life* magazine had included him in its "People" section with a photograph of him looking out of one of the embassy windows. Part of the caption read, "Now he seldom appears at a window, for Peru's army dictatorship would like to shoot at Haya—with a gun, not a camera."[127] The article also refers to the fact that the Odría government was not respecting the right of sanctuary, which "is especially sacred in Latin America." The Odría government attempted to restrict circulation of the magazine in Peru.[128] Haya's friend Germán Arciniegas, the Colombian intellectual, pointed out in a 1954 article that the case had achieved the opposite of what President Odría wanted by publicizing the name of Haya, who was written about in newspapers worldwide: "The name Haya has grown to the highest point in popularity and good fame."[129]

Some years after his release, while living in Sweden, Haya emphasized to Sánchez the importance of using the asylum case to help legitimize the party in Peru. Criticizing Sánchez for not making enough of this case in his forthcoming book, Haya wrote, "The interpretation must be clear and based on a syllogism: As the head of Aprismo, that is, the Party, I was accused of being a common delinquent. My acquittal is that of the Party. Sustaining this thesis with vigor (it emanates from the accusations), there will be no judge that makes any move against us in Lima."[130] In Haya's estimation, the case was never given the importance in Peru that it had internationally.

After he was released from the embassy, Haya traveled to Mexico. On May 7, 1954, former Mexican president Emilio Portes Gil presided at a banquet for three hundred people held at a restaurant in Mexico City to honor Haya. In his speech, Portes Gil "reiterated that aprismo was the only philosophy that fit the reality of America."[131] The banquet received front-page coverage in many Mexican newspapers, according to attendee Manuel Vázquez Diaz, who was a member of APRA's first Mexican cell back in 1928. On May 8, the Brazilian magazine O Cruzeiro published an interview with Haya, conducted in Mexico, in which Haya provided an outline of the principles of APRA that was much more democratic than the earliest formulation of Aprismo of 1928. Haya emphasized the protection of individual rights within countries and the sovereignty of countries.[132]

As Nelson Manrique has pointed out, from the moment Haya took refuge in the Colombian embassy to his permanent return to Peru in 1969 after years of self-imposed exile in Europe, he remained distant from Peruvian politics, with the exception of his two runs for president in 1962 and 1963. When he did return to Peru, he did so to the adulation of his followers. He sometimes returned to celebrate the Día de la Fraternidad, his birthday. Haya would remain abroad, primarily in Europe, for most of the next fifteen years, with only brief periods of residence in Peru.

The years in Europe allowed him to dedicate his time to writing on a variety of issues having more to do with global politics than with the intricacies of Peruvian politics. He visited the Scandinavian countries and wrote travel articles about Sweden and Norway. He wrote extensively about a trip to Greenland. His articles on European politics express a growing admiration of European social democracy. He wrote a large number of articles on global political issues, with titles such as "Nehru, guia del buen camino" and "Está triunfando la diplomacia rusa."

Europe also freed Haya of some of the constraints on the expression of his sexuality that limited him in Peru as leader of a major party. People who knew him in Europe report that he visited gay bars. The Peruvian writer Julio Ramón Ribeyro, who lived in Paris, encountered Haya on a couple of occasions. On one occasion in 1966, Ribeyro tells that Haya had been beaten up by some strangers and suggests that the altercation may have originated in a gay bar: "Some say they were leftist students. This seems unlikely, because I have links with them and I would have known. Others say that it was a problem of a group of pansies, because the cafés that Haya frequents are of that sort."[133] The French intellectual André Coyné, who was openly gay and was also allegedly the lover of Peruvian Cesar Moro, publicly recounted his own experiences of going to "boy bars" with Haya both in Paris and in Japan.[134]

Rumors claim that Haya had an Italian lover who even visited him in Lima at one point. The rumors say that eventually the lover had to leave because of pressure from the party.[135] Rumor also claims that Haya's longstanding lover while in Peru was his personal secretary and bodyguard Idiaquez, who accompanied him for most of his life. His political enemies used the claim that Haya was homosexual against him. In a recent essay that suggests that Haya was homosexual, journalist Toño Angulo Daneri relates the experience of a photographer who was given a tip so that he could photograph Haya and Idiaquez in a hotel room together. The door had been left open for him. When he arrived, he found the two together in the bedroom, Haya about to go to bed. At the time, Haya was eighty-three. The photographer described the scene not as sexual but as endearing. He froze and never took the photograph. As further evidence of Haya's homosexuality, Angulo Daneri also points to the fact that Haya, particularly as he aged, liked to be surrounded by young male disciples.[136]

To this day, the subject remains a sensitive one for Apristas. When Angulo Daneri presented his book with an essay on Haya's homosexuality at the Trujillo Book Fair in 2005, a group of Aprista militants threw an egg at him and attempted to attack him.[137] Members of the audience gathered around him to protect him from further aggression. In a 2001 television interview, former president Alan García, when asked about the topic, reflected on his own prejudices about homosexuality and on gay rights as an important social movement and then claimed that he had lived with Haya and never seen any signs of his being gay. He explains the fact that Haya remained single his whole life by pointing out that Haya knew that party leaders who got married and had a family would be less dedicated to the party. García describes this as a "misogynistic" attitude. He also describes how painful it was to him and others to see political cartoons that depicted Haya dressed like a woman.[138]

Educator and Democrat? The Last Decade

When Haya returned to Peru in 1969, the military government of General Juán Velasco Alvarado had implemented a set of nationalist reforms that seemed to be taken directly from APRA's original program. These included agrarian reform and nationalizations. The shift in Peru to the left seems to have encouraged Haya to embrace some of his original ideas. He now allowed, for the first time in decades, the republication of his earlier book *El antimperialismo y el APRA*. His enemies have accused him of political fickleness for embracing his more radical political ideas at a time when it was politically convenient for him to do so.

During these years, Haya became the venerated elder statesman who held court at the party headquarters, La Casa del Pueblo, located on Alfonso Ugarte Avenue in downtown Lima. He was a great conversationalist and had numerous stories to tell listeners about his long life both in Peru and abroad. He lectured and met with followers who came to see him. Now that he would clearly never become president of Peru, Haya increasingly inhabited the role of teacher. He also held court at his home, Villa Mercedes, located on the outskirts of Lima in Ate. Over the course of his life, Haya continued to relish his role as teacher. The businessman Raffo, who became a friend of Haya's, describes how he met Haya in 1945 at a gathering of young students:

> I met Haya through [Carlos Enrique] Melgar who took me to a meeting. It was 1945 and APRA had just emerged from hiding. The encounter with Haya impressed me greatly and influenced the way

I viewed politics. Haya had a great ease with words and dominated the stage. He knew where he wanted to lead each and every one of us. He was 50 years old and had reached maturity in hiding. . . . The meetings with Haya were held at a crossroads of Paseo Colón, near Plaza Bolognesi and a cinema called Rívoli, if I am not mistaken. At that time the premises of Alfonso Ugarte did not exist.[139]

One last political door now opened up for Haya after General Francisco Morales Bermúdez took power in 1975 and initiated the transition back to democratic rule. In a gesture intended to end the historic enmity between APRA and the military once and for all, Morales Bermúdez put an end to the military commemorations of those who died fighting APRA's 1932 uprising in Trujillo. When Morales Bermúdez convoked elections to name delegates for a constituent assembly that would write a new constitution for Peru, APRA's continued strength as a party became evident when it won over one-third of the votes.

As leader of his party, Haya was now entitled to preside over the Constituent Assembly and would take the first elected position of his life. However, Luis Bedoya Reyes, head of the Partido Popular Cristiano (Christian Democratic Party), tells of the behind-the-scenes scheming by members of APRA's traditional enemies, the parties of the Communist Left. The leaders of the leftist parties that had had an unusually strong showing offered to form a block with Bedoya to become a majority and to back him as president of the Constituent Assembly. According to Bedoya's account, he refused because he saw Haya as a venerable elder statesman who deserved the position. He described Haya's eyes welling up with tears when he realized that he had survived the politicking and been elected president of the Constituent Assembly.[140]

Haya's entry into the congressional building was a moment of great emotion and symbolism. After half a century of attempting to gain political power, he now set foot in the Peruvian Congress to preside over the writing of a new constitution. The man whose party had been vilified for decades by the Peruvian military now walked down the Hall of the Pasos Perdidos, an imposing hallway leading to the chambers, accompanied by two officers (*edecanes*) assigned to accompany him, and received honors from the military. Almost four decades later, Luis Alva Castro, who, as Haya's secretary at the time, had witnessed that moment, teared up when he described Haya's entry into the building.[141] Alva Castro would later hold a number of high-ranking positions in both subsequent APRA governments, including

Older Haya giving a speech, probably in 1957 (Armando Villanueva Papers, courtesy of Lucía Villanueva).

minister of economy and finance and prime minister (head of the cabinet in the Peruvian political system).

Haya continued to cultivate an ascetic image, one of service to the country and to his party. As president of the Constituent Assembly, he refused the official government vehicle he was entitled to and continued to use his own small car.[142] The myth of Haya continues to this day both among his disciples and surviving followers and among the younger members of the party. Aprista Consuelo Torres Tello keeps photographs of Haya, together with religious images and candles, in a small altar she has mounted in a room in her home. She has in her possession a death mask of him as well.[143] Young members of the party continue to speak with awe of Haya. His followers continue to celebrate his birthday as the Day of Fraternity.

The caudillo-based party structure continued after Haya's death. García became the party's new caudillo. While García continued to infuse the party with personalism, he was never able to rival Haya on this front. Despite García's achievement of winning the presidency twice, no cult of personality developed around him. After a disastrous showing in his attempt to win the presidency for what would have been a historic third time in 2016, García has stepped down as head of the party. No new caudillo has yet emerged, although it is rumored that he may try again to run for president in 2021. The future of the party is certainly in question at the moment. While some observers have begun to pronounce its demise, others mention the often-cited saying "El APRA nunca muere" (APRA never dies).

CHAPTER FIVE

Broken Promises
The Women of APRA

> I am just beginning to speak, now I am speaking about certain
> things in the committees when I go; I am speaking about the worth
> of the Peruvian woman ... when she belongs to something beloved
> like the Aprista Party.
>
> —CONSUELO TORRES TELLO

> The political woman needs to do everything intelligently, must be
> flirtatious, but only moderately flirtatious.
>
> —CONSUELO TORRES TELLO

> Leaders devised gender-related programs that suited their
> perceived political ends.
>
> —SANDRA McGEE DEUTSCH

Lindomira Peirano was only twelve when she heard Víctor Raúl Haya de la
Torre speak in the main square of Cajamarca in 1931. The young political
candidate, recently returned from Europe, drew large crowds as he campaigned for president: "Everybody must be well prepared ... must study,"
she recalled him telling his enthusiastic supporters. She also recalled his
words about women: "We must give women the vote, that is what most
caught my attention and what I most liked. One always thinks: Why should
I be subjected to men's issues, they need to also consider women."[1] Haya's
message that year gained even greater poignancy when Peruvian women
witnessed a woman, Magda Portal, campaigning for him in Cuzco, Arequipa,
Puno, and towns all along the coast. As a founding member of the American Popular Revolutionary Alliance (APRA) and the only woman to hold a
permanent seat on the party's executive committee, Portal was one of the
first women in Latin America to go out on the campaign trail. She commented on how "the very presence of a woman had a great impact since
this phenomenon had not occurred before, as women were always restricted
to domestic functions."[2] She even suggested that she became as well known
as Haya during these early years, claiming that "with time, the people

recognized me and discovered me during the large popular marches, chant-
ing my name—the name of a woman—as much as they chanted that of
V. R. Haya de la Torre."[3]

At a time when women still lacked the right to vote in Peru, the Partido
Aprista Peruano (PAP) was the first to recruit women into its ranks. By
doing so, the party inaugurated a new era in the political history of women
in Peru. APRA's position on women stood in stark contrast to that of the
many suffrage movements at the time. While the Apristas elected to the
Constituent Assembly supported women's suffrage, party ideologues, led by
Portal herself, argued to delay suffrage until women had developed a revolutionary consciousness, lest they cast a conservative vote. She criticized the
suffragist movement as "bourgeois" and claimed that it would have little impact on the history of women in the long run. "What, then, can the vote be
in female hands, if it is not inspired by a new social and political concept?
What it has been in the hands of men throughout the history of bourgeois
and capitalist democracy. What is urgent is not for women to vote, but to
know who to vote for."[4] She also made the argument in her 1931 article
"El voto femenino deber ser calificado."[5] Portal expressed great faith in
women's revolutionary potential. In her essay *Hacia la mujer nueva* (1933),
she argued that women would be among the most interested in rising up
against the social order that oppressed them, and APRA would thus have
ready supporters among women.

The issue of women's suffrage for Apristas became moot for the next decade and a half, as the proscribed party was unable to participate in elections. Prevented by political circumstances from pursuing the issue of
women's rights, Apristas faced a decade of political persecution that helped
to equalize the experiences of men and women. Together with men, women
participated in underground activities such as distributing propaganda,
fought in some Aprista insurrections, faced incarceration for their political
activities, and in some cases were forced to go into exile.

Once the party regained temporary legal status and helped to bring President José Luís Bustamante y Rivero to power as part of a coalition government, women's issues once again came to the forefront. In 1946 the party
held the First National Convention of Aprista Women, and in 1948 the second party congress addressed the issue of women's political rights. Yet the
party now failed to institutionalize what had been occurring in practice during a decade of female participation in party affairs. Haya himself spoke
out against granting women equal rights within the party structure. When
the party denied women full participation in party affairs, Portal walked

out of the congress in disgust.[6] General Manuel Odría eventually granted women the vote in 1955 during his presidency to ensure what was perceived as being a conservative vote.

Haya's position in 1948 reflects the prejudices of a culture that continued to reject a public role for women. Portal pointed to these cultural prejudices in a letter to her friend Anna Melissa Graves in which she stated that women in America "suffer the prejudices of the Middle Ages" and are seen as "white slaves, toys for pleasure." Women like herself faced two sets of enemies: social injustices and social prejudices. Portal claimed that these prejudices "can still be found amongst our own compañeros! Difficult, my dear friend, but we do what we can." While rejecting any feminist label, Portal claimed that women could change the world drastically. "I believe," she wrote to Graves, "that if women took an active part in the affairs of the world, they would drastically change the face of humanity."[7] To make her case, Portal also relied on a traditional view of motherhood as politically empowering: women's love of their children would make them into a force for peace.

In her analysis of twentieth-century gender politics in Latin America, Sandra McGee Deutsch has argued that "leaders devised gender-related programs that suited their perceived political ends."[8] Haya's reaffirmation of male leadership and abandonment of the party's early revolutionary stance on women reflected the party's overall more conservative posture as he rejected its revolutionary past in efforts to gain political legitimacy in Peru. His stance also reduced the threat of any kind of challenge to his power from Portal, one of the few people in the party who dared to criticize him. His position therefore reinforced the party hierarchy and kept power in his own hands and that of its male leaders. Haya's reaffirmation of a male-dominated order, although not unusual for the times, takes on an added significance in light of Haya's own unconventional personal life as a political leader who never married. In fact, allegations of his homosexuality have led his followers to list a number of women with whom he allegedly had romantic relationships.

While Portal stands out as the most prominent woman in the early history of the party, numerous women of different social classes contributed to the day-to-day activities that made the PAP the best-organized and strongest political force in Peru for many decades.

Women's Rights and Class Issues in Peru and Latin America

The first women to participate in the public sphere during the nineteenth century were of middle- and upper-class origin. They did so through their writing—the very act of writing gave women a voice outside the domestic sphere—and their participation in literary gatherings (*tertulias*) that also addressed political issues. Clorinda Matto de Turner commented through her fiction on issues of national importance, such as the role of the Indian in national life.[9] Another, Juana Manuela Gorriti, an Argentine writer who had settled in Peru, ran one of the most notorious *tertulias*. As in Peru, educated women throughout Latin America at the time sought a public voice in their societies' affairs.

Women also began to make some inroads into education during the nineteenth century. Some upper-class women received tutoring at home or attended religious schools. Some working-class women also received an education in schools established by charitable societies. The drive for expanding public education to women, however, came primarily from middle-class women. It went further in some countries than others—Argentina was at the forefront in the process of educational reforms. Governments throughout the region began to establish schools known as normal schools, primarily oriented to training women as teachers. Chile became the first country to admit women into higher education.[10] Argentina and Chile, which pioneered women's educational efforts, had fairly homogenous populations, unlike the more complex population in Peru, which had a heavily indigenous component.[11] In Peru schools were restricted to urban areas and were more heavily controlled by the Catholic Church than in other parts of the continent, even as late as the 1950s.

By the twentieth century, a number of female journalists had begun to write about political issues. Angela Ramos, Angélica Palma, María Wiesse, and Doris Gibson were among the most prominent.[12] The importance of women writers in Peru parallels trends in other parts of the continent—the driving forces for such a movement, which spurred a greater feminist consciousness, were not only the process of modernization in these societies but also the transnational networks that brought women together and allowed them to have a voice in international forums, unconstrained by the problems of discrimination in national contexts.[13]

International gatherings, such as the First International Feminist Congress, which was held in Buenos Aires in 1910, brought women of different social classes and political views together. The resolutions coming from this congress included approval of Uruguay's Divorce Law and a demand for equal pay for equal work. As Francesca Miller points out, Latin American feminism differed from feminism in the United States and northern Europe in that it did not seek as great a level of equality between the genders and instead embraced women's roles as mothers and wives.[14] Two feminist congresses took place in Merida in 1916 that brought discussion of women's suffrage to the forefront. Despite the discussions, women were not given the right to vote in the Mexican Constitution of 1917. Miller makes an important distinction between battles for legal reforms that were part of a process of secularization and the battle for the extension of political rights: "The drive to revise the civil codes should be distinguished from the extension of political rights to new groups in society. The civil codes governed interfamilial relationships."[15] Latin American women also participated in organizations that included U.S. feminists, such as the Pan-American Woman Suffrage Alliance.

By the early twentieth century, some changes became apparent in the public discourse regarding the role of women in society. Margarita Zegarra analyzes theses written at San Marcos University that emphasize the importance of women's education. One of these theses points to the fact that women in Europe were quickly able to take the place of men in a number of occupations during World War I. Esther Festini, one of the first women to graduate from San Marcos, wrote a thesis in 1901 that reflected the conservative nature of some of these arguments. Festini argued for women's education and civil rights but remained guarded about woman's participation in the broader political sphere and continued to see her main influence as being in the home.[16] Yet the drive for educating women consisted of a few lone voices at the time in Peru.

Unlike in countries such as Chile and Argentina, the drive for political reform in Peru was tied not to the expansion of public education for women but to the struggle for civil rights. The 1852 Civil Code in Peru treated women legally as minors, as they were either under the protection of their fathers or their husbands. One of the key figures in the struggle for women's political rights in Peru was María Jesús Alvarado. In a conference at the prestigious Geographic Society of Lima in 1911, she may have publicly introduced "the woman question" in Peru with her lecture titled "Feminism," in which she argued that women had the same capacities as men and called for social reforms to grant women equality of opportunity. Her thinking was framed in the context of positivism: she did not call for abrupt changes but rather saw the incorporation of women as equals as part of the broader process of social evolution. In 1914 she founded a women's rights organization, Evolución Femenina, made up primarily of professional women. This organization attempted, unsuccessfully, to alter the legal status of women as determined by the 1852 Civil Code. The conservatism of Peruvian politics can be gauged by the fact that Evolución Femenina's first successful struggle was for women to be accepted as full members of the Sociedades de Beneficencia Pública, social welfare institutions. This right was won in 1922.

In 1915, Evolución Femenina founded a school called Moral y Trabajo, a trade school for working-class women. Among the skills taught were proper hygienic measures for women and their babies—a sign of the school's participation in the hygienist discourse of the period. Alvarado also participated in the temperance movement—she was the second vice president of the Sociedad Nacional de Temperancia.[17] Alvarado had international connections and had attended the First International Feminist Congress in Buenos Aires in 1910. At the 1924 Pan-American Women's Conference in Lima, Alvarado proposed that women be given full legal equality and faced opposition from the Catholic Women's League. That year, the Augusto B. Leguía regime deported her for political activism. Zegarra considers Alvarado "possibly the most advanced Peruvian intellectual in her proposals for changes in women's condition."[18]

In 1924, Zoila Aurora Cáceres, a writer, founded another women's rights organization, Feminismo Peruano, with the goal of seeking equal political rights for women. The daughter of Mariscal Andrés Avelino Cáceres, leader of the Peruvian resistance during the War of the Pacific and president of Peru (1886–90), Zoila Aurora Cáceres had studied at the Sorbonne in Paris. She made use of the press to disseminate the organization's ideas. Her campaign put the proposition of a woman's right to vote on the agenda, making it a necessary topic of debate during the 1931–33 Constituent Assembly.[19]

Although the organization consisted primarily of upper- and middle-class women, Cáceres also reached out to working-class women and began to organize women workers, particularly telephone operators and seamstresses working for the state.[20] Working-class women had already been participating in labor protests. In 1916, some women lost their lives in a labor protest in the town of Huacho. Women also fought for the eight-hour workday alongside men in 1919. Cáceres continued to fight for women's right to vote into the early 1940s.

In 1908 less than 1 percent of adult women were working in white-collar jobs in the city of Lima.[21] The numbers of women increased over the course of the next decades, with women working in telegraph, post, and telephone offices, as well as in commercial, banking, and insurance companies. The 1940 census counted forty thousand women in white-collar jobs, about 20 percent of the white-collar workforce, in Lima and the adjacent port of Callao.[22] Not surprisingly, women earned half and sometimes less than half the salary that men earned. Most of the women entering the workforce as white-collar workers (*empleadas*) came from the upper sectors of society: "Contemporary observers pointed out time and again that these new *empleadas* were typically young, light-skinned, fairly well educated, and still living with their parents."[23]

APRA and Women's Rights, 1931–1934

Initially, on August 20, 1931, at the PAP's first party congress, held at the Teatro de Lima, located in the Barrios Altos neighborhood in Lima, Apristas fully embraced women's political rights. The congress included a Declaration of Women's Rights, a document drafted by the women's section of the party, presided over by Portal. It demanded full legal equality for women, the right to vote, and the right to hold public posts, as well as equality of pay with men and independent civil status for women after marriage.[24] The party's program for Peru (*programa mínimo*) recognized women's rights, stating, "We will recognize a woman's political rights and her ability to take on public positions to which she has been named or elected. We will establish the independence of women in the exercise of their civil rights within marriage. We will establish equality before the law of all kinds of children."[25] Yet in his speech to this congress, Haya made no mention of women's issues.

The first party congress had been preceded by a series of smaller congresses that met in the provinces to help formulate party policy. Apristas participated in open conversations to help formulate party policy. Lewis Taylor considers this "the beginning of a new form of 'conducting politics' in Cajamarca: there was significant participation from the people of Cajamarca, a public and democratic discussion took place about the country and its problems."[26] At the first departmental congress of the PAP in Cajamarca, women actively participated in political debates. Luisa Araujo Bazán, one of the founders of the women's Aprista cell in the city, gave the final address at this congress and called on the delegates to ensure that "the sphere of action of women should expand from the home to society."[27] Luis Heysen organized the Regional Aprista Congress of Southern Peru.

Haya with women by his side and the upheld arm that was the APRA salute, probably during the 1931 campaign. Behind him with glasses is Carlos Manuel Cox (Armando Villanueva Papers, courtesy of Lucía Villanueva).

In his campaign speeches, Haya addressed both men and women. Indeed, Graciela Zurita recalls a talk she heard Haya give at the party headquarters in Trujillo when she was a young girl: "There were men and women all together there to listen to a lecture by Víctor Raúl when he returned from exile."[28] She recalls that soon thereafter the party established two separate locations for men and women. The work of Portal was invaluable in drawing women to the party at this early stage. Party leader Manuel Seoane described Portal's activities in the following terms: "She went from province to province, persisting in her work, bringing in more and more women until finally the movement became large and important. Her task was to organize the women recruits, to give direction to their specific needs and demands. She held meetings, gave classes, founded brigades to deliver social services. She overcame obstacles and resolved conflicts. She pressed forward, encouraging, leading.... She studied the problems of women, and for the first time in the history of Peru she put forward at the First Party Congress a platform of women's demands."[29] The PAP began to reach out to working- and middle-class women. Together with a number of labor organizations, the party supported the August 1931 telephone operators' (*telefonistas'*) strike, which had become the focus of public attention in the election year. Telephone operators working for the Compañía Peruana de Teléfonos, a subsidiary of ITT (the International Telephone and Telegraph Corporation), earned a meager forty-five soles a month and were often not even allowed to get up for bathroom breaks. The attention to the issue worked in favor of the telephone operators, whose wage was raised to eighty soles.[30] The incident also demonstrated that the PAP had begun to make inroads in the labor movement.

Following the 1931 election, the Aprista congressmen in the Constituent Assembly scaled back the party's original proposals by advocating a restricted vote for women: only women who worked outside the home and women who had an education should be allowed to vote. The proposal reflected Apristas' fear that middle-class women who remained at home would cast a conservative vote. A faction argued that women should be given the unrestricted right to vote. Luis Alberto Sánchez, congressman for Lima, cited Bertrand Russell's argument that a woman needed go outside the home to gain her political rights. Sánchez also rejected the notion that a woman working in the home was a true worker. Aprista congressman Seoane, also representing Lima, made a similar argument, linking the right to vote to a person's economic activity.[31] On the other hand, the Unión Revolucionaria, Luís Sánchez Cerro's party, supported women's unrestricted right to vote. The members of the Socialist Party also supported this position.

The arguments against women's suffrage reflected the persistence of traditional views of women as being more prone to emotions than men. Manuel Ignacio Frisancho, a congressman from Puno, argued that "women[,] as they are psychologically more sentimental and emotional than men, had been assigned the home and the family, and it was there that woman had to 'affirm her virtues'; for their part, men, being 'more intellectual,' were prepared for the 'struggle for life.' "[32] Others argued that women were too influenced by the Catholic Church and therefore would not have political independence. The 1933 Constitution that resulted from the assembly continued to define citizenship as male but granted women the right to vote in municipal elections. Women finally enjoyed this right decades later when the first municipal elections were held in 1963. It ceased to be momentous, as women had already been granted the vote in national elections in 1955.

While women had been denied full political rights in Peru, APRA continued to incorporate women into its ranks. Portal set a remarkable example of how a woman could consolidate power within the party. She had begun to make a name for herself as an effective propagandist after she joined the APRA cell in Mexico in 1928, when APRA functioned as a transnational network of exiles. This setting freed Portal of many of the constraints for women in a national setting and gave her many of the same opportunities as men. In 1929, she traveled to Cuba, Puerto Rico, the Dominican Republic, and Colombia to lecture on anti-imperialism. During these years, Haya apparently treated her as he would any other member of the party, judging her character according to her willingness to make personal sacrifices on the party's behalf. By her own account, she gave up poetry when Haya asked her to do so in order to focus on studying political economy. She describes a dramatic moment that occurred while picnicking with friends when she tore to pieces a book of her own poems and threw them into a river.[33] While she would later continue to write and publish poetry, her party activities clearly detracted from her career as a poet. Her prominent role in party leadership, her writings, and her life of sacrifice for the party, which included time in jail, all contributed to an international prominence that few in the party shared. In 1935, while she was in jail, the Argentine journal *Claridad* dedicated an entire issue to her.

Once the PAP was established, Portal headed the Sección Femenina, which organized biweekly conferences to discuss women's issues at the central party headquarters on Belen Street in Lima.[34] She held the position of secretary general and was also the only permanent female member of the party's executive committee. Even after the party became illegal in 1932, the Sección Femenina continued to function. It organized the Comité Pro Presos (Committee to Support Those in Jail), which offered assistance to jailed Apristas, and particularly to Haya during his time in jail. The Sección Femenina also participated in international propaganda efforts and corresponded with women abroad. In August 1932, for example, it sent a letter to the Argentine women's organization América Nueva thanking them and asking them to persist in petitioning for the liberation of Haya from jail.[35] On March 10, 1933, the Sección Femenina issued a statement to the foreign press condemning the current war with Colombia.

While Portal recognized that women faced social obstacles as a result of their gender, in her view social class took precedence over gender. Portal recognized that women were in a worse situation than men for a number of reasons, including the fact that they were not afforded equal protection before the law: "The Peruvian woman, both middle and working class, suffers the consequences of social inequality much more acutely that her male companion."[36] The problem of women's rights, she argued, would be resolved as part of a more general revolutionary transformation. Portal expressed this view in her 1933 essay *Hacia la mujer nueva* where she wrote, "Aprismo will zealously defend women because Aprismo is not concerned with her gender but rather sees here a part of the exploited class, and this exploitation occurs in greater proportions than that suffered by men."[37] Because of their situation, women would be among the most committed to seeking a revolutionary transformation: "The aprista call, with its broad program to vindicate people's rights, with its realistic conception of our social and economic situation, needed to find in women, enthusiastic and decisive militants, as women are among the most committed to the task of destroying a social system based on the most flagrant inequality that so cruelly subjects her to despotism and humiliation."[38] Portal did not object to giving women the vote, and she celebrated the fact that the Constitution of 1933 granted women the right to vote in municipal elections as an Aprista victory, referring to it as "the first feminine triumph."[39] She also lamented that this right was in fact being denied, as no municipal elections were scheduled. Yet in her view, women's issues would be resolved as part of a broader revolutionary process. For example, she expressed admiration for the Peruvian activist and journalist Miguelina Acosta Cárdenas for having fought for the rights of the working class generally, rather than focusing specifically on women's issues.[40]

Portal was quite critical of some of the women who had preceded her. She considered the work of Alvarado an isolated effort to address a specific issue, that of women's position in charitable organizations. She criticized her predecessors as upper-class women with little impact on working women. She did not laud the organizational work of Cáceres and instead accused her of having failed in her drive to obtain the vote for women. The issue in this case may have been one of rivalry. As Kathleen Weaver points out, "Cáceres' highly effective labor organizing may have competed with Aprista efforts to expand its base in the trade union movement."[41]

A focus only on women's suffrage might, according to Portal, open up the doors for literate upper- and middle-class women to support conservative candidates. The experience of other countries, such as Spain, demonstrated that women's husbands and the Catholic Church influenced them and made them more conservative: "The Peruvian woman's cultural level, her prejudices, her undoubted dependence on male influence, and often on clerical influence, mean that the female vote becomes a way of consolidating conservative rather than revolutionary ideas."[42] Portal addressed the issue of religion and reaffirmed that APRA was not against the Catholic Church. The issue was of particular relevance for women, who were considered to be more religious than men: she reassured them that it was possible to be both an Aprista and a Christian.[43]

Hers was therefore a very particular kind of feminism—in fact, she did not consider herself a feminist—not uncommon among some revolutionary women of this period. Women's rights, she believed, were part of a broader revolutionary process, and she "resisted inclinations to place women's experiences at center stage."[44] Portal stood closer to many European Socialists than she did to the suffragist movements of the English-speaking world. Her position resembled that of revolutionaries for whom "women's issues became secondary to the more important goal of working-class revolution because solution of the 'woman question' supposedly would accompany the revolutionary transformation of society."[45] Among the thinkers she admired was the Russian Alexandra Kollontai, who rejected suffragist movements for their upper-class origins. According to Portal's proposal, APRA thus played a crucial role in the process of educating women to fight for their own rights. Her position echoes the broader Aprista view of the party as a mechanism of education in revolutionary values. Yet she also claimed that women would not fully understand the Aprista doctrine, displaying a certain condescension. The working woman "does not have enough culture to penetrate the philosophical doctrine of the new revolutionary tendency; her inexperience in the struggle, her absolute dissociation from politics and the ignorance of class contradictions, make her a totally unprepared element, but likewise, able to receive, without preconceived prejudices, new ideas that will open wide horizons of justice of which she was unaware."[46] She attributes this state of mind of women to the influence of both religion and what she refers to as a feudal-bourgeois mentality.

By creating the "New Woman," Aprismo would break these mental shackles. This New Woman, while asserting her equality with men, needed also to retain certain feminine qualities. Portal refers specifically to female sexuality: "Our women will not become flappers, a type of creature who is asexual, completely free and a bit unaware, as she accepts all of the flatteries of capitalist civilization and withstands its oppressions with no other protest than that of rejecting its sexual demands. Rather she will be a woman who is sure of herself, who has taken the path of heroic struggle and who, by taking this path, has begun to enjoy previously unknown rights which in turn she will not abuse or turn into licentiousness."[47] Portal defines femininity not only as retaining sexuality but also as affirming motherhood, which she refers to as the foundation "of authentic femininity."[48]

As Haya did not write at any length on the issue of women, we must turn to another Aprista author to capture a male perspective on women's issues within the party. In his book *Aprismo femenino peruano*, published a year after Portal published *Hacia la mujer nueva*, Aprista Rómulo Meneses reaffirmed some of Portal's ideas on the need to frame women's issues in the context of a broader revolutionary transformation. Yet he also expressed longstanding prejudices about women's limitations regarding participation in the public sphere. A supporter of APRA from its earliest years, Meneses had been jailed during much of the Sánchez Cerro government and released under the amnesty granted by President Oscar Benavides. He would later be elected to Congress in 1945. Meneses presented men and women as facing the problems of exploitation: "The doctrinal and economic principles of aprismo as a political-social movement of the oppressed classes cannot differentiate between the sexes nor can these principles recognize any problems between men and women beyond those stemming from the unequal exploitation to which they are exposed."[49] Meneses thus recognized the fact that historically women had been subject to greater exploitation than men.

Unlike Portal, he continued to promote stereotypical views of women as the weaker sex. He claimed that many women probably joined Aprismo at first only because it was fashionable. As members of the weaker sex, they were still not politically ready to exercise their rights. The party "does not promise great economic and social conquests for the weaker sex, precisely because it cannot help but recognize its weakness in the process of consciousness of political struggle."[50] He describes the middle-class women who support APRA as "fearful, fainthearted, apathetic; she remains unconcerned with larger social issues if she doesn't find the atmosphere and the stimulus to become interested in them." These middle-class women would need to make a huge effort to overcome what he saw as their innately frivolous tendencies. He claimed that "that same woman who is exploited and impoverished, prefers frivolity, parties, the movies to the struggle for her own improvement."[51] And when it came to women in the provinces and indigenous women, Meneses had an even more dismal view. These women lacked political consciousness and lacked the will, he claimed, to be incorporated into the political realm.[52]

Belonging to APRA would help middle-class women overcome these inherent weaknesses. Placed in the right environment, they would become interested in political issues.[53] Meneses was encouraged by how the times of persecution had transformed what he considered superficial commitments and forced many women to make sacrifices for the party. In particular, he praised the women who worked in Asistencia Social and the Red Cross, as well as the feminine brigades.[54]

Meneses expressed hope in the prospects of lower-middle-class women, whom he considered a key to the PAP's success. Within what he called the petit bourgeoisie, Meneses distinguished two different sectors: small-property-owning women with an "instinctive" sense of class consciousness, and a more intellectual sector drawn to leftist parties and needing to develop a sense of class consciousness. The first group included women working in commerce—for example, women with their own stands at marketplaces and the owners of small restaurants and *chicherías* (primarily in the Andean region, these were pubs that served *chicha*, a traditional alcoholic beverage made from fermented corn), as well as landowners and owners of small urban properties and shops. The second group included domestic servants, seamstresses, teachers, students, and the daughters of the small-property owners who belonged to the first group.

Historical experience demonstrated how much APRA needed the political support of the first category of women. Meneses referred to the support Sánchez Cerro received specifically from marketplace vendors (*placeras*) when he staged his revolution in Arequipa against Leguía in 1930: "Here is how the Supply Markets commanded by the innumerable *comadres* of the miserable general of the Hippodrome, were transformed during the midnight and early morning hours, into clubs of electoral propaganda and political rant."[55] However, these women did not have a revolutionary class consciousness, and they therefore supported the wrong candidate, according to Meneses. It is these women whom he believed needed to be won over by APRA: "Being as it is, an alliance of manual and intellectual workers, we must not lose sight for an instant that in this alliance the former have primacy and that our mission is to educate them, prepare them, train them so that only thus can they become the power, the soul and the true strength of the Party."[56] Meneses thus frames his arguments in the classic terms that portrayed the party as a vehicle for educating the masses and creating a revolutionary consciousness among them.

Aprista Women during Times of Persecution, 1934–1945

Women fought alongside men to build the PAP, though most of them are now forgotten to history. They participated in all aspects of party organization, helping with fund raising, taking messages back and forth, organizing events, and assisting party members in need—women in particular played an important role in assisting Aprista prisoners. In 1932 when the party was first proscribed, Aprista women occupied a party building to challenge the government order to shut it down, marched through the streets of Trujillo to protest Haya's imprisonment, and staged a hunger strike in prison.[57] They wrote public letters to the members of the Constituent Assembly calling for the release of Aprista prisoners.

Graciela Zurita, who was only twelve at the time, recalls the participation of women during the Trujillo insurrection. Women fought "together with the men and also from the houses, as they ran to take them and to pull and heal them, sometimes dead and sometimes badly wounded."[58] She also recalls a woman from Trujillo's high society who secretly supported the party: "There was a Mrs. Eloisa Flor de Morales of Trujillo's high society, the 'chic' people, she was an Aprista and she secretly helped the party and she also partook of the conversations; she was very Aprista to the end, until she died."[59] The experience of battle and persecution brought the different social classes together.

Political persecution equalized the experiences of Aprista men and women by subjecting them to similar dangers. Throughout Peru, Aprista women participated in party activities. A group of Aprista women in the city of Ayacucho belonged to a woman's cell—"célula femenina Aprista."[60] The following piece of propaganda makes no distinction between the genders and places women alongside men in the struggle for social justice: "The APRISTA WOMAN knows that she must always be the honorable COMPAÑERA of party militants and of the struggle. As much in painful losses as in victory, she will always be at her brother's side, arm in arm in this INCESSANT AND TENACIOUS struggle that demands all of our efforts, all of our energy, and all of our sacrifices. In this holy task, the APRISTA WOMAN marches reliably and radiantly on the precipitous route that leads toward the Conquest of SOCIAL JUSTICE, armed with the unbreakable FAITH that ONLY APRISMO WILL SAVE PERU.[61]

Numerous women shared the experience of persecution, although not all such experiences are as well documented as that of Portal. In 1932, Portal's mother was arrested and jailed when she refused to reveal the whereabouts of her daughter. In 1934, Portal was also arrested and jailed, and she reported that even after her release she remained under constant surveillance by the *soplones*, members of the government security forces: "I am a half prisoner whose steps are watched," she wrote to Graves.[62] As a precaution, Portal kept her Remington typewriter outside her home, which she left when she needed to write.

The women whose stories we know reveal how much the party relied on both men and women for its success. Juanita González de Vélez, from Abancay, daughter of a Peruvian mother and a Chinese immigrant, was one of the first women to join the party. González had met Haya through her brother, a student at the Escuela de Bellas Artes. Haya was a student leader at the time and had not yet founded APRA. González had participated in handing out political propaganda and been jailed. She later married an Aprista, José Armando Velez Orozco, and became involved in party activities. In 1931 she joined the Comando Femenino. Her house became a meeting place during the years of persecution. In 1933, she left Peru with her two-year-old son and traveled to Chile to join her husband and other Aprista exiles. She returned to Peru in 1936 and continued to support the party by helping to distribute letters written by exiled leaders to their counterparts in Peru. This activity led to her capture and imprisonment in the Santo Tomás prison. She was pregnant at the time. When she was due to have the baby, she was taken to a hospital to give birth and subsequently returned to prison. After her release she continued to work for the party, helping to support, as many women did, jailed Apristas by bringing them food, letters, and care packages. Her house continued to function as a meeting place for Apristas, and Haya sometimes even lectured there.[63]

Consuelo Torres Tello, from the town of Monsefú in the department of Lambayeque, met Haya when she was thirteen after he had just returned from exile in Europe. She recalls having heard him speak: "I listen to the *jefe* speak and he speaks about poverty and the change he hoped to make in his country in which people were suffering persecution, jail, exile and death. And he said he had returned after a period of time, because he had been deported. They even denied him his own country, they tried to take away, one could say, even the fact that he was Peruvian."[64] Her father participated in the Trujillo insurrection and, once the period of political persecution began, he was involved with underground organizing.

The family home became a place for secret meetings among Apristas. Torres, a teenager at the time, recalls a meeting the day Manuel Arévalo, the APRA labor leader, was captured in Trujillo: "Then and that day they arrested Manuel Arévalo, and at my home, with my father there was an important meeting of revolutionaries. . . . We were working there; well, I was a bit far away because they wouldn't let me near but I was curious and watching everything." Arévalo was captured on February 7, 1937, tortured, and later murdered on February 15. Following Arévalo's capture, another important Aprista leader, Alfredo Tello Salavarría, remained hidden in the home of Consuelo Torres. With the police surrounding the area, he asked the young Torres to get a car to help him escape. She did so and had to argue with the police, pretending that a relative of hers was gravely ill and that she needed the car to take him to the hospital. Tello Salavarría managed to barely escape, despite the heavy police surveillance. Torres later called the escape miraculous and cited Haya's claim that the party had its miracles: "So [Tello Salavarría] passes by the place where they are . . . and all surrounded, he heads toward Mansiche and he is ok, he came out, what a miracle, the boss said there are miracles in the Party in the APRA there are great miracles! And so it is, the miracle is faith, that faith, that will to not take a step back." Torres says that Tello Salavarría recognized that he owed her his life. "Alfredo was saved, so he always in the meetings said: I have the life I owe it to the *compañera* Consuelo."[65]

A few days later, Tello Salavarría returned disguised as a peasant, wearing a poncho and a hat and riding a donkey, to try to convince Torres's father that they should attempt to rescue the captured Arévalo. Her father dissuaded him. "This man is crazy," she recalls her father saying. The police soon captured both Consuelo Torres and her father. The man in charge of the department of La Libertad, Prefect Colonel Armando Sologuren y

Vélez, knew that she was helping her father in his party activities, "that I helped him and supported the clandestine party grassroots organizations." She spent three months in a Trujillo prison. Claiming that women in politics must be smart and also flirtatious, Torres goes on to tell how she flirted her way out of jail, "because the political woman needs to do everything intelligently, must be flirtatious, but only moderately flirtatious." When she was in jail, her captors attempted to extract information from her about APRA activities. She refused until she had had time to make up a story that she was able to tell to Prefect Sologuren: "The Prefect starts to ask me, to smother me with questions, and I told him a lie; so then I lifted my leg, like this, like this, I lifted my leg, but dresses back then were long; so when I lifted my leg, you could see my leg, a great revolutionary and you could see her leg, ha ha ha, and the Prefect looked at me, I could see him looking at me and I used great wisdom." He told her that he liked her and she said he could come meet her at her home if he granted her freedom. When he arrived, she refused to have sex with him. He took out a gun and she told him to go ahead and kill her since this would simply implicate him and make people wonder what he was doing at that address: "And I told him 'shoot' 'you shoot'; but tomorrow the news will be out that the Prefect has shot a woman here; he became frightened upon seeing the strength of my personality; you must be decisive, son, die or live, but without taking a single step back."[66]

Realizing that if her home was searched they would find materials connecting her to the party, Torres invoked the spirit of Arévalo: "Then I began to implore Manuel Arévalo, you have been here, do not abandon me, do not abandon me." She had outsmarted the prefect and managed to retain her freedom. After that, she continued to support Aprista activities, acting as a messenger: "Later, Alfredo Tello [Salavarría] assigned me to take a message to Chiclayo. When I got to Chiclayo, I immediately delivered the message at the marketplace to some Aprista *compañeros* who had shops there; I immediately delivered them and then returned to the house where I was staying." As she recalled these events, Torres made a poignant comment about the importance of women in the party: "I am speaking about the worth of the Peruvian woman . . . when she belongs to something beloved like the Aprista party."[67]

Torres was imprisoned a second time for her activities, this time at the Santo Tomás prison for women in the district of Chorillos in Lima. The prison held a number of Aprista women, the most prominent of whom was Portal, who spent a year there. Torres recalls the moment she entered the prison: "So I went in that small door, and the nun made me recline and told me to commend myself to God, I commend myself to God; she holds my arm, come this way, she puts me with the common criminals, with the sick, with the drug addicts, that is where she puts me. The bed was made of cement with a straw mat on top, and the nuns put me in the room of a woman who has just died of tuberculosis, and the mattress had books on it, and that is what she gave me to sleep on."[68] The experiences of jailed Aprista women are important to remember in order to have a complete picture of the ways in which women supported the party. Women have primarily been remembered for their role in supporting their jailed male relatives—taking them food and probably also sneaking in messages relevant to the party's operation. As it was for other Aprista prisoners, social class was a factor in the different treatments women received while in jail.[69]

When I interviewed her in 2007, when she was almost eighty-nine years old, Torres recalled a photograph of Haya that he had inscribed for her in recognition of her time in jail. He had written, "To *compañera* Consuelo Torres Tello for having withstood with bravery her honorable imprisonment." She recalled having helped to hide Haya on a number of occasions during the times of political persecution. On one occasion she met him at one of his hiding places.

> I arrived at his hiding place, in the year . . . it was at the end of the
> year [19]40; I arrived at the hiding place. . . . You had to cross rivers,
> sandy, dark, barking dogs where the Jefe was hidden, in an adobe
> house. . . . I think I can see it . . . an adobe house, there were two, two
> at the door to receive me; adobes houses, without light, with a lamp
> lit and inside where the Jefe was, sitting at a rustic table the kind they
> had in those days, with a candle and when I entered that little tiny
> room, the Jefe stood up, and said "turn around *compañera*" he said,
> he hugged me, I told him "*compañero* here I am again, I'm at your
> service."[70]

Among the mementos she still keeps of Haya is a death mask. She also was aware of the allegations of his homosexuality and disapprovingly says, "You know the bad things they say about the Jefe. . . . You know, you understand me."[71]

Torres dedicated her life to social work with women. In 1957, she founded the first Club de Madres (Mothers' Club) in El Agustino.[72] The club provided meals for children, many of them Quechua-speaking immigrants, who were beginning to arrive in greater numbers in the city of Lima. El

Agustino was the first of many migrant settlements that would begin to transform the face of Lima. While Torres has received recognition for her social work from the Peruvian government and from UNICEF, she speaks of not having received the recognition she feels she deserves from the party.

Another woman connected to APRA, Lindomira Peirano, was drawn to APRA at a young age. Born in Cajamarca in 1919 to a middle-class family, Peirano tells that her father, who was of Italian descent, held government positions and was named subprefect of the town where she was born. He worked for customs when the family moved to Lima. Peirano heard Haya for the first time when he campaigned in Cajamarca in 1931. She was only twelve years old at the time, but she recalls that she and a friend skipped school so that they could go listen to him in the main square of the town, the Plaza de Armas, where he spoke in favor of giving women the vote. She recalls Haya as "a very good, a very proper, a very human man."[73] Once the family moved to Lima, she found a way to join the party without the knowledge of her family: "So here in Lima we had the opportunity to live on Washington Street, downtown, near Paseo Colón. And just on the other block there was an Aprista Party headquarters. Then, I would escape for a little while in the evening to go and listen and I had myself registered. . . . At the entrance there was a lady who was registering and giving orders."[74]

Peirano had joined the Federación Aprista Juvenil, the party's youth organization, and heard lectures given by Armando Villanueva, then general secretary of the youth organization, as well as Ramiro Prialé and Andrés Townsend Ezcurra. All three would go on to become prominent party leaders. Six young girls attended the meetings: "There we would get together with the youth and we would continuously receive lectures. There were good people who directed and watched us."[75] Peirano recalls the names of Susana Medrano, Carmela Araujo, and a somewhat older girl from Callao with the last name Razuri. Peirano recalls the party efforts to discourage any kind of amorous relationship, as these were seen as damaging to party loyalty. Her recollection of the disciplinary process is worth quoting at length:

> They watched us to the millimeter, . . . We had to be there at the party headquarters but with great seriousness. Some fell in love; they judged them, both the boy and the girl. . . . You know that the young people did not have much control. Then, when they arrived, instead of entering the room, they stayed behind the gates of old houses

kissing, hugging each other. And that's why they were judged. . . .
They were put on trial in front of everyone. They said: you were with
such and such a person on such and such a day, such an hour and
disrespecting things here. You've been hugging, kissing. I was afraid.
I barely greeted the boys, that was it. . . . They subjected us to
discipline and the shame by telling about our intimacies in front of
the whole world. I was very ashamed. I took good care of myself. I
had my friends in the street, on Paseo Colón but there in the Party,
not one.[76]

While watchful of amorous relationships, the party also organized excursions and other activities that would have appealed to the youths. Peirano recalls excursions to the beach and playing volleyball.

Peirano tells that she stuck with the party through good times and bad, those of legality and those of persecution. During times of persecution, she recalls having helped to distribute *La Tribuna*, the party's then-clandestine newspaper. She also visited the prisons as part of a group of Aprista women who were supporting prisoners. The lawyers representing the prisoners would inform Aprista women of what the prisoners required: "In the party there was the Lawyers Corps. At the time doctor Carlos Alberto Eyzaguirre was head of that group. They had knowledge because the families were going to see how they could help them. Then he was aware that so-and-so was missing pants, that he had no underwear, no soap, no toilet paper. Then the corps of women, we would go. The ladies went and of the young women, I was the one who went."[77] Her testimony reveals how much the party depended on well-organized networks during the time when Apristas were persecuted.

She described an incident with the police in which she was lucky to avoid being arrested and thrown in jail. One day the police arrived at her house just as she was reading a register with the names of Aprista women: "I had the list and I put it on the table. My grandmother brought the clothes she had just washed and put them on top of it, and then the police arrived. I was so scared that they would take the list and then arrest all the people in that sector. They also would have taken me because they would have realized that I was a party leader." They did confiscate a book by Portal that Peirano had been reading and had left on her bedside table. The dialogue that she recalls with the police seems almost friendly and presents the confiscation as a pure formality given the fact that they had not found any other incriminating evidence: "Then they told me: we will take this little book.

Ok, I said. We need to justify to our superiors that we have been here, they said. Go ahead and take it." The book had been inscribed by Portal, who gave it to Peirano.[78]

Peirano recalled Portal, whom she referred to as "the number one woman in the party." She had not worked directly with Portal, who was in charge of organizing adult women and not the youngsters. Here Peirano is likely recalling her early years with the Federación Aprista Juvenil: "The young girls were separated.... Magda was a very harsh woman, very harsh. One couldn't just be by her side easily.... Unfortunately, Magda had a brusque personality. And so the young girls who went there to talk, she pushed us away."[79]

Despite their lack of voting power on internal party matters, women joined the party in large numbers throughout Peru. Rosa Miranda, born in 1929, recalls how she was drawn to the party as a young high school girl in the town of Huanta, Ayacucho, in 1943: "Well, as I said, when I was studying in high school I had a friend whose uncle was very Aprista; he was even in El Frontón because they arrested him during the time of the revolt. She knew more than I did because in her house they probably spoke to her uncle. She is the one who took many of us girls to go hear the lectures that a cousin of hers gave."[80] The uncle, Emilio Bendezu, was a leader of the Juventud Aprista Peruana, the renamed Federación Aprista Juvenil. Miranda continued to support the party, as did many other women. Her husband, Carlos Miranda, recalls an incident under the Bustamante government when a group of Aprista women saved him from being beaten up by the supporters of an opposition political candidate: "We were doing propaganda one time when Alejandro Carrillo Rosa was the candidate. On one corner was a small group and they were going to give me the beating of the century because I was on my own. Then a group of Aprista women appeared and they started slapping them and chased them away and I was unharmed."[81] In 1962 Rosa Miranda campaigned for Haya's presidential run by going out into the countryside to convince people to vote for APRA, including Quechua speakers: "In Quechua and Spanish, if people spoke Spanish we would speak to them in Spanish. But mostly at that time in the countryside people spoke Quechua; even now in the countryside Quechua is spoken, but less so, because the children of peasants no longer want to speak Quechua."[82]

APRA impacted the lives of women in other ways. Those who married Aprista leaders also bore the brunt of responsibility for raising a family alone when their husbands were imprisoned. Carlos Miranda recalls a relative of his who was in that position: "I had a cousin who was married to a party leader, her name was Carmen Rosa. That woman fought. The husband was a leader, they captured him and sent him to El Frontón, to the Panopticon; she had to take care of her home, to her duties as a mother. She was my mother's niece, she was very beloved, and so she and my mother stuck together."[83]

While Torres, Miranda, González, Peirano, and Zurita de Cueva came from either working- or middle-class families, some women belonging to the country's upper classes also supported the party. Marcela Pinillos Ganoza belonged to one of the wealthy landowning families of Trujillo, was a cousin of Haya, and was educated by a tutor: "When Marcela turned eighteen, people commented on her good education and her progressive ideas, unlike her friends, who had trained to be housewives, Marcela did not hold back in giving free reign to her desires and she put sports before other activities that were considered mainly feminine."[84] Pinillos had not been able to join the crowds that welcomed Haya when he arrived in Trujillo in August 1931: "Marcela would have wanted to be there to witness the triumphant arrival of her cousin, but the strict behavior norms prevented her from leaving the house and getting lost in the crowds. A woman could not do that."[85] She was able to hear him speak because the balcony of her house looked out on Trujillo's main square, a further sign of her family's status. Pushing the boundaries of acceptable feminine behavior that restrained most women of her class, Pinillos got involved in her cousin's campaign and soon found herself warming up crowds in preparation for Haya to speak. She continued to support the party when it was proscribed by acting as a messenger—her upper-class status and the fact that she had not officially joined the party shielded her from suspicion. She even knew how to shoot a gun and may have used one during the Trujillo insurrection. She was later discovered with propaganda and arrested. Her surname may have saved her from being executed.[86] She was sent instead to Lima and there continued to support the party by bringing Haya meals while we was imprisoned. Her activity on behalf of the party ended when she married a Swiss émigré who had recently arrived in Peru.

Women in Exile and the Feminization of Exile, 1934–1945

Political exile represented another equalizing experience for men and women. Examining the issue of feminine exile generally, Ricardo Melgar

Bao argues that it helped to break down gender barriers: "The emergence of feminine exile fractured and broke down the masculinization of politics, which relied on the sentence of expatriation."[87] Like men, women who went into exile belonged primarily to an educated middle class with the connections necessary to make a new life abroad. Yet, as Melgar Bao points out in his study of Mexican exiles, we know little about the contributions of these women to the party:

> The invisibility of Aprista women in Mexico in the documentation of the CAP [Aprista Committee] of Mexico is remarkable. Three of them are referred to as wives: Angélica Sotomayor as the wife of Alfredo Saco and the wives of Guevara y Enríquez are not mentioned by name. Finally, Lola Voysset is identified as Aprista, but without specifying her marital status or occupation. Undoubtedly, Aprista women in exile were much more numerous. We have found out nothing about their activities, except for a fraternal honorary invitation to "Lica" Saco, as they liked to call Angélica Sotomayor, to the founding congress of the Confederacion de Estudiantes Socialistas Unificados de México (CESUM) in 1937.[88]

The experience of Portal remains the best documented. While living in Chile from 1939 to 1945, she continued to participate in political activities on behalf of her party.

During the 1930s, Santiago became a hub in the Aprista transnational networks and an important locus for the dissemination of APRA propaganda. The publishing house Editorial Ercilla published Aprista books, including the long-delayed first edition of Haya's *El antimperialismo y el APRA* (1936). Even before leaving Peru, Portal had been involved in discussions about propaganda in Chile. In a letter written from Lima shortly after her release from prison, Portal encouraged Sánchez, then living in Chile, to expand Ercilla's propaganda work. She held up the Spanish publishing house Cenit, known for its publication of Marxist works, as an example. She also referred to the need to distribute books without political constraint, a difficult task in Peru given the government's persecution of APRA.[89]

Portal was able to find somewhat greater financial stability in Chile. Her contacts with the Socialist Party, which she joined, included Salvador Allende and his wife, Hortensia Bussi Allende.[90] Her Chilean connections helped her to get employment with the Chilean Ministry of Education. One of her tasks at the ministry was writing radio plays for the Radio Escuela

Experimental, which was affiliated with the Chilean Ministry of Education's Dirección General de Educación Primaria. Her radio work ranged from historical topics such as Tupac Amaru II to talks on social mores, such as the effects of modernity on the traditional family. While in Chile, she also returned more deliberately to her own poetry, and toward the end of her stay she published a book of poems, *Costa sur*. She also maintained her interest in women's issues, joined the Asociación de Mujeres Socialistas, and published a book on Flora Tristan, the nineteenth-century French Socialist and feminist, who had Peruvian family roots.[91]

While her role within APRA in Chile was not as prominent as that of exiled leaders Seoane and Sánchez, Portal represented the party at a number of public events.[92] Her correspondence demonstrates that she remained active and in touch with leaders in Lima. As in all of her correspondence with men, her tone is one used between equals. In an exchange with Sánchez before her arrival in Chile, she ends her letter with the wish that he "receive a strong handshake from your *compañera* and friend."[93] He seemed likewise to value her opinion on party strategy, asking for her advice and support. "I believe we must stop the attacks from the sidelines to concentrate our fire on the fascism of Benavides, the antidemocratism of [Carlos] Concha and his group, etc. . . . not waste ammunition," wrote Sánchez, and then added, "Don't you agree? I believe that agreement on these issues is essential for a good campaign to come."[94] A 1945 telegram to Benavides requesting permission to return to Peru for the coming elections is signed by all three Aprista leaders: Seoane, Portal, and Sánchez.[95]

Portal remained engaged in strategic discussions about furthering APRA's Latin American presence. In October 1940, she was on the organizing committee of the First Congress of Democratic and Popular Parties of Indo-America, sponsored by the Chilean Socialist Party in Santiago with participation by exiled Apristas. In a letter to Haya, she informed him that the Chilean Socialist Party had accepted the resolutions of the congress affirming continental unity.[96] In his reply, dated July 7, 1941, he criticized her for not having sent enough propaganda to Lima about the activities of the congress. He reproached her, sometimes harshly, for not promoting APRA's continental program more forcefully, suggesting that she should have tried to hold a similar congress in Mexico. "You, the ex-delegates of that Congress," wrote Haya, "should have protested against the postponement of the second congress. You should have said that no national issue is worth as much as the continental issue that the Congress would confront.

Say something to indicate that exiled Apristas are not only involved in routine, personal, and casual tasks, but that they are preoccupied with maintaining the continental meaning of our work."[97] He expressed disappointment that exiled Apristas such as Sánchez and Seoane were not sufficiently dedicated to the continentalist mission.

Portal responded with equal forthrightness. She remained committed to the work of forging continental unity, but her life experience and in particular her two and a half years outside Peru had helped her gain a better understanding of the international scene than Haya possessed. To begin with, she argued, the cause of Apristas outside Peru had reached a low point: people were tired of hearing about their persecution and about the fact that they were in jail. Her insights stemmed from her recent letter-writing campaign to release her husband from prison in Peru. The Aprista cause had become like the complaints of a beggar, which may move people on the first day, she wrote, but bore them on the second day, and by the third day lead people to kick him out the door. She also warned that the United States would much rather see a divided than a united Latin America. In the seven years that Haya had been living in hiding, he had become isolated from issues outside Peru. Gabriel del Mazo, the Argentine student leader who corresponded extensively with Portal, worried also about Haya's becoming isolated: "His continentalist view seems diminished, after he promoted it strongly during his youth. The lack of contact prevents him from being stimulated and from assessing the experiences of other peoples."[98]

Portal admonished Haya that remaining in Peru would mean that he could not understand the bigger picture. She urged him to leave the country in order to reinvigorate the party's continentalist program: "I am convinced that you are the only person who can promote a New Indoamerican Policy, effectively moving toward the union of the 20 republics."[99] The party was strong enough in Peru and did not need him there. Besides, Portal wrote, he must be exhausted and in need of contact with different people and points of view. During that period, Haya was still in hiding, traveling from one safe house to another. He replied firmly in the negative, arguing that his enemies wanted him to leave Peru and claiming that President Manuel Prado Ugarteche had offered him up to one million (he doesn't specify the currency) to do so, but Haya felt that this would weaken the party. He claimed to be neither exhausted nor isolated. His series of justifications indicates that he took Portal's critique seriously. The exchange also reveals a growing tension between them.

Haya and His Women?

Haya expressed disdain for Aprista exiles, whom he condemned in gendered terms by accusing them of "feminine weakness" and of "sensualization," as they allegedly lived easy lives abroad, in contrast to the sacrifices of those who had remained in Peru. In hindsight, it seems ironic that he should have framed the issue in such traditional gender terms, given his own untraditional place in terms of gender expectations in Peru. He never married, and no evidence exists to show that he ever participated in a heterosexual relationship. Numerous accounts suggest that he viewed marriage as a distraction for party members—getting married translated into a decreased commitment to a party that demanded complete commitment and loyalty. This disparagement of the institution of marriage could perhaps have been related to his alleged homosexuality.

Apristas have countered the claim of homosexuality by attempting to prove that Haya had a number of female lovers. In her book titled *Las mujeres de Haya*, journalist María Luz Díaz refers to some of these women, including a German woman named Alice Hoehler with whom Haya allegedly had a child. Hoehler was the daughter of the family that lodged Haya while he lived in Berlin.[100]

These accounts attempt to defend a traditional male virility by pointing to a number of relationships that Haya, over the course of his life, had with women, some of whom reportedly were in love with him. The first woman Haya is alleged to have had a relationship with was Ana Billinghurst, daughter of Guillermo Billinghurst, president of Peru from 1912 to 1914. Their friendship began while Haya was living in Lima during his twenties. At the time, she had a fiancé, whom she later married. Aprista accounts claim that following the death of her husband, caused by an opium overdose (opium had become a fashionable drug in Lima), Ana Billinghurst sought Haya out in Berlin. No evidence supports this claim.[101]

A woman who was allegedly in love with him and who wrote about him was the journalist Maria Luisa García Montero. She had met Haya as a young girl but had encountered him again in the 1950s. She then allegedly became obsessed with him later in life. At the time, she was a journalist and had a reputation in Lima as a passionate woman "who took the bulls by the horn" and who was attracted to famous and powerful men.[102] She described herself by saying that "more than a journalist, I am a writer and more than a writer, a woman who feels strongly, who trembles, enjoys, suffers and is dignified that way as a human being capable of assimilating the very essence of life."[103] García Montero had a chance encounter with Haya when he saw her while he rode in a car, recognized her, stopped the car to ask her who she was, and told her to call him. Although she doesn't state the date and even admits that the memory may be inaccurate and a combination of earlier memories, she claims that Haya was shy and therefore did not pursue her: "As private as he is, timid and unfamiliar with Don Juan–like experiences, he probably did not dare to insist."[104] In the book she published, with chapters on different famous men she had known, she openly expressed her desire for Haya and her schemes to seduce him. Her desire was revived toward the end of 1960 when she attended a lecture he gave at the Casa del Pueblo, the party headquarters: "That same night I got interested in Víctor. I liked the virile gesture of his oratory. I though he was too voluptuous, also cerebral and Dionysian, full of erotic exuberances with his ornamental and pantheistic gestures."[105] She was not discouraged in her efforts by a party member who explained to her that Haya remained voluntarily celibate because he feared that marriage would detract from his work as party leader: "His celibacy contributed to make him more interesting and worldly."[106] She did not comment at all on his alleged homosexuality and rather claimed that "for man to define himself he needs a woman."[107] When she approached him after another of his lectures at the Casa del Pueblo, she claims he invited her to Trujillo to participate in the yearly festivities for his birthday, the Día de la Fraternidad, on February 22. She concludes her account by claiming to have made a deep connection with him based simply on the way he looked at her: "It was a look that said it all, so subtle that it reflected a whole array of spiritual affinities worthy of being kept forever."[108] Yet even in this description, so revealing of her desire for him, there is no inkling of any erotic feeling on his part.

At least two of the women in Haya's life helped him financially: Billinghurst and Graves, the latter helping to pay for his studies in England. García Montero may also have contributed: "There are those who claim that María Luisa Montero was probably a patron of APRA and may have connected him with some wealthy individuals. . . . While it remains unknown whether they were large sums of money, such as those that Ana Billinghurst at some point contributed, she certainly contributed to Víctor Raúl Haya de la Torre."[109] While exact amounts remain unknown, Haya's magnetic personality seems to have helped him to gain support from some of the women whom he met at different stages of his life.

APRA and Women's Rights, 1945–1955

As a revolutionary party, APRA had initially called for a radical transformation in the role of women, putting them on an equal footing with men in party affairs. Although the party leaders continued to be predominantly male, women fought alongside men during the years of political persecution. However, as the country's main political force, when it attained partial legal status (the party still was not allowed to run a presidential candidate) in 1945, how would APRA proceed on the issue of women's political rights?

McGee Deutsch has written about the relationship between gender and politics in Latin America and argued that the distance between word and deed "leads one to question the revolutionary character of the governments under study": Mexico (1910–24), Argentina (1946–55), Chile (1970–73), and Cuba (1959–).[110] In one example of her argument that "leaders devised gender-related programs that suited their perceived political ends," she writes that "the gendered rhetoric and policies of Mexican revolutionaries also served as a paradigm for the preferred political and social order. The Carrillos' innovative views on gender relations were a model for the democratic socialism they envisioned. The emphasis that Alvarado and Carranza placed on control and order in their gender and familial notions symbolized the hierarchical political and economic order that prevailed in Mexico by the 1920s."[111] Ideas about women's equality helped to shape politics but lived alongside traditional views: "However contradictory to reality, the idea that men and women had immutable personalities persisted."[112] She points out that the Cuban and Chilean movements proposed greater changes in the status of men and women than did those of Mexico and Argentina, a fact that is not surprising considering that both Chile and Cuba were Socialist revolutionary governments, in contrast to the populist governments of Mexico and Argentina. How does APRA fit into the pattern that McGee Deutsch establishes?

Women continued to fill party positions when APRA regained its legal status under the government of President Bustamante (1945–48). For example, Peirano held an official position as national subsecretary of social assistance and had an office at party headquarters. She recalls talking to party leader Prialé and reflects on the fact that she had the respect of party leaders due to her commitment to the party: "I would arrive at 7:30 or 8 and *don* Ramiro Prialé was in the other office outside the main party headquarters. He was at his desk and since he saw that I was so young he apparently liked me. So I arrived and would say: Ramirito, good evening. He would say: *cholita*, come here, sit here, let's talk, don't go to your office yet. So we talked for a long time. I was always held in high esteem as people could see that I had always tried to be correct, upright and polite."[113] Although the term *cholita* is the diminutive of the word *chola*, a pejorative term for people of indigenous descent, in this context it becomes a term of endearment.

Between November 14 and 24, 1946, the First National Convention of Aprista Women met to discuss women's issues within the party. Women from all parts of Peru came to Lima for this event. In her address to the convention, Portal, who had now returned from Chile, acknowledged the numerous contributions of women to the party over the past decade and a half. She referred to some Aprista women by name, listing Carmen Rosa Rivadeneyra, Josefina del Valle, and Rosa Michelini de Casas as women who had, like Portal, served on the party's executive committee. She also acknowledged Francisca Steward, Carmen Saldías, Alicia de Suarez, Jesús Evangelista, and many others who had served time in the Santo Tomás women's prison, and stated that María Olivia Grados had been a courageous organizer.[114] In her speech, Portal urged women to get involved in party activities.[115]

Portal criticized the party's practice of limiting the role of women to proportional representation on party delegations and committees.[116] According to Portal's own account, a clash occurred with Haya at this event when he took the podium and affirmed that a woman's main role was in the home. Recalling this event many years later, she wrote, "I was outraged. 'Don't talk about what you don't understand,' I said to him under my breath. 'They didn't come to hear this.' Haya continued, his face flushed with anger, then finally he was finished, turning away from the podium in an almost violent way."[117] It is quite telling that in his three-volume biography of Haya, Aprista historian Roy Soto Rivera omits any reference to this event. In his account of the important events of the year 1946, with regard to women, Soto Rivera points only to the role of women in organizing Christmas celebrations for poor children.[118]

What had happened? Haya's conservative stance on women coincides with his shift toward more-conservative positions in both national and international politics as he sought to gain full legal recognition for his party. Haya had marked APRA's emergence from underground activities with a public speech to thousands in Lima's Plaza San Martín in which he reassured Peru's business community of his commitment to capitalism and wealth creation. On the international front, Haya aggressively pursued ties with the United States and had dropped the anti-imperialist line. He needed to keep his grip on the party in the face of the criticism of members on the left, including Portal, who disagreed with these shifts. His relegation of women to a secondary position within the party may have been closely linked to a concern with giving the tremendously popular Portal a position of power within the party.

Tensions between Portal and Haya had worsened two years later when the party held the second Aprista party congress, between May 27 and June 3, 1948. At this event, according to Portal's recollection, Haya declared that "women, since they do not yet have the vote in Peru, cannot be considered authentic members of the Aprista Party. Women can only be sympathizers."[119] Haya denied Portal's request that women be given the vote within the party structure. Following a public clash with Haya, who shut down debate on the issue, Portal protested by walking out of the congress. Two years later in an accusatory pamphlet, her voice was full of recrimination regarding these events:

> They agreed on what I considered to be the greatest disloyalty for the aprista woman, denying her the right to be a member of the Party "as long as she lacked political rights" and restricting these rights in the future, since the Statutes established the right of women to vote politically at 24 years of age and that of men at 18 years of age. In this way the Party of the People rewarded women for more than 20 years of loyal commitment, women who had not made any distinctions in age or sex to fight for the conquest of liberty, justice and democracy for all Peruvians.[120]

Haya's clash with Portal at this congress and his unwillingness to grant women full power within the party probably also has personal roots. Portal had initially been quite close to Haya, and their correspondence demonstrates the degree to which she was able to speak frankly to him about a number of different issues. The initial closeness between them slowly was replaced by a more distant and eventually antagonistic relationship. The reasons for this distancing must remain speculative. The fame of Portal may have proved threatening as she gained international prominence as a political activist within APRA. When she was jailed in 1935, the Argentine journal *Claridad* dedicated a whole issue to her. When she finally left Peru in 1939, tired of the political persecution and of hiding from the police, she was received like a heroine in Bolivia, Argentina, and Chile. Other evidence also points to the role of personal factors. For reasons that remain unclear, Haya had not attended the wake of Portal's daughter Gloria, who committed suicide in 1947. Anecdotal evidence points to a judgmental Haya, angry at an alleged illicit sexual relationship between Gloria and a member of APRA's leadership.

While APRA's shift to the right may have contributed to Portal's estrangement from the party during these years, it must be remembered that she was no longer a fiery revolutionary in her twenties but rather a fifty-year-old woman with a more mature understanding of the workings of political life. Her regular column titled "El pueblo y su raiz" (The people and its roots) in the party newspaper *La Tribuna* expressed concerns about the need for popular education and the erosion of certain traditional values as a result of modern life. In an installment in the series, an article titled "El piropo callejero," she complained of how the once-chivalrous custom of publicly flattering a woman for her beauty had degenerated from flirtation into lewd exclamations.[121] She may have been following *La Tribuna*'s now more moderate editorial line, but the series also expressed a more critical assessment of social change than that in her earlier writings.

Following the October 3, 1948, Callao uprising led by Aprista sympathizers in the Peruvian navy, the party once again was outlawed. Together with numerous other Apristas, Portal went into hiding. Two years later she faced a military tribunal that included her among those accused of participating in the Callao uprising. Portal received a reduced sentence and was released after the trial. While she was in detention, she had written a condemnatory pamphlet that also marked her very public departure from APRA. Titled *¿Quienes traicionaron al pueblo?*, the pamphlet reclaimed the party's revolutionary tradition and defended its numerous uprisings over the years. Portal accused the APRA leadership of having betrayed the cause of the people. She attacked party leaders for failing to defend these efforts: "Traitors and cowards—-Judases of the People—who at the last hour abandoned and negated those who bravely and romantically attempted more than one tragic adventure—San Lorenzo, Huaráz, Cajamarca, Loreto, Trujillo, Huancavelica, Callao—to bring their party to power and to fulfill the postulates of social justice that had been inscribed in its fighting banners."[122]

In this final pamphlet, Portal strikes at the cherished cult of martyrdom. She subtly calls into question traditional notions of male virility by portraying Aprista men presenting themselves as victims: "Once again they adopt the discredited approach of martyrdom, persecution, and clandestine existence. The posture of victims seems to be what best suits the Aprista gentlemen, both those persecuted as well as those jailed and deported."[123] In addition, she notes, the party's martyrs were all men. Referring to the 1948 party congress, she writes, "Its greatest success was to build a cenotaph for the martyrs—males—of the Party!"[124] In her break from APRA, Portal displayed the same rhetorical boldness that had characterized her earlier writings and lectures. Apristas had lost their most prominent female leader. In the eyes of party stalwarts, she had become a "traitor" and was now all but erased from party history.

The departure of Portal coincided with a new period of political persecution under Odría. Apristas once again faced persecution, jail time, and exile. Portal herself felt endangered and feared retaliation by the party. She left briefly for Argentina but only spent a few months there and then returned to live in Peru, now disconnected completely from APRA. Ironically for her and probably other Apristas, they would watch as women were finally granted the vote by General Odría in 1955.

Aprista Women, 1956–1979

The departure of Portal and the upheaval that resulted in the party following the 1948 insurrection also created setbacks for women. When Odría granted women the vote, APRA lost any possibility of remaining at the forefront of the struggle to incorporate women fully into politics. Peruvian women voted in a national election for the first time in 1956. The lack of connection between the struggles of women for political rights and the gesture "from above" by Odría leads Elsa Chaney to conclude, "The conferring of the vote on women by General Odría in 1955 caught most women by surprise; it came as a gift for which they had not expended any large amounts of energy."[125] The new law granted the vote to women who could read and write and were twenty-one years or older, or eighteen years or older if they were married.

Following the 1956 elections, the PAP congressional delegation included one woman, María Colina de Gotuzzo, out of seven women elected to the Congress from different parties. She was reelected in 1963, this time one of only two women in Congress. When Haya presided over the Constituent Assembly in 1978, not a single Aprista woman represented the party.[126] Yet by extending the vote to all Peruvians—including those who were illiterate— the Constituent Assembly took an important step in enfranchising Peruvian women. In 1980, the PAP had a woman senator elected, Juana Castro, and four congresswomen: Antonieta Zevallos de Prialé, Gladys Laos, Ilda

Urizar, and Beatriz Seoane. Castro was a shantytown (*pueblos jóvenes*) organizer. As Sara Beatriz Guardia points out, while these women all made
important contributions in their roles in the Senate and Congress, little is
known about the work of women within the party at the time.[127] In 1985,
the PAP increased its female representation by one: four congresswomen
(Ilda Urízar, Berta Gonzales Posada, Mercedes Cabanillas, and María An-
gelats Quiroz) and two senators (Castro and Judith de la Matta).[128]

Examining formal participation in national politics by women may only
provide part of the story of female participation in APRA. The importance
of family networks as building blocks for the party calls for a more careful
analysis of the role of women at different levels of the party. As Sarah Radcliffe points out, "It has been suggested that the Apra party offers women
opportunities which are not available in other political parties, and which
stem from a tradition of family activism in the party."[129] She gives the example of Mercedes Cabanillas, who was education minister during Alan
García's first government, as an example of a woman who had been able to
gain experience as a result of her activities within the party. Chaney points
out that "for the young woman of an Aprista family, joining the party made
sense even though women were not yet allowed to vote. The party offered
a way of life, and the idealistic young girl found social action outlets, rec-
reation, and friends all within the party milieu."[130]

It is not surprising that during the years of military government (1968–
80), when political parties had little impact on public issues, feminists
pushed ahead with their agenda through nongovernmental organizations.
An attempt to coordinate the work of such organizations occurred in 1979
with the establishment of the Comité Coordinador de Organizaciones Fem-
inistas. This short-lived organization attempted for six years to coordinate
the activities of nongovernmental organizations such as Flora Tristán, Manuela Ramos, Alimuper, Mujer y Cambio, Mujeres en Lucha, and Creativi-
dad y Cambio. They promoted a number of important issues related to
women's labor rights, reproductive rights, and legal equality. As Peru returned to democracy in 1980 and political parties once again became relevant to national life, these organizations continued to pursue their work
outside the structure of formal political parties, which they found constrain-
ing, as political parties were addressing numerous issues and could not
concentrate exclusively on furthering women's rights. The relevance of
APRA to the project of furthering women's issues becomes part of the larger
story of the relation between political parties and nongovernmental organizations that often preferred to pursue their own agendas outside the con-

Welcoming for Haya in Huanta, Ayacucho (author's collection).

text of political parties. In her study of low-income organizations in Peru during the first years of APRA's first government, Radcliffe points out this rejection of party affiliation, as with the women organizing the Vaso de Leche program (providing glasses of milk for children in Lima's poorer neighborhoods), who were not interested in being absorbed by APRA.[131]

Despite APRA's early leadership on the women's rights issue, in the final analysis, when it came to legal changes in favor of women, the party has become more a follower than a leader in championing the cause of women in Peru. McGee Deutsch has pointed to the gap between rhetoric and reality when it came to revolutionary and reformist movements in twentieth-century Latin America. In the case of APRA, the reluctance to allow women full participation even in the party seems surprising. Early on, the lack of full rights for women was due to a particular policy position that subsumed the women's rights issue under the more general struggle to bring a revolution to Peru. However, the Aprista position during the 1940s may be explainable more as a result of Haya's concerns about rivalry with Portal than by reference to ideological tenets regarding women. It can also be seen as part of the general move in a more conservative direction, as APRA sought not to rock the boat in its quest for full legality. Following the enfranchisement of literate women in 1955 and of illiterate women in 1980, an increasing number of women have represented APRA, thus following a general trend in Peruvian society that has brought women more fully into the political arena.

Nonetheless, despite APRA's disappointing record at the policy level, women of different social classes and from all parts of Peru played a crucial role in the building of the party. From Peirano, who was drawn to the party when she heard Haya talk about women's rights, to Portal, who campaigned, wrote, and organized tirelessly for the party, to Torres, who went to jail for her connection to APRA, to the thousands of other women whose stories have not yet been told, Aprismo inaugurated a new stage in the political history of women in Peru and Latin America. For all its broken promises to women, APRA remains the first party to have actively incorporated women into its ranks in an array of roles.

Conclusion

During a conversation at a café in the neighborhood of San Borja in Lima, I commented to the son of one of the American Popular Revolutionary Alliance's (APRA's) most important historic leaders that I believed Víctor Raúl Haya de la Torre's economic and political ideas remained relevant to the present times in Peru. I was unable to finish making my point, as he interrupted me by asking, "Which Haya de la Torre? The Haya of *El antimperialismo y el APRA* or the later Haya?" The notion that there are two Hayas illustrates the fact that many Peruvians are still coming to terms with the trajectory of a revolutionary party that deliberately shifted to the center, and some would even claim the Right, of the Peruvian political spectrum. Persecuted and forced to operate underground for almost three decades, Haya had allied with former enemies in his quest for legitimacy and ultimately power. The father of my interlocutor that day had been instrumental in brokering the agreement in 1956 known as the *convivencia*, which restored APRA as a legal party, with President Manuel Prado Ugarteche, who had persecuted Apristas during his first government (1939–45). Yet hadn't such alliances been merely tactical? Or did they undermine the party's basic identity as the Partido del Pueblo, the Party of the People? The Apristas who began to leave the party had a clear answer to that question. Luis de la Puente Uceda founded the short-lived Apra Rebelde before joining the Communist Party. Other Apristas were drawn to the ranks of newly formed Communist parties and to the promise of a new revolution inspired by Fidel Castro and his unlikely rise to power in Cuba.

Are there two Hayas? In this book, I have suggested that in fact there are many more than two, that Haya was a man like any other, full of contradictions. There was Haya the young student, who traveled from provincial Trujillo to Lima and was captivated by his links to international Protestant networks, the Haya who gave lectures titled "Christ." There was Haya the Marxist, who was inspired by Vladimir Lenin and Harold Laski, the latter of whom he took classes from at Oxford. There was the Haya so deeply impressed by the Mexican Revolution that he invented a political program based on spreading this revolution to the rest of Latin America. There was the Haya who lived in hiding in Lima as leader of a persecuted party yet also remained in contact with the U.S. embassy and met with visiting U.S. citizens. There was the Haya whose party had blemished its relationship with the Peruvian military yet who was forever hopeful that he would be able to seduce a general or two to stage a coup and bring APRA to power. There was the Haya who for decades courted the United States, offering his party first as a bulwark against Fascism and then as the best alternative to Communism in Peru. There was Haya the disappointed politician, who lived for an extended period in Europe, enamored of Scandinavian social democracy, and who returned only reluctantly to Peru to dirty his hands in politics. There was Haya the party builder, so obsessed with propaganda that he even used Peru's currency to spread the word by writing "APRA" on sol bills that passed through his hands. There was Haya the educator of the people, who hated to be challenged as he imparted, with a certain condescension, his wisdom and knowledge to his followers. In addition, there was Haya the elder statesman, holding court at his office on the second floor of the Casa del Pueblo, the party headquarters, lecturing to the party's youths, an embodiment of the party and the political doctrine he had created.

And of course there was the Haya that people would continue to whisper about, the gay Haya, the one who never married, the one for whom his followers were constantly seeking to invent romantic relationships, the Haya who reprimanded his followers for engaging in "sensual" behavior but who was fond of the company of young men and most likely had male lovers. He is rumored to have had a relationship with Jorge Idiaquez, his bodyguard and secretary for many decades. Cultural norms on homosexuality change across time and place. Haya had visited New York in 1927, a time when the city had a flourishing gay world, and from 1929 to 1931 he had lived in Berlin, a city with a remarkable openness toward homosexuality. No such openness was possible for Haya in the Peru of the 1930s and 1940s, although this may not have mattered to a man who spent most of these decades living in hiding. However Haya lived and experienced his sexuality during these years, once the real possibility of his running for president emerged in the 1960s, it became clear that homophobic accusations would follow him into a more visible political role. Well aware of how public talk of his sexuality could be used against him, Haya must have been affected by this in his political decision making, and it may have played a role in his reluctance to continue fighting for the presidency when he narrowly won the popular vote in 1962.

The question to ask is not whether Haya was homosexual but rather how his sexual identity affected his life at different times and in different places. As George Chauncey points out about New York in the pre–World War II years, "It was not a world in which men were divided into 'homosexuals' and 'heterosexual.' This is, on the face of it, a startling claim, since it is almost impossible today to think about sexuality without imagining that it is organized along an axis of homosexuality and heterosexuality."[1] This raises a larger, unanswerable question: Did the fact of his sexuality play a role in keeping him from becoming Peru's president?

Had I finished making the point that I had begun to make that day in the café in San Borja, I would have insisted on the congruence between the two Hayas. I would have expressed the admiration I undoubtedly feel for the Haya who in 1928 wrote *El antimperialismo y el APRA*, calling on all Latin American countries to develop strong national states capable of imposing the necessary constraints on foreign capital in order to redistribute wealth and guarantee prosperity for all members of society. That Haya never implemented such ideas himself does not diminish his accomplishment in spreading these ideas throughout the continent. At a time when Peru continues to implement a model primarily inspired by neoliberal economics, Haya's early ideas have something to tell us. I would also have expressed admiration for Haya's continentalism, his attempts to perpetuate Simón Bolívar's dream of a united Latin America. I find his internationalism refreshing at a time when nationalism seems once more to be on the rise. Haya's claim in 1945 that "we cannot declare ourselves to be proudly insular and close our borders, and say that nothing in the external world interests us during a period of growing interdependence"[2] is undoubtedly instructive in the era of President Donald J. Trump's call for closed borders and walls and of Britain's departure from the European Union.

Yet to seek inspiration from Haya only as the ideologue of anti-imperialism or as the proponent of a united Indo-America or as a democratic populist is to overlook his often-contradictory selves. I have come to believe that it is precisely the many Hayas, with their many contradictions, who can speak to us most strongly today. To attempt to understand how and why he led his party through complicated twists and turns in his quest for power, a course that may ultimately have made APRA unrecognizable ideologically, is to ask deeper questions about Peruvian and Latin American society and resistance to social change. To understand his and his party's championing of women while they kept them in a secondary role is to inquire more broadly about gender roles and attitudes in Latin America. To follow his thought and actions in relation to the United States is to examine the contradictions of U.S. policy in the region. In an era that has for the first time seen a Peruvian politician openly announce that he is gay, attitudes may again be changing, to the point that discussion of Haya's sexuality could illuminate the persistence of homophobia and serve as an inspiration to politicians and others to more openly express their sexual identities.

Haya can be many things to many people and can speak powerfully to our times. His relationship to democracy can interest scholars of Latin American populism, as it demonstrates that "the relationship between populism and democracy cannot be established in abstract but depends, rather, on the political context in which populism and democracy interact."[3] It can also be inspirational for proponents of democracy in Latin America. After all, here was a revolutionary politician who drew great inspiration from the Mexican Constitution of 1917 in the 1920s, who supported democracy against Fascism in the 1940s, who expressed great admiration for European social democracy in the 1950 and 1960s, and who at the end of his life placed his signature on Peru's 1979 Constitution, over whose drafting he presided as president of the Constituent Assembly that year. The Constitution was part of Peru's return to democracy after twelve years of military rule.

Most poignantly, Haya impressed those who knew him personally. During the last years of his life, when Haya had returned to live in Peru, he traveled daily to the Casa del Pueblo, the party headquarters on Avenida Alfonso Ugarte, and there held court as a teacher. He lectured and met with his followers at the Casa del Pueblo and stayed up talking, as had always been his habit, into the late hours of the night. Lindomira Peirano recalls a warmth in her encounters with him, almost as though she were sitting down with a member of her family: "I liked to listen to Victor Raul. He would sit in his office and tell me: sit down, sit down *compañerita*; don't leave until we've had tea. The tea was served at around 12 at night. But I was going to tell the boss that I'm leaving. I could not do that; I stayed until the end. He went out and took his car." Peirano made the long trip from her home in Chosica, about an hour east of Lima, by taking a *colectivo*—a car that functioned as a communal taxi, filling up with passengers to travel an established route. Her husband expressed the traditional male concern for what others might think when they saw her out so late at night: "And my husband said to me: What will people say that you come back at 1 or 2 in the morning from Lima and they do not know where you are going?" To which she replied, "Look: I do not care what people say, my conscience is what counts."[4] Peirano had continued to make the trip to party headquarters into her early nineties, many decades after Haya's death.

Peirano recalls Haya as a generous man who, despite the fact that he had little money, would dig around in his pockets when approached by a beggar. He would travel east along Peru's Central Highway from where he lived in Villa Mercedes to Chosica for lunch, driven in a car by Idiaquez. Haya once gave Peirano a gift: "I have a plastic bracelet with my name. He came to lunch here at Chosica, there in the restaurant of a couple that was in the corner. He came Mondays for lunch. There was a little man at the door who made some plastic wristbands and one night: *compañera* Lindomira, excuse me that it is very simple, a little reminder." She recalls that Haya liked tamales, and that she sometimes ordered them from a woman who made them in Chosica and delivered them to Villa Mercedes, where Haya lived during the last decade of his life. She recalled, "Sometimes the *jefe* would have women's meetings. He was giving talks, he was entertaining. He had a memory, like he remembered everything that had happened in Switzerland."[5]

Near the bend of the river in the region of Chanchamayo in the jungle areas of Cusco, there is a large rock. The local people have dubbed it Haya de la Torre because of its apparent resemblance to his distinctive face, with its aquiline nose and sharp features. That his name still echoes in this remote area so long after his death and so far from his place of birth, Trujillo, says something about the way that Haya captivated for many decades the imagination of a whole country and about how his memory has lived on to this day. What the inhabitants of the region say and think about the man after whom they named the rock, or whether they even know who he is today, is a different matter. But the story of the ways in which his life and that of his party helped to shape twentieth- and twenty-first-century politics in both Peru and Latin America is one of many stories that remains to be fully told today.

Notes

Introduction

1. A number of scholars have researched the history of APRA in Peru. Peter Klaren wrote the classic book on the origins of APRA, *Modernization, Dislocation, and Aprismo*. In a more recent monograph on APRA, *Usted fue Aprista*, Nelson Manrique explores the history of the party. For the quasi-religious nature of allegiance to APRA, see Klaiber, *Religion and Revolution in Peru*, and Vega Centeno, *Aprismo popular*. For Haya's early years, see Planas, *Mito y realidad*. For a biography that emphasizes Haya's connection to spiritualism, see Pike, *Politics of the Miraculous*. For histories of the party from an Aprista perspective, see Murillo Garaycochea, *Historia del APRA*, and Soto Rivera, *Víctor Raúl*. For further studies of APRA, see Valderrama et al., *El APRA*, and Bonilla and Drake, *El APRA*. For studies of APRA in different regions of Peru, see Taylor, "Origins of APRA in Cajamarca"; Nugent, *Modernity*; Heilman, "We Will No Longer Be Servile"; Heilman, "To Fight Soviet Agents"; Wilson, *Citizenship and Political Violence*. On the anarchist roots of APRA, see Hirsch, "Anarcho-syndicalist Roots." On the middle-class origins of APRA, see García-Bryce, "Middle-Class Revolution." For APRA's connection to the labor movement, see Pareja Pflucker, *Aprismo y sindicalismo*, and Drinot, "Creole Anti-Communism."

2. Charles Anderson, "Theory of Latin American Politics," 7.

3. Stein, *Populism in Peru*, 7.

4. Roberts, "Parties and Populism," 38.

5. Roberts defines critical junctures as "watershed periods of political change, when political institutions across a range of countries adjust—in different ways—to a common set of societal pressures and challenges." Ibid., 42.

6. Some scholarship has already taken steps in this direction—for example, Robert Levine's study of Getulio Vargas: Levine, *Father of the Poor*, and, for an earlier period, Sobrevilla, *Andrés de Santa Cruz*.

7. Alexander, " Latin American Aprista Parties."

8. For Chile, see Drake, *Socialism and Populism in Chile*. For the influence on the Alianza Revolucionaria de la Juventud Unida in Panama, see Pearcy, "Panama's Generation of 31," 711. For Peronismo, the claim is made by Haya in a letter to Luis Alberto Sanchez, November 8, 1952, cited in Pike, *Politics of the Miraculous*, 235–36. The topic deserves further research.

9. Ameringer, *Democratic Left in Exile*, 20.

10. Alexander, interview with the author. For a reference to Betancourt denying any influence from Haya in the Agrupación Revolucionaria de Izquierda group that preceded Acción Democrática, see Alexander, *Rómulo Betancourt*, 55.

11. The pioneering scholarship of Ricardo Melgar Bao paved the way for a new generation of historians to explore the centrality of these networks to Aprismo. See Melgar Bao, *Redes e imaginario del exilio*. For more recent studies, see Bergel, "Manuel Seoane y Luis Heysen," and Bergel, "Nomadismo proselitista y revolución"; Dorais, "Coming of Age in Exile" and "Indo-America"; Sessa, "Los exiliados como 'traductores.'" For a focus on how these networks empowered both APRA's most active female leader and women more generally, see García-Bryce, "Transnational Activist." The most recent study of these networks, from the perspective of historical sociology, is Iglesias, *Du pain et de la Liberté*, and Iglesias, "Redes políticas transnacionales."

12. Halperín Dongui, *Historia contemporánea de America Latina*, 395. Unless otherwise stated, translations are my own.

13. The contested meaning of the Mexican Revolution became evident in the propaganda wars that followed the revolution. The United States attempted to undermine the legitimacy of the event, while various Mexican governments defended it in the broader Latin American forum. See Yankelevich, *Miradas australes*.

14. Aprismo did not offer a method of revolution in the same way as the Cuban Revolution—as Harry Kantor has pointed out, "The Aprista ideology has its weaknesses, the most conspicuous being its neglect of a method of achieving power, but it is an impressive attempt to create a political program suitable to Latin American conditions." Kantor, *Ideology and Program*, 115.

15. Haya de la Torre, *El antimperialismo y el APRA*, in *Obras completas*, 4:167.

16. Kantor, *Ideology and Program*, 115.

17. Alexander, interview with the author. Charles Ameringer also points to Betancourt's rejection of the label *Aprista* in favor of the more general *national revolutionary*. Ameringer, *Democratic Left in Exile*, 31.

18. Caballero, *Latin America and the Comintern*, 9.

19. Anderson, "Theory of Latin American Politics," 20.

20. McClintock, "Populism in Peru," 207.

21. Roberts, "Parties and Populism," 44.

Chapter One

1. See García-Bryce, "Haya de la Torre."

2. Haya de la Torre, "What Is the APRA?," 756. See also Alexander, *Aprismo*, 97.

3. Lenin, "Imperialism, the Highest Stage of Capitalism," in Tucker, *Lenin Anthology*, 204–74.

4. See Yankelevich, *Miradas australes*.

5. Yankelevich, *La revolución mexicana*, 14.

6. Werlich, *Peru*, 200.

7. Haya de la Torre, Berlin, to unknown recipient, October 2, 1930, cited in Eduardo Enriquez, *Haya de la Torre*, 84.

8. For a study of these networks more generally, see Pita González, *La Unión Latino Americana*.

9. Weaver, *Peruvian Rebel*, 78.

10. The following four paragraphs are taken from my article García-Bryce, "Transnational Activist."

11. Carr, "Radicals, Revolutionaries and Exiles," 29.

12. These networks thus help to expand earlier scholarly conceptions of politics based on national "imagined communities," as described by Benedict Anderson, and public spheres, as described by Jurgen Habermas. Benedict Anderson, *Imagined Communities*; Habermas, *Structural Transformation*.

13. Pakkasvirta, *¿Un continente, una nación?*

14. For an analysis of the relationship between APRA and middle-class identity, see García-Bryce, "Middle-Class Revolution."

15. Pita González, *La Unión Latino Americana*, 19.

16. Ibid., 69.

17. Kersffeld, "La Liga Antiimperialista," 145.

18. Klaiber, "Popular Universities." See also McNicoll, "Intellectual Origins of Aprismo."

19. Haya de la Torre to Esteban Pavletich, London, July 10, 1926, Armando Villanueva Papers.

20. Sánchez, *Haya de la Torre y el APRA*, 68,

21. At almost the same time, Chinese students participated in the Chinese May Fourth Movement (1919), which represented an important step in student involvement in political issues in China.

22. Tracing some of Haya's ideas back to the Argentine University Reform movement, Carlos Altamirano writes, "APRA (American Popular Revolutionary Alliance) . . . is an example of the most successful, but certainly not the only one of the many political vanguards that emerged throughout Latin America stimulated by the University Reform Movement." Altamirano, general introduction to *Historia de los intelectuales*, 10.

23. Planas, *Mito y realidad*, 19.

24. Gutierrez Sánchez, *Haya de la Torre y los protestantes liberales*, 42.

25. Soto Rivera, *Víctor Raúl*, 1:62.

26. Melgar Bao, "Redes y espacio público transfronterizo," 73.

27. Pedro Ugarteche, interview with Steve Stein, February 13, 1971, cited in Stein, *Populism in Peru*, 120.

28. Haya de la Torre, "Carta desde la prisión (3 de octubre de 1923)," in *Por la emancipación de América Latina: Artículos, mensajes, discursos (1923–1927)*, in *Obras completas*, 1:10. The reference to *la gran transformación* (the great transformation) is interesting in light of more recent Peruvian history, as Abimael Guzmán, the leader of the Shining Path, used identical language to refer to the Maoist revolution he sought to bring to Peru.

29. "Víctor Raúl Haya de la Torre, Presidente de la Federación de Estudiantes del Perú, desterrado por el Presidente Leguía, ha sido invitado por Vasconcelos para que cotinúe en la Universidad de México sus estudios interrumpidos ha poco," *Heraldo de Cuba* 12, no. 304 (November 1, 1923), facsimile published in Alva Castro, *Peregrino de la unidad continental*, 2:11.

30. Melgar Bao, "Redes y espacio público transfronterizo," 78.

31. Expediente 121-E-P-18, Archivo General de la Nación, Lima, Peru, cited in ibid., 74.

32. Vasconcelos, *El desastre*, 93.

33. Gonzalez A., "Las cartas de Haya de la Torre."

34. Haya de la Torre, "La unidad de America Latina es un imperativo revolucionario del mas puro carácter económico," *Córdoba*, February 20, 1924, in *Obras completas*, 1:11.

35. Melgar Bao, "Redes y espacio público transfronterizo," 78.

36. Yankelevich, *Miradas australes*, 20.

37. Vasconcelos, *La raza cósmica*. Later Vasconcelos would veer increasingly to the right.

38. Carr, "Radicals, Revolutionaries and Exiles"; Delpar, *Enormous Vogue of Things*.

39. Melgar Bao, "Redes y espacio público transfronterizo," 83.

40. Haya de la Torre, "Excombatientes y desocupados," in *Obras completas*, 3:18.

41. Melgar Bao refers to these as "redes vasoncelianas," the network of intellectuals and politicians connected to Vasconcelos.

42. Zaïtzeff, "Diálogo epistolar," 45.

43. Melgar Bao, "Redes y espacio público transfronterizo," 80.

44. Ibid., 88.

45. Ibid., 84.

46. Haya de la Torre, *Por la emancipación de América Latina*, 1:36–37.

47. Ibid., 37.

48. These observations appear in a piece titled "Emiliano Zapata, apostol y martir del agrarismo mexicano," part of his *Apuntes de viaje* (1924). It is not clear whether it was published at the time or was part of a private notebook. Haya de la Torre, *Por la emancipación de América Latina*, 1:35–38.

49. Melgar Bao, "Redes y espacio público transfronterizo," 79. Haya's connections to Freemasonry deserve further research.

50. Valderrama et al., *El APRA*; Planas, *Mito y realidad*.

51. Haya de la Torre, "Discurso ante el Primer Congreso Nacional del Partido Aprista Peruano," in *Obras completas*, 5:38.

52. Haya de la Torre, "Excombatientes y desocupados," 3:17.

53. A copy of the letter is reproduced in ibid., 20.

54. Melgar Bao, "Redes y espacio público transfronterizo," 85–86.

55. Lunatcharski to Haya, September 23, 1924, cited in Soto Rivera, *Víctor Raúl*, 1:83.

56. Haya de la Torre, "Excombatientes y desocupados," 3:17.

57. Haya de la Torre, "Impresiones sobre la Rusia Soviética," *Obras completas*, 2:431.

58. Haya de la Torre, "Carta a un universitario argentino," London, June 1925, in *Obras completas*, 1:80.

59. Romain Rolland to Haya de la Torre, Villeneuve (Vaud), Villa Olga, March 15, 1926, in *Por la emancipación de América Latina*, 1:5–6.

60. Planas, *Mito y realidad*, 32–34.

61. Schlesinger, "Left Out," 44.

62. Planas, *Mito y realidad*, 35.

63. Anna Melissa Graves to Magda Portal, November 17, 1935, Box 1, Folder 1, Magda Portal Papers.

64. The extent of his connection remains unclear, but he wrote a number of letters on the club stationary.

65. Haya de la Torre to Luis Heysen, London, January 29 [year unknown], Armando Villanueva Papers.

66. Bergel, "Manuel Seoane y Luis Heysen," 135–36.

67. Haya de la Torre to Esteban Pavletich, November 15, 1926, Armando Villanueva Papers.

68. "Desde Londres: Declaraciones de Haya de la Torre a 'La Tribuna de Cantón' por el corresponsal en Inglaterra Chon-Sgeik," Lima, May 5, 1927, Armando Villanueva Papers. The place is obviously a mistake made during the transcription of the original document. It is not clear where or whether this interview that was translated into Spanish was published.

69. Pedro Planas refers to an article titled "El APRA y el Kuomintang" that was published in a number of Latin American journals at the time, but not in Haya's complete works.

70. Haya de la Torre, *El antimperialismo y el APRA*, in *Obras completas*, 4:105.

71. Haya de la Torre to Manuel Ugarte, Oxford, March 28, 1927, in Ugarte, *El epistolario de Manuel Ugarte*, 59–60.

72. Soto Rivera, *Víctor Raúl*, 1:87.

73. Ravines, *Yenan Way*, 19.

74. [Author unclear] to Carlos Manuel Cox, Paris, July 10, 1928, Armando Villanueva Papers.

75. Taracena Arriola, "La Asociación General de Estudiantes Latinoamericanos," 74.

76. Ibid., 68.

77. "Memorandum Left at Embassy Prepared by APRA Protesting against Certain Acts of the Government of the United States in Haiti," December 21, 1929, 810.43 APRA 47, National Archives, College Park, Maryland.

78. "Copies of June 1 Edition of Publication of APRA in which Articles Attacks Electric Bond and Share Co and the United Fruit Co.," June 11, 1930, 810.45 APRA 47, National Archives, College Park, Maryland.

79. Carlos Manuel Cox to Luis Heysen, Mexico, February 18, 1928, Armando Villanueva Papers.

80. Iglesias, *Du pain et de la Liberté*.

81. Hatzky, *Julio Antonio Mella*, 226–28.

82. Caballero, *Latin America and the Comintern*, 24, 38–39.

83. Ibid., 70–71.

84. Ibid., 69.

85. Melgar Bao, "Cominternismo Intelectual."

86. Carlos Manuel Cox to Luis Heysen, Mexico, February 18, 1928, Armando Villanueva Papers.

87. Hatzky, *Julio Antonio Mella*, 308.

88. Ravines, *Yenan Way*, 27-8.

89. Quoted in Alba, *Politics and the Labor Movement*, 126.

90. Mothes, "José Carlos Mariátegui und die Komintern," 83–100, quoted in Hatzky, *Julio Antonio Mella*, 319.

91. Drinot, "Creole Anti-Communism"; Heilman, "To Fight Soviet Agents."

92. Haya de la Torre to Esteban Pavletich, April 15, [1926?], Armando Villanueva Papers.

93. Eudocio Ravines to Luis Heysen, Paris, March 22, 1927, Armando Villanueva Papers.

94. See García-Bryce, "Middle-Class Revolution."

95. Haya de la Torre, *El antimperialismo y el APRA*, 4:163.

96. Haya de la Torre, London, to Luis Heysen, September 26, [1925?], Armando Villanueva Papers. He actually uses the diminutive *maestrito de acción*, or "little teacher of action."

97. Ibid.

98. Haya de la Torre to Esteban Pavletich, April 15, [1926?], Armando Villanueva Papers.

99. Ibid.

100. There is an extensive literature on this debate. See Barba Caballero, *Haya de la Torre*, and Luna Vegas, *Mariátegui*.

101. Planas, *Mito y realidad*, 77.

102. Hatzky points to the inconsistencies in Mella's attack, as he was pursuing very similar goals to those of Haya. Hatzky, *Julio Antonio Mella*, 306–7.

103. As Pedro Planas has pointed out, "By the end of 1935, he already had a different philosophical position, definitely less Marxist than that of 1928." Planas, *Mito y realidad*, 78. He points to the article "El Aprismo es una doctrina completa y un método de acción-realista" (in the Chilean journal *Atenea*, 1930) and to the book *Teoría y táctica del Aprismo* (1931), which included this article, as direct sources of Haya's thinking at the time.

104. Haya de la Torre, *El antimperialismo y el APRA*, 4:73.

105. "Debating Union to Hold First Meeting Tuesday," *Harvard Crimson*, October 20, 1927.

106. Haya de la Torre to Eudocio Ravines, Washington, September 27, 1927. Cited in Iglesias, "Réseaux transnationaux," 171.

107. Haya de la Torre to Carlos Manuel Cox and Esteban Pavletich, New York, October 2, 1927, Armando Villanueva Papers.

108. Published literature, including Planas, dates the founding of the Mexico APRA cell to 1927 when Haya returned to Mexico. The evidence is somewhat contradictory: Haya mentions the founding of the Mexico cell in a November 15, 1926, letter to Pavletich. The letter in Armando Villanueva's private archive contains a handwritten pencil notation, probably by Villanueva, dating the founding of the Mexico cell to October 1926. Haya de la Torre to Esteban Pavletich, Oxford, November 15, 1926, Armando Villanueva Papers. But in another letter, to Cox and Pavetich from New York, Haya says he plans to go to Mexico to found the APRA

section there. Haya de la Torre to Carlos Manuel Cox and Esteban Pavletich, New York, October 2, 1927, Armando Villanueva Papers.

109. Haya de la Torre, London, to Luis Heysen, September 26, [1925?], Armando Villanueva Papers.

110. Haya de la Torre, "What Is the APRA?," 758.

111. Haya de la Torre, "Carta a un universitario argentino," 1:84.

112. Haya de la Torre, *El antimperialismo y el APRA*, 4:118.

113. Ibid., 122.

114. Ibid., 118.

115. Ibid., 122.

116. Ibid., 125.

117. This was a common vision of Latin American history among theorists such as Haya and Mariátegui that has since been dispelled by a historiography that makes a clear distinction between the economic systems established under colonial rule and the feudal system of medieval Europe.

118. Haya de la Torre, *El antimperialismo y el APRA*, 4:164.

119. Ibid., 166.

120. Ibid.

121. Ibid., 167.

122. Ibid., 170.

123. Haya de la Torre, Oxford, to Esteban Pavletich, December 21, 1926, Armando Villanueva Papers.

124. Haya de la Torre to Luis Heysen, March 27, 1928, Armando Villanueva Papers. This issue requires more research to determine the extent of such contacts.

125. Roy Soto Rivera makes this connection. Soto Rivera, *Víctor Raúl*, 1:293.

126. For more on these plans, see Manuel Seoane to Luis Heysen, July 21, 1928, Armando Villanueva Papers.

127. "El Plan de Mejico," in Ricardo Martinez de la Torre, *Apuntes para una interpretación Marxista del Peru*, 2:289–93.

128. There is still some dispute about the facts, with Planas treating this portion of the plan as factual and Nelson Manrique questioning it. See Manrique, *Usted fue Aprista*.

129. Portal, *América latina frente*.

130. "Hay que hacer 'Nuestra' la revolución Mexicana," *Patria* (Havana), June 18, 1938, facsimile published in Alva Castro, *Haya de la Torre*, 2:135.

131. Manuel Seoane to Luis Alberto Sánchez, November 18, 1951, Luis Alberto Sánchez Papers.

132. Quoted in Soto Rivera, *Víctor Raúl*, 1:92.

133. José María Zeledón, "La conferencia de Haya de la Torre," *Repertorio Americano* 17, no. 15 (1928): 229, quoted in Oliva Medina, *Dos peruanos en Repertorio Americano*, 63.

134. On the homoerotic possibilities implicit in such friendships, see Macías-González, "Las amistades apasionadas," 19–48.

135. Bridi to Haya de la Torre, Berlin, January 9, 1932. Federico More Papers. I have been unable to establish Bridi's full identity.

136. Bridi to Haya de la Torre, Berlin, March 3, 1934. Federico More Papers.

137. Bruno to Haya de la Torre, Berlin, March 3, 1934, Federico More Papers. I have been unable to establish Bruno's full identity. Bruno spells the name "Bridi" as "Bridy."

138. Haya de la Torre, "El Programa: 23.8.31," in *Revolución sin balas*, 28.

139. Basadre, *Historia de la República*, 10:229–50.

140. Melgar Bao, *Redes e imaginario del exilio*, 73.

141. Gabriel del Mazo to Magda Portal, May 26, 1940, Box 1, Folder 4, Magda Portal Papers.

142. Haya de la Torre, *El antimperialismo y el APRA*, 4:113.

143. Haya de la Torre to Luis Alberto Sánchez, August 1935, Letter 876, Luis Alberto Sánchez Papers.

144. Haya de la Torre to Magda Portal, July 7, 1941, Box 1, Folder 5, Magda Portal Papers.

145. Magda Portal to Haya de la Torre, June 20, 1941, Box 1, Folder 5, Magda Portal Papers.

146. See Iglesias, "Réseaux transnationaux," and Melgar Bao, *Redes e imaginario del exilio*.

147. "Orden de regreso de los deportados, Lima 14 de abril de 1939," Document 15 in Davies and Villanueva, *Secretos electorales del APRA*, 38–39.

148. León de Vivero, New York, to César E. Pardo, Valparaiso, May 5, 1939, Document 28 in Davies and Villanueva, *Secretos electorales del APRA*, 57–58.

149. Ravines, *Yenan Way*, 19.

150. Manuel Seoane to Luis Alberto Sánchez, October 12, 1949, Letter 1711, Luis Alberto Sánchez Papers.

151. Manrique, *Usted fue Aprista*, 128.

152. Moreno Mendiguren, *El APRA es un partido internacional*.

153. Haya de la Torre, Geneva, to Luis Alberto Sánchez, February 4, [1955?], in *Correspondencia*, 2:199.

154. Ibid., 198.

155. Manrique, *Usted fue Aprista*, 187.

Chapter Two

1. We still lack an academic study that focuses on the party's insurgent wing and activities. Aprista historian Percy Murillo Garaycochea refers to this insurgent tradition in his book *Historia del APRA*. In his recent study of APRA, Nelson Manrique also covers this topic. Manrique, *Usted fue Aprista*.

2. Kantor, *Ideology and Program*.

3. Manrique, *Usted fue Aprista*, 75.

4. Víctor Villanueva, *La sublevación aprista*, 41.

5. Davies and Villanueva, *300 documentos*, 13.

6. Víctor Villanueva, *La sublevación aprista*, 18.

7. Charles Anderson, "Theory of Latin American Politics," 1.

8. Dispatch 11,385, January 2, 1945, FW 832.00/1-245 CS/HS, National Archives.

9. James, *Lenin's Terror*, 184.

10. Hughes-Hallet, *Gabriele d'Annunzio*.

11. Haya de la Torre, London, to Esteban Pavletich, July 10, 1926, Armando Villanueva Papers.

12. Manrique disputes the amount of support that Iparraguirre received and claims he received virtually no support once he arrived in Peru and quickly ended up in jail. Manrique, *Usted fue Aprista*, 79–81.

13. Haya de la Torre to Luis Heysen, March 27, [1928?], Armando Villanueva Papers.

14. "Plan de México," Anexo 3, in Planas, *Mito y realidad*, 117.

15. Planas, *Mito y realidad*, 74.

16. Both letters cited in Flores Galindo, *Haya de la Torre*, 31, 37.

17. Ibid., 89.

18. Haya de la Torre, Berlin, to unknown recipient, [1930?], Armando Villanueva Papers.

19. Klaren, *Peru*, 273.

20. For an account of the campaign, see Stein, *Populism in Peru*, 101–28, 158–87.

21. Ibid., 185.

22. See García-Bryce, "Middle-Class Revolution," and Parker, *Idea of the Middle Class*, 152–84.

23. Haya de la Torre, "Discurso ante el Primer Congreso Nacional del Partido Aprista Peruano," in *Obras completas*, 5:36.

24. Giesecke, "Trujillo Insurrection," 151.

25. Ibid., 151.

26. Quoted by Vega Centeno, *Aprismo popular*, 114.

27. Hansen, "New Political Options," and Hansen, "Neue politische Optionen."

28. Haya de la Torre, "Discurso," 5:35.

29. Historian Jorge Basadre considered the elections to have been fair, although he recognizes that irregularities occurred, such as the elimination in the final tally of votes of those from Cajamarca, where APRA had strong support, and states that it is ultimately impossible to verify whether fraud occurred on a large scale. Basadre, *Historia de la República*, 10:186–87. See also Stein, *Populism in Peru*, 189–98.

30. Stein, *Populism in Peru*, 199.

31. Haya de la Torre, *Construyendo el aprismo*, 172–75.

32. Giesecke, "Trujillo Insurrection," 152–53.

33. Ibid., 154–55.

34. Haya de la Torre, *Construyendo el aprismo*, 84–92.

35. *Juicio seguido contra el Sargento Primero Alfonso Pinedo Sanduro y otros poe el delito de rebellion, Lima, 8 de enero de 1934*, p. 5, Archivo Histórico Militar. This portion of the testimony is dated January 6, 1934.

36. Giesecke, "Trullijo Insurrection," 166.

37. Ibid., 155.

38. Ibid., 157.

39. Ibid., 159.

40. Ibid., 141.

41. Murillo Garaycochea, *Historia del APRA*, 209.

42. Ibid., 209–10.

43. Giesecke, "Trujillo Insurrection," 276.

44. Murillo Garaycochea, *Historia del APRA*, 209–11.

45. Luis Alberto Sánchez, Panama, to Gustavo Jimenez, May 8, 1932, Letter 1178, Luis Alberto Sánchez Papers.

46. Rebaza Acosta, "La Revolución de Trujillo," 2:57. A total of twelve Apristas and sixteen soldiers were wounded in the attack.

47. One of the first aerial bombings of civilians in history may have occurred in 1914 during the Mexican Revolution.

48. *El Comercio*, July 15, 1932, quoted in Echague, "Lo que vi," 2:239.

49. Giesecke, "Trujillo Insurrection," 223.

50. For an account of the repercussions of the Trujillo insurrection in twentieth-century Peruvian political culture, see García-Bryce, "Revolution Remembered."

51. Basadre has tended to agree with the APRA version that the killings were not the direct responsibility of Aprista insurgents but rather performed by rogue elements within APRA. Basadre, *Historia de la República*, 10:237.

52. Haya de la Torre, "El proceso Haya de la Torre," in *Obras completas*, 5:247.

53. Quoted in Soto Rivera, *Víctor Raúl*, 1:180.

54. Haya de la Torre, "El proceso Haya de la Torre," in *Obras completas*, 5:311.

55. Ibid., 307.

56. Ibid., 310.

57. Ibid., 321.

58. I will henceforth use the names Peruvian Aprista Party and APRA interchangeably to refer to the Peruvian branch of this international party. Strictly speaking, Peruvian Aprista Party is the correct name to use; however, the party is referred to as APRA in Peru.

59. Giesecke, "Trujillo Insurrection," 279

60. Soto Rivera, *Víctor Raúl*, 1:246.

61. Víctor Villanueva, *El Apra en busca del poder*, 117–39.

62. Basadre, *Historia de la República*, 10:242.

63. Ibid., 243. Basadre does not include information about the statement's source.

64. Chávez Vargas, interview with the author.

65. Basadre, *Historia de la República*, 10:247.

66. Gustavo Jimenez to Luis Alberto Sánchez, April 26, 1932, Letter 1177, Luis Alberto Sánchez Papers.

67. Luis Alberto Sánchez to Gustavo Jimenez, May 8, 1932, Letter 1178, Luis Alberto Sánchez Papers.

68. Gustavo Jimenez to Luis Alberto Sánchez, April 26, 1932, Letter 1177, Luis Alberto Sánchez Papers.

69. Gustavo Jimenez to Luis Alberto Sánchez, June 20, 1932, Letter 1181, Luis Alberto Sánchez Papers.

70. Gustavo Jimenez to Luis Alberto Sánchez, April 26, 1932, Letter 1177, Luis Alberto Sánchez Papers.

71. Ibid.

72. Ibid.

73. Gustavo Jimenez to Luis Alberto Sánchez, July 31, 1932, Letter 1183, Luis Alberto Sánchez Papers.

74. Ibid.

75. Haya de la Torre, *El antimperialismo y el APRA*, in *Obras completas*, 4:108.

76. Juan Gargurevich, *Historia de la prensa peruana*, 157.

77. A full list can be found in Víctor Villanueva, *Ejército peruano*, 412.

78. Armando Villanueva, interview with the author, July 20, 2005.

79. Murillo Garaycochea, *Historia del APRA*, 331–35.

80. Ibid., 333.

81. *Juicio seguido contra el Sargento Primero Alfonso Pinedo Sanduro y otros por el delito de rebellion, Lima, 8 de enero de 1934*, p. 5, Archivo Histórico Militar. This testimony is dated January 6, 1934.

82. Ibid.

83. Giesecke, "Trujillo Insurrection," 137.

84. Aguilar, interview with the author.

85. *La verdad sobre el APRA* (n.d., n.p.), 61.

86. Ibid., 35.

87. Tirso Molinari Morales, *El fascismo en el Perú*, 164.

88. See Whitney, *State and Revolution in Cuba*.

89. Víctor Villanueva, *Ejército peruano*, 226.

90. Giesecke, "Trujillo Insurrection," 138–39.

91. Murillo Garaycochea, *Historia del APRA*, 356.

92. Viejo [Haya], Lima, to Perales (pen name for Colonel César Pardo), La Paz, September 6, 1936, Archivo Pardo, in Davies and Villanueva, *300 documentos*, 89.

93. Ibid.

94. Pardo to Haya, July 22, 1936, Archivo Pardo, in Davies and Villanueva, *300 documentos*, 61.

95. Pardo to Haya, August 31, 1936, Archivo Pardo, in Davies and Villanueva, *300 documentos*, 78.

96. Haya de la Torre to "The Three Musketeers," August 30, 1936, Archivo Pardo, in Davies and Villanueva, *300 documentos*, 73.

97. Víctor Villanueva's version of the events was that Haya organized the uprising and had struck a deal to let Benavides leave the country and that the relationship between Haya and Benavides went back to the time when they had both had Sánchez Cerro as a common enemy. Víctor Villanueva, *La sublevación aprista*, 21–23. He also points to the fact that one of Haya's "hiding places" was the home of Augusto Benavides Canseco, the cousin of President Benavides. Davies and Villanueva, *300 documentos*, 298.

98. Werlich, *Peru*, 218.

99. Soto Rivera, *Víctor Raúl*, 1:346.

100. Davies and Villanueva, *300 documentos*, 19.

101. Soto Rivera, *Víctor Raúl*, 1:347. The author cites no sources for this encounter.

102. Pike, *Politics of the Miraculous*, 120.

103. Davies and Villanueva, *300 documentos*, 21.

104. Ibid., 22.

105. Proclama de Rodriguez, Archivo Benavides, Document 17-39, in Davies and Villanueva, *300 documentos*, 325.

106. Haya de la Torre to Pardo, February 1939, Letter 1021, Luis Alberto Sánchez Papers.

107. Víctor Villanueva, *La sublevación aprista*, 26.

108. Víctor Villanueva, *Ejército peruano*, 246.

109. For a study of this period, see Portocarrero Maisch, *De Bustamante a Odría*.

110. The phrase in Spanish rhymes: "Con Bustamante, ni para atrás ni para adelante."

111. Haworth, "Peru," 170.

112. Klaren, *Peru*, 291.

113. Werlich, *Peru*, 240.

114. Klaren, *Peru*, 292.

115. Velasquez, interview with the author.

116. Weekly Political Report, June 23, 1947, 823.00/6-2347, National Archives.

117. Weekly Political Report No. 1728, Lima, June 23, 1947, 823.00/6-2347, National Archives.

118. Haya de la Torre, "A la opinión pública chilena: Manifiesto de Raúl Haya de la Torre," December 1944, clipping, 823.00/1-245, National Archives.

119. Claude G. Bowers Santiago, to the secretary of state, January 2, 1945, 823.00 /1-245, National Archives.

120. Víctor Villanueva, *Ejército peruano*, 248.

121. Víctor Villanueva, *La sublevación aprista*, 24–25.

122. Werlich, *Peru*, 244.

123. Masterson, *Militarism and Politics*, 119.

124. Víctor Villanueva, *La sublevación aprista*, 151–54.

125. Haya de la Torre, "Mensaje al III Congreso Nacional del Partido Aprista Peruano, July 27, 1957," in *Obras completas*, 1:354.

126. Víctor Villanueva, *La sublevación aprista*, 20–21.

127. Ibid., 41.

128. Ibid., 42–43.

129. Ibid., 51.

130. Ibid., 46.

131. Ibid., 54.

132. Ibid., 56.

133. Masterson, *Militarism and Politics*, 112.

134. Ibid., 113.

135. Ibid., 116.

136. Víctor Villanueva, *El APRA y el ejercito*, 89.

137. Masterson, *Militarism and Politics*, 120.

138. Ibid., 124.

139. Ibid., 135.

140. Ibid., 150.

141. "Significativo homenaje rindió la ciudadanía a los Institutos Armados al conmemorarse el 1er. aniversario del alzamiento aprista en el Callao, el 3 de Octubre del año pasado," *Revista Militar del Perú* 46, nos. 9–10 (September–October 1949): 16.

142. López Jiménez, "Configuraciones de partidos."

143. Masterson, *Militarism and Politics*, 164.

144. Ibid., 165.

145. Ibid., 142.

146. Ibid., 138.

147. Ibid., 139.

148. Ibid., 162.

149. Ibid., 170.

150. Ibid., 172.

151. Ibid., 174.

152. Haya de la Torre, "El discurso del 'veto' del 4 de julio de 1962, Casa del Pueblo," in *Obras completas*, 5:455.

153. Masterson, *Militarism and Politics*, 233.

154. Ibid.

155. Ibid.

156. Ibid., 234.

157. Morales Bermúdez, interview with the author.

158. Townsend Ezcurra, *50 Años de Aprismo*, 150.

159. Alva Castro, interview with the author.

160. "Ollanta Humala dijo que Armando Villanueva lo llamó para dar golpe contra Toledo," *Diario Correo*, February 20, 2013, http://diariocorreo.pe/politica/ollanta-humala-dijo-que-armando-villanueva-l-184622/.

Chapter Three

1. C. Van H. Engert to the Secretary of State, Venezuela, January 11, 1929, 810.43 APRA 16, National Archives.

2. Cerdas, *Sandino*.

3. Fred Dearing to Frank B. Kellogg, September 7, 1931, 810.43 APRA 102, National Archives.

4. Manrique, *Usted fue Aprista*, 62.

5. Schwartzberg, *Democracy and U.S. Policy*, 62.

6. Ibid., 100.

7. Haya de la Torre, "Discurso programa, 23 de agosto, 1931," in *Obras completas*, 5:61.

8. Haya de la Torre, *La defensa continental*, 11–12.

9. Schwartzberg, *Democracy and U.S. Policy*, 124. For more information on Haya's connection to the United States, see Pike, *Politics of the Miraculous*, 187–98, and Dorais, "Indo-America."

10. Haya de la Torre, "Teoria y táctica del Aprismo," in *Obras completas*, 1:193.

11. Haya de la Torre, "The Introduction to Continental Defense," in Alexander, *Aprismo*, 294.

12. Haya de la Torre, *El antimperialismo y el APRA*, in *Obras completas*, 4:148.

13. Haya de la Torre, "Teoria y táctica del Aprismo," 1:194–95.

14. Haya de la Torre to Luis Alberto Sánchez, May 21, 1953, in Haya de la Torre and Sánchez, *Correspondencia*, 2:66.

15. Dorais, "Indo-America," 36.

16. Weaver, *Peruvian Rebel*, 22.

17. Dorais, "Indo-America," 35–81.

18. Gutierrez Sánchez, *Haya de la Torre*, 69.

19. Ibid., 130.

20. See Lazitch, *Biographical Dictionary of the Comintern*, 514–15.

21. "Debating Union to Hold First Meeting Tuesday," *Harvard Crimson*, October 20, 1927.

22. Haya de la Torre, Washington, D.C., to Eudocio Ravines, September 27, 1927, cited in Iglesias, "Réseaux transnationaux," 171.

23. Haya de la Torre, "Teoria y táctica del Aprismo," 1:198.

24. Pike, *Politics of Miraculous*, 191.

25. Alexander, *Aprismo*, 25.

26. "To the Diplomatic and Consular Officers in Latin America and Mexico from the Secretary of State," November 21, 1928, 810.43 APRA 1, National Archives. This document is a draft written for the Secretary of State to send out; the author is unknown.

27. Reedy, *Magda Portal*, 147.

28. Dispatch 1492, R.M. de Lambert to Secretary of State, San Salvador, February 2, 1929, 810.43 APRA 21, National Archives.

29. Dispatch 2122, Guatemala, September 28, 1928, 810.43 APRA 14, National Archives.

30. Haya de la Torre, "Teoria y táctica del Aprismo," 1:195–96.

31. Roy Davis to the Secretary of State, Costa Rica, February 15, 1929, 810.43 APRA 24, National Archives.

32. Dispatch 650, April 22, 1931, 823.00/673, National Archives.

33. "Haya de la Torre llegó a Talara e inicio su campaña presidencial," *El Tiempo* (Talara), July 19, 1931, clipping, 823.00/726, National Archives.

34. Haya de la Torre, "Discurso programa," 5:60.

35. Haya de la Torre, "Discurso ante el Primer Congreso Nacional del Partido Aprista Peruano," in *Obras completas*, 5:39.

36. Haya de la Torre to Luis Alberto Sánchez, received March 24, 1937, in Haya de la Torre and Sánchez, *Correspondencia*, 1:305–6.

37. Pilar Chocano (Oscar Chocano's daughter), personal communication with the author, Lima, July 2004.

38. Atala, interview with the author; Pike, *Politics of Miraculous*, 120.

39. Haya de la Torre to Luis Alberto Sánchez, March 1937, in Haya de la Torre and Sánchez, *Correspondencia*, 1:307–8. I have been unable to establish the identity of "P" in this letter.

40. "Alianza Popular Revolucionaria Americana—APRA, Peru" from J. Edgar Hoover, Director FBI, to Adole Berle, Assistant Secretary of State, June 12, 1943, 810.43 APRA 258, National Archives.

41. *Acción Aprista* (Trujillo), May 19, 1934, clipping in dispatch 3430, Fred Dearing to Secretary of State, May 25, 1934, 810.43 APRA 202, National Archives.

42. Dispatch 4482, Louis G. Dreyfus to Secretary of State, April 1, 1936, 810.43 APRA 207, National Archives.

43. Dispatch 4868, Louis G. Dreyfus to Secretary of State, December 23, 1936, 810.43 APRA 211, National Archives.

44. Dispatch 4959, Louis G. Dreyfus to Secretary of State, February 13, 1937, 810.43 APRA 212, National Archives.

45. Informal translation of "President Roosevelt Will Not Come to Peru," *Cuaderno Aprista*, September 1938, enclosure in dispatch 649, Louis G. Dreyfus Jr. to Secretary of State, September 13, 1938, 810.43 APRA 224, National Archives.

46. Dispatch 649, Louis G. Dreyfus Jr. to Secretary of State, September 13, 1938, 810.43 APRA 224, National Archives.

47. "Comité Nacional de Acción del Partido Aprista Peruano, Secretaría Nacional de Organización, Directiva para los Comités Sectorales de toda la República y en especial para los de Lima, Callao y Balnearios," Enclosure 1, Lima, October 21, 1938, 710H/149, National Archives.

48. Dispatch 710, "VIII Inter American Conference: Aprista Plans," to Louis G. Dreyfus Jr., Chargé d'Affaires, to the Secretary of State, Lima, October 21, 1938, 710H/149, National Archives.

49. Haya de la Torre, "Pan Americanism or Inter Americanism," in Alexander, *Aprismo*, 313.

50. Ibid., 312.

51. Haya de la Torre, "On the Inter American Democratic Front," in Alexander, *Aprismo*, 321.

52. Ibid., 322.

53. Haya de la Torre, "Pan Americanism or Inter Americanism," 313.

54. Ibid.

55. Haya de la Torre, "Latin American Unity and the Yankees," in Alexander, *Aprismo*, 260.

56. Pike, *Politics of Miraculous*, 192.

57. Davies and Villanueva, *Secretos electorales del APRA*, 17–19.

58. September 8, 1938, 823.00/1315, National Archives, reproduced in Davies and Villanueva, *Secretos electorales del APRA*, 18.

59. Ibid., 19.

60. Ibid., 18.

61. Inman, *Latin America*, 164.

62. Ibid.

63. Ibid., 165.

64. Frank, *South American Journey*, 383.

65. Laurence Duggan to Cordell Hull, memorandum, November 18, 1942, 810.43 APRA 259, National Archives.

66. Dispatch 11,385, January 2, 1945, FW 832.00/1-245 CS/HS, National Archives.

67. Dispatch 1728, June 23, 1947, 823.00/6-2347, National Archives.

68. Confidential telegram, August 19, 1947, 823.00/8-1847, National Archives.

69. Conway Forbes to the Viscount Halifax, Foreign Secretary, Lima, July 19, 1940, FO317, Box 24221, File A3679, Public Records Office, Kew, England.

70. Haya de la Torre, "El 'Buen Vecino': ¿Garantía definitiva?," in *La defensa continental*, in *Obras completas*, 4:259.

71. Ibid., 261.

72. Dispatch 47, December 14, 1938, 810.43 APRA 219, National Archives.

73. Secret Dispatch 2380, "Activities of the APRA," January 11, 1945, 823.00/1-1145, National Archives.

74. Haya de la Torre, "El 'Buen Vecino,'" 4:261.

75. Dispatch 6301, R. Henry Norweb to the Secretary of State, March 12, 1943, 810.43 APRA 255, National Archives.

76. Manrique, *Usted fue Aprista*, 180.

77. Haworth, "Peru," 184–85.

78. Arturo Sabroso to George Meany, Lima, March 10, 1952, Archivo Arturo Sabroso.

79. Haya de la Torre, "El plan económico del Aprismo, 9 de octubre de 1945," in *Discursos*, in *Obras completas*, 5:363.

80. Ibid., 368.

81. Ibid., 381.

82. Dispatch 2124, "Interview with Haya de la Torre re: Present Political Situation," Ambassador Prentice Cooper to the Secretary of State, Lima, November 3, 1947, 823.00/11-347, National Archives.

83. Secret Dispatch 852, Ambassador Prentice Cooper to the Secretary of State, Lima, December 2, 1947, 823.00/12-247, National Archives.

84. "Memorandum of Interview with Haya de la Torre," Charles Ackerman, Chargé d'Affaires, to the Secretary of State, Lima, May 23, 1947, 823.00/5-2347, National Archives.

85. Ibid.

86. Ibid.

87. Soto Rivera, *Víctor Raúl*, 2:547.

88. Letter reproduced in Alegría, *Gabriela Mistral intima*, 73.

89. For a full description of the interaction between Mistral and Haya, see Crow, "Writing Indo-America."

90. Quoted in Manrique, *Usted fue Aprista*, 180.

91. Haya de la Torre, "My Five Year Exile," 152.

92. Ibid., 154–57.

93. Ibid., 157.

94. Haya de la Torre to Luis Alberto Sánchez, May 21, 1953, in Haya de la Torre and Sánchez, *Correspondencia*, 2:67.

95. United Press International, "World Court Backs Colombia in Sheltering Outlaw," *Pittsfield Berkshire Evening Eagle*, June 14, 1951, 7.

96. "Begins Fifth Year of Custody in Embassy," *Fort Pierce (Fla.) News Tribune*, January 4, 1953.

97. Information on the life of Frances Grant taken from Perrone, "Biographical Sketch of Frances Grant."

98. Ibid.

99. Ibid.

100. Kantor, *Ideology and Program*, iii.

101. Ibid., 68.

102. Ibid., 114.

103. Ibid., 125.

104. Ibid., 124.

105. Ibid., 60.

106. Ibid., 120.

107. Haya de la Torre, "Discuso en el dia de la Fraternidad Campo de Marte," February 18, 1972, in *Obras completas*, 7:372.

108. Haya de la Torre, "My Five Year Exile,"164.

109. United Press International, "Peruvian Exile Remains in Mexico City," *Brownsville (Tex.) Herald*, June 13, 1954, B7.

110. Haya de la Torre to Luis Alberto Sánchez, February 4, 1955, in Haya de la Torre and Sánchez, *Correspondencia*, 2:200–201.

111. Ibid., 199.

112. We still lack Haya's complete collected works. The seven-volume *Obras completas* published by Editorial Mejía Baca during Haya's lifetime does not in fact do justice to the title. Luis Alva Castro has compiled articles by Haya, many of which do not appear in the *Obras completas*, in a series of books.

113. "A Tamer Rebel Comes Home," *Life*, August 12, 1956.

114. Current Intelligence Bulletin, Document 8, August 16, 1956, approved for release January 29, 2003, CIA-RDP 79T00975A002700080001-3, National Archives.

115. Haya de la Torre, "Estados Unidos Frente al Mercado Comun Latinoamericano," *La Tribuna*, 1959, in *Obras completas*, 1:407–9.

116. Phil Newsom, UPI, "Haya de la Torre Center of Political Storm in Peru," *Lima (Ohio) News*, July 12, 1962, 8.

117. Haya de la Torre, "Discursos del Dia de la Fraternidad, 25 de febrero, 1961," in *Discursos*, in *Obras completas*, 5:438.

118. Quoted in Schwartzberg, *Democracy and U.S. Policy*, 120.

119. Haya de la Torre, "Mensaje a la Europa Nórdica," in *Obras completas*, 3:248–52.

120. Oswaldo Nuñez, personal communication with the author, Lima, Barranco, October 25, 2017.

121. Morales Bermúdez, interview with the author.

122. Alva Castro, interview with the author.

Chapter Four

1. Cotler, *Clases, estado y nación*, 235.

2. Sánchez, *La vida del siglo*, 405.

3. Chauncey, *Gay New York*, 1–29.

4. Manuel Seoane to Haya de la Torre, April 27, 1939, Document 23 in Davies and Villanueva, *Secretos electorales del APRA*, 47–52.

5. Bederman, *Manliness and Civilization*, 10–15.

6. Gustav-Wrathall, *Young Stranger*, 4–6.

7. This myth was debunked by Mariano Valderrama and Pedro Planas. Valderrama et al., *El APRA*; Planas, *Mito y realidad*.

8. Haya de la Torre, "Cartas prisioneros Apristas," *Obras completas*, 7:204.

9. Haya de la Torre, "A la célula del APRA del Cuzco," Berlin, February 25, 1930, in "El proceso Haya de la Torre," in *Obras completas*, 5:261. While this letter was most likely written by Haya, it does not bear his signature and is allegedly authored by the International Executive Committee of APRA.

10. Ibid., 262.

11. Ibid., 266.

12. Ibid., 263.

13. Ibid., 268.

14. Sánchez, *Vida del siglo*, 410.

15. Chávez Vargas, interview with the author.

16. Manrique, *Usted fue Aprista*, 96–97.

17. Haya de la Torre, "A la célula," 5:268.

18. Sánchez, *Testimonio personal*, 353.

19. Basadre, *Historia de la República*, 10:159.

20. Murillo Garaycochea, *Historia del APRA*, 118.

21. Seoane, *Obras Apristas*, cited in Murillo Garaycochea, *Historia del APRA*, 108.

22. Magda Portal, autobiography manuscript 10, n.d., unnumbered box, Magda Portal Papers.

23. Murillo Garaycochea, *Historia del APRA*, 182–83.

24. Haya de la Torre, "Cartas prisioneros Apristas," 7:208.

25. Gutierrez Sánchez, *Haya de la Torre*, 99.

26. Ibid., 101.

27. The connection between the YMCA and gay culture is a subject worth pursuing for Latin America. In New York, YMCA guesthouses became meeting places for gay men. Chauncey, *Gay New York*, 156–58.

28. Haya de la Torre, "Cartas prisioneros Apristas," 7:212.

29. Ibid., 212–13.

30. Ibid., 212.

31. Ibid., 236.

32. Ibid., 245.

33. Carlos Manuel Cox eventually published the letters in 1946, during APRA's brief period of legality. Haya de la Torre and Cox, *Cartas*.

34. Haya de la Torre to Manuel Checa, Incahuasi, Chile, February 10, 1939, Document 4 in Davies and Villanueva, *Secretos electorales del APRA*, 23–24.

35. Haya de la Torre, "Cartas prisioneros Apristas," 7:216.

36. Ibid., 246.

37. Ibid., 245.

38. Haya de la Torre, "La oración admirable," 315.

39. Klaiber, *Religion and Revolution in Peru*, 135.

40. Ibid.; Vega Centeno, *Aprismo popular*.

41. Klaiber, *Religion and Revolution in Peru*, 151.

42. *Libertad* (Lima), August 1933, 2, quoted in ibid., 152.

43. Melgar Bao, *Redes e imaginario del exilio*, 69.

44. Lucho de las Casas (Luis Felipe de las Casas's son), personal communication, August 2007.

45. Gadea, *My Life with Che*, 128.

46. Torres Tello, interview with the author.

47. Partido Aprista Peruano, *Juventud Aprista Peruana*, 3.

48. Armando Villanueva, interview with the author, July 2008.

49. Ibid.

50. Ibid.

51. Ibid. Surco is the name of a district in the city of Lima.

52. Armando Villanueva, interview with the author, July 2008.

53. Mae Hoyle de Armijo, personal communication, May 18, 2007, Las Cruces, New Mexico.

54. Nugent, *Edge of Empire*, 236.

55. *Juicio seguido contra el Sargento Primero Alfonso Pinedo Sanduro y otros poe el delito de rebellion, Lima, 8 de enero de 1934*, 5, Archivo Histórico Militar.

56. Haya de la Torre, "La Reforma Universitaria," in "Teoria y táctica del Aprismo," in *Obras completas*, 1:213–14.

57. Bergére, *Sun Yat Sen*, 105.

58. Klaiber, "Popular Universities," 694.

59. Haya de la Torre, "Discurso ante el Primer Congreso Nacional del Partido Aprista Peruano," in *Obras completas*, 5:40.

60. Klaiber, "Popular Universities," 700.

61. Ibid., 694.

62. Soto Rivera, *Víctor Raúl*, 1:57.

63. Klaiber, "Popular Universities," 701.

64. *La Prensa*, March 18, 1922, 2, cited in ibid., 704.

65. Klaiber, "Popular Universities," 715.

66. French, *Peaceful and Working People*; García-Bryce, *Crafting the Republic*, ch. 3.

67. González Vigil, *Importancia de la educación popular*.

68. García-Bryce, *Crafting the Republic*, 89–90.

69. Soto Rivera, *Víctor Raúl*, 1:59.

70. Para la célula de La Plata, dependiente de la de B.A. (COPIA) [For the La Plata cell, dependent on the Buenos Aires cell (COPY)], May 1927 [date handwritten in pencil, probably by Armando Villanueva]; Circular del No. 1 del Comite Ejecutivo de la A.P.R.A., Armando Villanueva Papers.

71. Klaiber, "Popular Universities," 712.

72. Ibid., 715.

73. Ibid., 704.

74. Ibid., 715.

75. Stein, "Paths to Populism in Peru," 118.

76. Soto Rivera, *Víctor Raúl*, 1:285.

77. Ibid., 286.

78. Drinot, "Creole Anti-Communism."

79. Velasquez, interview with the author.

80. León Seminario to Luis Alberto Sánchez, March 6, 1953, Letter 1223, Luis Alberto Sánchez Papers.

81. Gadea, *My Life with Che*, 128.

82. Soto Rivera, *Víctor Raúl*, 1:129. The three men in charge of the *dorados* were Carlos Lizarzaburu, Dr. Alfonso Mac Gubin, and Buenaventura Machuca.

83. Werlich, *Peru*, 206.

84. Haya de la Torre, "El proceso Haya de la Torre," 5:284.

85. Publicaciones del Partido Aprista Peruano, *El proceso Haya de la Torre*, 164.

86. Ibid., 148–83.

87. "Moción aprobada por unanimidad en el Senado de Colombia," Bogotá, July 26, 1932, in ibid., 161.

88. "Haya de la Torre, Reported Death Of," February 24, 1933, 810.43 APRA 177, National Archives.

89. Haya de la Torre, "Cartas prisioneros Apristas," 7:211.

90. Magda Portal to Anna Melissa Graves, January 16, 1936, Box 1, Folder 2, Magda Portal Papers.

91. Anna Melissa Graves to Magda Portal, December 3, 1936, Box 1, Folder 2, Magda Portal Papers.

92. Quoted in Britton, *Carleton Beals*, 151.

93. Alfredo González Prada to Luis Alberto Sánchez, New York, December 30, 1937, Letter 725, Luis Alberto Sánchez Papers.

94. Soto Rivera, *Víctor Raúl*, 1:318.

95. Ibid., 318–19.

96. Haya de la Torre to Luis Alberto Sánchez, May 13, 1936, Luis Alberto Sánchez Papers.

97. Haya de la Torre to Luis Alberto Sánchez, May 6, 1936, in Haya de la Torre and Sánchez, *Correspondencia*, 1:258. Throughout the correspondence, there are references to individuals in code that remain to be deciphered.

98. Anna Melissa Graves to Magda Portal, December 3, 1936, Box 1, Folder 2, Magda Portal Papers.

99. Rebolledo, "Reseña," 263.

100. Alfredo González Prada to Luis Alberto Sánchez, New York, June 5, 1939, Letter 758, Luis Alberto Sánchez Papers.

101. Sánchez, *Haya de la Torre*, 9.

102. Ibid., 10–11.

103. Ibid., 144–45.

104. "Debating Union," *Harvard Crimson*, October 20, 1927.

105. Cossío del Pomar, *Haya de la Torre*, 20.

106. Quoted in ibid., 37.

107. Quoted in ibid., 57.

108. Quoted in ibid., 83.

109. Cossío del Pomar, *Haya de la Torre*, 104.

110. Ibid., 86.

111. Ibid., 93.

112. Ibid., 87.

113. Ibid., 140.

114. Ibid., 252.

115. Ibid., 148.

116. Ibid., 195–96.

117. Ravines, *Yenan Way*, 19.

118. Raffo, "Memorias," 26.

119. Ibid., 27.

120. Hidalgo, *Por qué renuncié al APRA*, 25.

121. Ibid., 25–26.

122. Ibid., 26–27.

123. Ibid., 27.

124. Ibid., 29.

125. *Notas cambiadas*, 11 (consulted in Peruvian Subject Collection, Box 1, Folder 4, Hoover Institution Library and Archives).

126. Soto Rivera, *Víctor Raúl*, 2:595.

127. "People: A Refugee Peruvian Leader Finds Dangerous Sanctuary," *Life* 26, no. 13 (March 28, 1949): 43.

128. Soto Rivera, *Víctor Raúl*, 2:620.

129. Quoted in ibid., 656.

130. Haya de la Torre, Stockholm, to Luis Alberto Sánchez, April 12, 1955, in Haya de la Torre and Sánchez, *Correspondencia*, 2:229.

131. Manuel Vázquez Diaz to Luis Alberto Sánchez, May 10, 1954, LAS Correspondence 1956, Luis Alberto Sánchez Papers.

132. Soto Rivera, *Víctor Raúl*, 2:665–67.

133. Ribeyro, *Cartas a Juan Antonio*, 149.

134. Angulo Daneri, *Llámalo amor*, 26–27.

135. Ibid., 42; Carlos Raffo Dasso, personal communication, July 29, 2014, Lima, Peru.

136. Angulo Daneri, *Llámalo amor*, 40–41.

137. "Periodista Toño Angulo Daneri fue agredido por apristas en Trujillo," *La República*, January 26, 2005.

138. "Alan García habla sobre homosexualidad y Haya de la Torre," YouTube video, 15:05, posted by "gaycitotv," January 3, 2013, https://www.youtube.com/watch?v=4FcSkyz2QO8.

139. Raffo, "Memorias," 4. The phrase "premises at Alfonso Ugarte" refers to the present-day party headquarters.

140. Bedoya Reyes, interview with the author.

141. Alva Castro, interview with the author.

142. Ibid.

143. Torres Tello, interview with the author.

Chapter Five

1. Peirano, interview with the author.

2. Magda Portal, autobiography manuscript 10, n.d., unnumbered box, Magda Portal Papers.

3. Ibid.

4. Portal, "Lo que urge," 6.

5. Portal, "El voto femenino," 7.

6. On Portal and APRA, see García-Bryce, "Transnational Activist." For biographies of Portal, see Weaver, *Peruvian Rebel*; Wallace Fuentes, *Most Scandalous Woman*; and Reedy, *Magda Portal*.

7. Magda Portal to Anna Melissa Graves, October 10, 1935, Box 1, Folder 1, Magda Portal Papers.

8. McGee Deutsch, "Gender and Sociopolitical Change," 270.

9. Denegri, *Damas escritoras*.

10. Miller, *Latin American Women*, 43–50.

11. On education, see Espinoza, *Education and the State*.

12. Balta, *Presencia de la mujer*.

13. García-Bryce, "Transnational Activist," 679.

14. Miller, *Latin American Women*, 74–76.

15. Ibid., 79.

16. Zegarra, "María Jesús Alvarado," 496–97.

17. Ibid., 506–9.

18. Ibid., 509.

19. Aguilar, "Via cruces de las mujeres peruanas," 283.

20. Weaver, *Peruvian Rebel*, 104.

21. Peru, Ministerio de Fomento, *Censo de 1908*, 914–925, cited in Parker, *Idea of the Middle Class*, 61.

22. Peru, Ministerio de Hacienda y Comercio, Dirección Nacional de Estadística, *Censo nacional de población de 1940*, vol. 5, *Departamento de Lima, ciudad de Lima, provincia constitucional del Callao* (Lima, 1944), pt. 1, pp. 102–3, pt. 2, pp. 30–31, cited in Parker, *Idea of the Middle Class*, 193.

23. Parker, *Idea of the Middle Class*, 193.

24. Weaver, *Peruvian Rebel*, 101.

25. Portal, *Hacia la mujer nueva*, 14.

26. Taylor, "Origins of APRA," 48.

27. *El Peru*, May 5, 1932, cited in ibid.

28. Cueva and Zurita de Cueva, interview with the author.

29. Manuel Seoane, "Escorzo de Magda Portal," *Claridad* (Buenos Aires) 15 (1935): 294, cited in Weaver, *Peruvian Rebel*, 100.

30. Parker, *Idea of the Middle Class*, 167–68.

31. Aguilar, "Via cruces de las mujeres peruanas," 274–75.

32. *Diario de los Debates del Congreso Constituyente de 1931, T.I. (28 de noviembre de 1931 a 23 de enero de 1932)*, 491, cited in ibid., 264.

33. For a discussion of various interpretations of this moment, see Wallace Fuentes, "Becoming Magda Portal," 336–43.

34. Portal, *Hacia la mujer nueva*, 20.

35. Sección Femenina del PAP, "Carta a las mujeres argentinas de 'América Nueva,'" August 1932, in ibid., 64–67.

36. Portal, *Hacia la mujer nueva*, 10.

37. Ibid., 8.

38. Ibid., 11.

39. Ibid., 7.

40. Ibid.

41. Weaver, *Peruvian Rebel*, 105.

42. Portal, *Hacia la mujer nueva*, 17.

43. Ibid., 24.

44. Unruh, *Performing Women*, 193.

45. Slaughter and Kern, *European Women on the Left*, 6.

46. Portal, *Hacia la mujer nueva*, 9.

47. Ibid., 52–53.

48. Ibid., 52.

49. Meneses, *Aprismo femenino peruano*, 20.

50. Ibid., 19.

51. Ibid., 37.

52. Ibid., 38.

53. Ibid., 36.

54. Ibid., 34.

55. Ibid., 42.

56. Ibid., 45.

57. Portal, *Hacia la mujer nueva*, 24–26.

58. Cueva and Zurita, interview with the author.

59. Ibid.

60. Heilman, *Before the Shining Path*, 93.

61. Quoted in ibid., 92.

62. Magda Portal to Anna Melissa Graves, May 29, 1936, Box 1, Folder 2, Magda Portal Papers.

63. Díaz, *Las mujeres de Haya*, 115–26.

64. Torres Tello, interview with the author.

65. Ibid.

66. Ibid.

67. Ibid.

68. Ibid.

69. Aguirre, "Hombres y rejas."

70. Ibid.

71. Ibid.

72. "Consuelo Torres: Madre de los cerros," BBC, accessed November 9, 2017, http://www.bbc.co.uk/spanish/specials/1535_consuelotorres/index.shtml.

73. Peirano, interview with the author.

74. Ibid.

75. Ibid.

76. Ibid.

77. Ibid.

78. Ibid.

79. Ibid.

80. Miranda and Miranda, interview with the author.

81. Ibid.

82. Ibid.

83. Ibid.

84. Díaz, *Las mujeres de Haya*, 130.

85. Ibid.

86. Ibid., 136.

87. Melgar Bao, "Exile in the Andean Countries," 106.

88. Melgar Bao, *Redes e imaginario del exilio*, 64–65.

89. Magda Portal to Luis Alberto Sánchez, April 21, 1936, Box 1, Folder 2, Magda Portal Papers.

90. Weaver, *Peruvian Rebel*, 135.

91. Portal, *Flora Tristán*.

92. See Reedy, *Magda Portal*, 213.

93. Magda Portal to Luis Alberto Sánchez, April 21, 1936, Box 1, Folder 2, Magda Portal Papers.

94. Luis Alberto Sánchez to Magda Portal, February 28, 1939, Box 1, Folder 3, Magda Portal Papers.

95. Manuel Seoane, Magda Portal, and Luis Alberto Sánchez to Oscar Benavides, telegram, January 8, 1945, Box 1, Folder 7, Magda Portal Papers.

96. Magda Portal to Haya de la Torre, June 20, 1941, Box 1, Folder 5, Magda Portal Papers. In his memoirs, party leader Armando Villanueva tells that the Congreso de Partidos Democráticos y Populares de Indoamérica was one of two such meetings organized by Seoane, at the time an exiled Aprista leader in Chile. Armando Villanueva and Thorndike, *La gran persecución*, 272.

97. Haya de la Torre to Magda Portal, July 7, 1941, Box 1, Folder 5, Magda Portal Papers.

98. Gabriel del Mazo to Magda Portal, May 26, 1940, Box 1, Folder 4, Magda Portal Papers.

99. Magda Portal to Haya de la Torre, June 20, 1941, Box 1, Folder 5, Magda Portal Papers.

100. Díaz, *Las mujeres de Haya*, 157.

101. Ibid., 77.

102. Ibid., 176.

103. García Montero Koechlin, *Detrás de la mascara*, 9.

104. Ibid., 8.

105. Ibid., 10.

106. Ibid., 17.

107. Ibid.

108. Ibid., 26.

109. Díaz, *Las mujeres de Haya*, 176.

110. McGee Deutsch, "Gender and Sociopolitical Change," 261.

111. Ibid., 270.

112. Ibid., 271.

113. Peirano, interview with the author.

114. Quoted in Weaver, *Peruvian Rebel*, 145–46.

115. Portal, *La mujer en el partido*.

116. Quoted in Weaver, *Peruvian Rebel*, 146.

117. "Magda Portal in San Francisco," B 19, Magda Portal Papers, Benson, University of Texas–Austin, quoted in Weaver, *Peruvian Rebel*, 147.

118. Soto Rivera, *Víctor Raúl*, 2:506.

119. Cited by Weaver, *Peruvian Rebel*, 155.

120. Portal, *¿Quienes traicionaron al pueblo?*, 27.

121. Portal, "El pueblo y su raiz," 12. *Piropo* has no real English equivalent; it is a flattering comment of a man to a woman on the street.

122. Portal, *¿Quienes traicionaron al pueblo?*, 29.

123. Ibid., 27.

124. Ibid., 20.

125. Chaney, *Supermadre*, 73.

126. Only two women participated, one for the Partido Popular Cristiano, the other for the Partido Obrero Marxista Revolucionario. Guardia, *Mujeres peruanas*, 99.

127. Ibid.

128. Ibid., 102.

129. Radcliffe, "*Asi es una mujer del pueblo*," 20.

130. Chaney, *Supermadre*, 120.

131. Radcliffe, "*Asi es una mujer del pueblo*," 25.

Conclusion

1. Chauncey, *Gay New York*, 12–13.

2. Alexander, *Aprismo*, 265.

3. De la Torre and Arnson, "Introduction," 34–35.

4. Peirano, interview with the author.

5. Ibid.

Bibliography

Archives

Austin, Tex.
  University of Texas Libraries
    Benson Latin American Collection
      Magda Portal Papers
College Park, Md.
  National Archives and Records Administration
    Records of the Department of State
  University of Maryland Libraries
    George Meany Memorial AFL-CIO Archive
Lima, Peru
  Archivo General de la Nación
    Documentos Prefecturas
  Archivo Histórico Militar
    Causas Criminales
  Archivo del Ministerio de Relaciones Exteriories
    Correspondencia Política Exterior
  Archivo Arturo Sabroso, Pontificia Universidad Católica del Perú
  Biblioteca Nacional del Perú
    Colección Hemeroteca
  Federico More Papers, private collection
  Armando Villanueva Papers, private collection
New Brunswick, N.J.
  Rutgers University Libraries
    Special Collections and University Archives
      Frances Grant Papers
Stanford, Calif.
  Stanford University
  Hoover Institution Library and Archives
University Park, Pa.
  Pennsylvania State University
    Special Collections Library
      Luis Alberto Sánchez Papers

Interviews

Aguilar, Alfonso. Interview with the author, Trujillo, July 2008.

Alexander, Robert. Interview with the author, New Brunswick, New Jersey, March 8, 2007.

Alva Castro, Luis. Interview with the author, Lima, January 6, 2016.

Atala, César. Interview with the author, Virginia, May 2006.

Bedoya Reyes, Luis. Interview with the author, Lima, January 5, 2016.

Chávez Vargas, Manuel. Interview with the author, Chimbote, July 8, 2005.

Cueva, Clodomiro, and Graciela Zurita de Cueva. Interview with the author, Lima, September 8, 2009.

Miranda, Carlos, and Rosa Miranda. Interview with the author, Lima, January 2010.

Morales Bermúdez, Francisco. Interview with the author, Lima, July 24, 2007.

Peirano, Lindomira. Interview with the author, Chosica, Peru, April 5, 2013.

Torres Tello, Consuelo. Interview with the author, Lima, July 5, 2007.

Velasquez, Alfonso. Interview with the author, Lima, August 5, 2003.

Villanueva, Armando. Interview with the author, Lima, July 20, 2005.

———. Interview with the author, Lima, July 2008.

Unpublished Primary Sources

Raffo, Carlos. "Memorias." Unpublished manuscript, n.d.

Published Primary Sources

Alegría, Ciro. *Gabriela Mistral intima*. Lima: Editorial Universo, 1968.

Alexander, Robert, ed. *Aprismo: The Ideas and Doctrines of Víctor Raúl Haya de la Torre*. Kent, Ohio: Kent State University Press, 1973.

Alva Castro, Luis. *Haya de la Torre: Peregrino de la unidad continental*. 2 vols. Lima: Fondo Editorial "V.R. Haya de la Torre," 1988, 1990.

Beals, Carleton. "Aprismo: The Rise of Haya de la Torre." *Foreign Affairs* 13, no. 2 (January 1935): 236–46.

Betancourt, Rómulo. *The Papers of Rómulo Betancourt*. Wilmington, Del.: Scholarly Resources, 2003. Microform.

Cossío del Pomar, Felipe. *Haya de la Torre: El Indoamericano*. Lima: Editorial Nuevo Día, 1946.

Davies, Thomas, Jr., and Víctor Villanueva. *300 documentos para la historia del APRA*. Lima: Editorial Horizonte, 1978.

———. *Secretos electorales del APRA: Correspondencia y documentos de 1939*. Lima: Editorial Horizonte, 1982.

Enriquez, Luis Eduardo. *Haya de la Torre: La estafa política mas grande de América*. Lima: Ediciones del Pacífico, 1951.

Frank, Waldo. *South American Journey*. New York: Duell, Sloan and Pearce, 1943.

García Montero Koechlin, María Luis. *Detrás de la mascara*. Lima: Editorial Latinoamericana, 1963.

González Vigil, Francisco de Paula. *Importancia de la educación popular*. Lima: Ediciones Horas del Hombre, 1948.

Haya de la Torre, Víctor Raúl. *Construyendo el aprismo: Artículos y cartas desde el exilio, 1924–1931*. Buenos Aires: Ed. Claridad, 1933.

——. *La defensa continental*. 3rd ed. Buenos Aires: Editorial Americalee, 1946.

——. "My Five Year Exile in My Own Country." *Life*, May 3, 1954, 152–66.

——. *Obras completas*. 3rd ed. Vols. 1–7. Lima: Editorial Mejía Baca, 1984.

——. "La oración admirable: A los héroes y mártires de la Revolución." *El Norte*, no. 3347, December 23, 1933. In *Trujillo 32*, 2:311–30. Trujillo: Trinchera de Mansiche, 1978.

——. *Revolución sin balas: 15 discursos de Haya de la Torre*. Lima: Okura Editores, 1984.

——. "What Is the APRA?" *Labour Monthly* 8, no. 12 (December 1926): 756–59. http://www.unz.org/Pub/LabourMonthly-1926dec-00756.

Haya de la Torre, Víctor Raúl, and Carlos Manuel Cox, *Cartas de Haya de la Torre a los prisioneros apristas*. Lima: Editorial Nuevo Día, 1946.

Haya de la Torre, Víctor Raúl, and Luis Alberto Sánchez. *Correspondencia*. 2 vols. Lima: Mosca Azul Editores, 1982.

Hidalgo, Alberto. *Diario de mi sentimiento (1922–36)*. Buenos Aires: Edición Privada, 1937.

——. *Por qué renuncé al APRA*. Lima: Imprenta Leomir, 1954.

Inman, Samuel Guy. *Latin America, Its Place in World Life*. Rev. ed. New York: Harcourt Brace, 1942.

Mackay, John. *The Other Spanish Christ: A Study in the Spiritual History of Spain and South America*. New York: Macmillan, 1933.a

Mariátegui, José Carlos, *Siete ensayos de interpretación de la realidad peruana*. Lima : Empresa Editora Amauta, 1952.

Martinez de la Torre, Ricardo. *Apuntes para una interpretación Marxista del Peru*. 2 vols. Lima: Universidad Nacional Mayor de San Marcos, 1974.

Meneses, Rómulo. *Aprismo femenino peruano*. Lima: Editorial Atahualpa, 1934.

Ministerio de Gobierno y Policia, Dirección de Publicidad, *La verdad sobre el APRA: Aprismo es comunismo*. Lima: Ministerio de Gobierno y Policia, Dirección de Publicidad, n.d.

Moreno Mendiguren, Alfredo. *El APRA es un partido internacional: Recopilación de los artículos publicados en "La Prensa" de Lima*. Lima: Impr. Lux, 1959.

Mujica Alvarez Calderon, Nicanor, and Francisco Mujica Serelle. *Nicanor Mujica Alvarez Calderon: Auto/biografía, memorias para un país desmemoriado*. Lima: Editado por Francisco Mujica Serelle, 2015.

Notas cambiadas entre el Ministro de Relaciones Exteriores del Peru y el Encargado de Negocios de Cuba, referentes al asilo de Fernando Leon de Vivero y Pedro Muñiz, 29 de diciembre de 1948, 19 de agosto de 1949. Lima: Imprenta Torres Aguirre, 1949.

Partido Aprista Peruano Federación Aprista Juvenil, *Juventud Aprista Peruana / Partido Aprista Peruano*. Editorial: Lima : Emp. Edit. La Tribuna, 1948.

Portal, Magda. *América latina frente al imperialismo y defensa de la revolución mexicana.* Lima: Editorial Cahuide, 1931.

———. *Flora Tristán: Precursora.* Santiago de Chile, Chile: Imprenta Nueva, 1944.

———. *Hacia la mujer nueva: El Aprismo y la mujer.* Lima: Editorial Cooperativa Aprista "Atahualpa," 1933.

———. *La mujer en el partido del pueblo.* Lima: Imprenta "El Condor," 1948.

———. "Lo que urge no es que las mujeres VOTEN, sino que sepan VOTAR." *La Tribuna,* November 16, 1931.

———. "El pueblo y su raiz: El piropo callejero." *La Tribuna,* February 24, 1946.

———. *¿Quienes traicionaron al pueblo?* Lima: Salas e Hijos, 1950.

———. "El voto femenino deber ser calificado." *APRA,* 2da época, no. 15 (December 31, 1931): 7.

Publicaciones del Partido Aprista Peruano. *El proceso Haya de la Torre: Documentos para la historia del ajusticiamiento de un pueblo.* Guayaquil, Ecuador: Imprenta La Reforma, 1933.

———. *Haya de la Torre y el APRA.* Lima: Ed. Universo, 1980.

Sánchez, Luis Alberto. *Haya de la Torre o el politico: Crónica de una vida sin tregua.* 2nd ed. Santiago: Ediciones Ercilla, 1936.

———. *Haya de la Torre y el APRA.* Lima: Ed. Universo, 1980.

———. *La vida del siglo.* Caracas: Biblioteca Ayacucho, 1988.

———. *Testimonio personal: Memorias de un peruano del siglo xx.* Lima: Ediciones Villasan, 1969.

Townsend Ezcurra, Andrés. *50 años de Aprismo.* Lima: Editorial e Imprenta DESA, 1989.

Tucker, Robert C., ed. *The Lenin Anthology.* New York: W. W. Norton, 1975.

Ugarte, Manuel. *El epistolario de Manuel Ugarte.* Buenos Aires: Archivo General de la Nación, 1999.

Vasconcelos, José. *El desastre: Tercera parte del Ulises Criollo.* México: Editorial Jus, 1968.

Villanueva, Armando, and Javier Landázuri García. *Los inicios.* Lima: Fundación Armando Villanueva del Campo, 2015.

Villanueva, Armando, and Guillermo Thorndike. *La gran persecución (1932–1956).* Lima: Empresa Periodística Nacional, 2004.

Villanueva, Guely. *Haya por Haya: apuntes para sus memorias.* Lima: Editorial del Congreso de la República, 2009.

Villanueva, Víctor, and Thomas Davies Jr. *Secretos electorales.* Lima: Editorial Horizonte, 1982.

Secondary Sources

Aguilar, Roisida. "Via cruces de las mujeres peruanas para salir de la marginación política, 1924–1956." In *"Nosotros también somos peruanos": La marginación en el Perú siglos XVI a XXI,* edited by Claudia Rosas Lauro, 323–61. Lima: Pontificia Universidad Católica del Perú, 2011.

Aguirre, Carlos. "Hombres y rejas: El APRA en prisión, 1932–1945." *Bulletin de l'Institut français d'études andines* 43, no. 1 (2014): 7–30.

Alba, Victor. *Politics and the Labor Movement in Latin America*. Stanford, Calif.: Stanford University Press, 1968.

Alexander, Robert. "The Latin American Aprista Parties." *Political Quarterly* 20, no. 3 (July 1949): 236–47.

———. *Rómulo Betancourt and the Transformation of Venezuela*. New Brunswick, N.J.: Transaction, 1982.

Aljovin, Cristobal, and Sinesio Lopez. *Historia de las elecciones en el Perú: Estudios sobre el gobierno representativo*. Lima: Instituto de Estudios Peruanos, 2005.

Altamirano, Carlos. General introduction to *Historia de los intelectuales en América Latina*. Vol. 1, *La ciudad letrada, de la conquista al modernismo*, 9–27, edited by Jorge Myers. Buenos Aires: Katz Editores, 2008.

Ameringer, Charles. *The Caribbean Legion: Patriots, Politicians, Soldiers of Fortune, 1946–1950*. University Park: Pennsylvania State University Press, 1996.

———. *Democratic Left in Exile: The Anti-dictatorial Struggle in the Caribbean, 1945–1959*. Coral Gables, Fla.: University of Miami Press, 1974.

Anderson, Benedict. *Imagined Communities: Reflection on the Origin and Spread of Nationalism*. London: Verso, 2006.

Anderson, Charles. "Toward a Theory of Latin American Politics." Occasional Paper No. 2, Graduate Center of Latin American Studies, Vanderbilt University, Nashville, Tenn., February 1964.

Angulo Daneri, Toño. *Llámalo amor, si quieres*. Lima: Aguilar, 2004.

Baeza Flores, Alberto. *Haya de la Torre y la revolución constructiva de las Américas*. Buenos Aires: Editorial Claridad, 1962.

Balta, Aida. *Presencia de la mujer en el periodismo escrito peruano*. Lima: Universidad San Martin de Porres, 1998.

Barba Caballero, Jose. *Haya de la Torre y Mariátegui frente a la historia*. Lima: Amauta, 1978.

Basadre, Jorge. *Historia de la República*. 11 vols. Lima: Editorial Universitaria, 1983.

Bazan Vera, Blasco. *La revolución de Trujillo: Asalto al cuartel O'Donavan en 1932, primera insurgencia civil del siglo XX*. Trujillo, Peru: Autor, 2003.

Bederman, Gail. *Manliness and Civilization: A Cultural History of Gender and Race in the United States, 1880–1917*. Chicago: The University of Chicago Press, 1995.

Bergel, Martín. "El anti-antinorteamericanismo en América Latina (1898–1930): Apuntes para una historia intellectual." *Nueva Sociedad* 236 (November–December 2011): 152–67.

———. "Manuel Seoane y Luis Heysen: El entrelugar de los exiliados Apristas peruanos en la Argentina de los veinte." *Políticas de la Memoria* 6/7 (Summer 2006–7): 124–42.

———. "Nomadismo proselitista y revolución: Notas para una caracterización del primer exilio aprista (1923–1931)." *EIAL: Estudios Interdisciplinarios de America Latina y el Caribe* 20, no. 1 (2009): 41–66.

Bergére, Marie-Claire. *Sun Yat Sen*. Translated by Janet Lloyd. Stanford, Calif.: Stanford University Press, 1994.

Bonilla, Heraclio, and Paul Drake, eds. *El APRA, de la ideología a la praxis*. Lima: Centro Latinoamericano de Historia Económica y Social; San Diego: Center for Iberian and Latin American Studies, University of California, San Diego, 1989.

Britton, John A. *Carleton Beals: A Radical Journalist in Latin America*. Albuquerque: University of New Mexico Press, 1987.

Caballero, Manuel. *Latin America and the Comintern, 1919–1943*. Cambridge: Cambridge University Press, 1986.

Carr, Barry. "Radicals, Revolutionaries and Exiles: Mexico City in the 1920s." *Berkeley Review of Latin American Studies*, Fall 2010, 26–30.

Cerdas, Rodolfo. *Sandino, el APRA y la Internacional Comunista*. San José, Costa Rica: Centro de Investigación y Adiestramiento Político Administrativo, 1980.

Chaney, Elsa. *Supermadre: Women in Politics in Latin America*. Austin: University of Texas Press, 1979.

Chang-Rodríguez, Eugenio. *Una vida agónica: Víctor Raúl Haya de la Torre*. With photos and text by Alberto Vera la Rosa and Tito Agüero. Lima: Fondo Editorial del Congreso del Perú, 2007.

Chauncey, George. *Gay New York: Gender, Urban Culture, and the Making of the Gay Male World, 1890–1940*. New York: Basic Books, 1994.

Clinton, Richard Lee. "APRA: An Appraisal." *Journal of Interamerican Studies and World Affairs* 12, no. 2 (April 1970): 280–97.

Conniff, Michael. *Populism in Latin America*. Tuscaloosa: University of Alabama Press, 1999.

Cotler, Julio. *Clases, estado y nación en el Perú*. 6th ed. Lima: Instituto de Estudios Peruanos, 1992.

Crow, Jo. "Writing Indo-America: Gabriela Mistral in Conversation with Peruvian Apristas." Paper presented at the Thirty-Fourth International Congress of the Latin American Studies Association, New York, May 27–30, 2016.

Dagicour, Ombeline. "Political Invention in the Andes: The Peruvian Case. An Essay on President Augusto B. Leguía's Strategies and Practices of Power during the Oncenio, 1919–1930." *Jahrbuch for Geschichtes Lateinamerikas/Anuario de Estudios Latinoamericanos* 51, no. 1 (2014): 59–86.

de la Torre, Carlos, and Cynthia J. Arnson. "Introduction: The Evolution of Latin American Populism and the Debates over Its Meaning." In *Latin American Populism in the Twenty-First Century*, edited by Carlos de la Torre and Cynthia J. Arnson, 1–35. Washington, D.C.: Woodrow Wilson Center Press, 2013.

———, eds. *Latin American Populism in the Twenty-First Century*. Washington, D.C.: Woodrow Wilson Center Press, 2013.

Delpar, Helen. *The Enormous Vogue of Things: Mexican Cultural Relations between the United States and Mexico, 1920–1935*. Tuscaloosa: University of Alabama Press, 1992.

Denegri, Francesca. *Damas escritoras: Las ilustradas del diecinueve*. Lima: Recreo, 2007.

Díaz, María Luz. *Las mujeres de Haya: Ocho historias de pasión y rebeldía*. Lima: Editorial Planeta, 2007.

Dorais, Genevieve. "Coming of Age in Exile: Víctor Raúl Haya de la Torre and the Genesis of the American Popular Revolutionary Alliance, 1923–1931." *Hispanic American Historical Review* 97, no. 4 (November 2017): 651–79.

——. "Indo-America and the Politics of APRA Exile 1918–1945." PhD diss., University of Wisconsin, Madison, 2014.

Drake, Paul. *Socialism and Populism in Chile, 1932–1952*. Urbana: University of Illinois Press, 1978.

Drinot, Paulo. "Creole Anti-Communism: Labor, the Peruvian Communist Party, and APRA, 1930–1940." *Hispanic American Historical Review* 92, no. 4 (November 2012): 703–36.

Echague, Felix. "Lo que vi y lo que sé de la revolución de Trujillo." In *Trujillo 32*, 2:139–225. Trujillo: Trinchera de Mansiche, 1978.

Epstein, Edward Charles. "Motivational Bases for Loyalty in the Peruvian Aprista Party." PhD diss., University of Illinois at Urbana-Champaign, 1970.

Espinoza, G. Antonio. *Education and the State in Modern Peru: Primary Education in Lima, 1821–c. 1921*. New York: Palgrave Macmillan, 2013.

Flores Galindo, Alberto, "Haya de la Torre," *Socialismo y Participación* 20 (December 1982): 29–40.

Fonseca Ariza, Juan. *Misioneros y civilizadores: Protestantismo y modernización en el Perú (1915–1930)*. Lima: Pontificia Universidad Católica del Perú, 2002.

French, William. *A Peaceful and Working People: Manners, Morals and Class Formation in Northern Mexico*. Albuquerque: University of New Mexico Press, 1996.

Gadea, Hilda. *My Life with Che: The Making of a Revolutionary*. New York: Palgrave Macmillan, 2008.

García-Bryce, Iñigo. *Crafting the Republic: Lima's Artisans and Nation-Building in Peru, 1821–1879*. Albuquerque: University of New Mexico Press, 2004.

——. "Haya de la Torre and the Pursuit of Power in Peru, 1926–1948: The Seven Paradoxes of APRA." *Jahrbuch for Geschichtes Lateinamerikas/Anuario de Estudios Latinoamericanos* 51, no. 1 (2014): 86–112.

——. "A Middle-Class Revolution: The APRA Party and Middle-Class Identity in Peru, 1931–1956." In *The Making of the Middle Class: Toward a Transnational History*, edited by A. Ricardo López and Barbara Weinstein, 235–52. Durham, N.C.: Duke University Press, 2012.

——. "A Revolution Remembered, a Revolution Forgotten: The Apristas Insurrection of Trujillo, Peru, 1932." *A Contracorriente* 7, no. 3 (Spring 2010): 277–322.

——. "Transnational Activist: Magda Portal and the American Popular Revolutionary Alliance (APRA), 1926–1950." *The Americas* 70, no. 4 (April 2014): 677–706.

Gargurevich, Juan. *Historia de la prensa peruana, 1594–1990*. Lima: La Voz Ediciones, 1991.

Giesecke, Margarita. "The Trujillo Insurrection, the APRA Party and the Making of Modern Peruvian Politics." PhD diss., University of London, 1993.

Gonzalez A., Osmar. "Las cartas de Haya de la Torre a Carlos Pellicer: Un revolucionario peruano le escribe a un poeta mexicano." *Pacarina del Sur* 4, no. 14 (January–March 2013), http://www.pacarinadelsur.com/home/huellas-y-voces /611-las-cartas-de-haya-de-la-torre-a-carlos-pellicer-un-revolucionario-peruano -le-escribe-a-un-poeta-mexicano.

Guardia, Sara Beatriz. *Mujeres peruanas: El otro lado de la historia*. Lima: Minerva, 2002.

Gustave-Wrathall, John Donald, *Take the Young Stranger by the Hand: Same-Sex Relations and the YMCA*. Chicago: The University of Chicago Press, 1998.

Gutierrez Sánchez, Tomás. *Haya de la Torre: El factor protestante en su vida y obra, 1920–1933*. Lima: Editorial Pankara, 2016.

———. *Haya de la Torre y los protestantes liberales (Peru: 1917–1923)*. Lima: Editorial Nuevo Rumbo, 1995.

Habermas, Jurgen. *The Structural Transformation of the Public Sphere: An Inquiry into a Category of Bourgeois Society*. 6th ed. Cambridge, Mass.: MIT Press, 1991.

Halperín Dongui, Tulio. *Historia contemporánea de America Latina*. Madrid: Alianza Editorial, 1993.

Hansen, Sönke. "Neue politische Optionen in Peru im Zeichen der Weltwirtschaftskrise: Das Beispeil der APRA in der liberalkonservativen Presse (1931–33)." MA thesis, University of Hamburg, 2006.

———. "New Political Options in Peru during the Great Depression: The Image of the American Popular Revolutionary Alliance (APRA) in *El Comercio* (1931–33)." Paper presented at the Twenty-Seventh International Congress of the Latin American Studies Association, Montreal, Canada, September 5–7, 2007.

Haworth, Nigel. "Peru." In *Latin America between the Second World War and the Cold War, 1944–1948*, ed. Leslie Bethel and Ian Roxborough, 170–98. Cambridge: Cambridge University Press, 1992.

Hatzky, Christine. *Julio Antonio Mella (1903–1929): Una biografía*. Santiago de Cuba, Cuba: Editorial Oriente, 2008.

Heilman, Jaymie. *Before the Shining Path: Politics in Rural Ayacucho, 1895–1980*. Stanford, Calif.: Stanford University Press, 2010.

———. "To Fight Soviet Agents in the Fatherland: Anti-Communism in Ayacucho's APRA, 1945–1948." *A Contracorriente* 9, no. 3 (Spring 2012): 94–120.

———. "We Will No Longer Be Servile: *Aprismo* in 1930s Ayacucho." *Journal of Latin American Studies* 38, no. 3 (August 2006): 491–518.

Hirsch, Steven. "The Anarcho-syndicalist Roots of a Multi-class Alliance: Organized Labor and the Peruvian Aprista Party, 1900–1933." PhD diss., George Washington University, 1997.

Hughes-Hallet, Lucy. *Gabriele d'Annunzio: Poet, Seducer, and Preacher of War*. New York: Alfred A. Knopf, 2013.

Iber, Patrick. *Neither Peace nor Freedom: The Cultural Cold War in Latin America*. Cambridge, Mass.: Harvard University Press, 2015.

Iglesias, Daniel. *Du pain et de la Liberté: Socio-histoire des partis populaires apristes (Pérou, Venezuela, 1920–1962)*. Villeneuve d'Ascq: Presses Universitaires du Septentrion, 2015.

———. "Redes políticas transnacionales y elites politicas partidarias: Sociología histórica de los lazos entre el Partido Apristas Peruano y el ARDI venezolano (1928–1935)." *Historia y Política: Ideas procesos y movimientos sociales* 23 (January–June 2010): 219–42.

———. "Réseaux transnationaux et dynamiques contestataires en exil: Sociologie historique des pratiques politiques des dirigeants des partis populaires apristes (1920–1962)." PhD diss., Univeristé de Paris Diderot, 2011.

Jacobsen, Nils. "Populism Avant La Lettre in Peru: Rebuilding Power in Nicolás de Piérola's Mid-Career, 1884–1895." *Jahrbuch for Geschichtes Lateinamerikas/Anuario de Estudios Latinoamericanos* 51, no. 1 (2014): 35–58.

James, Ryan. *Lenin's Terror: The Ideological Origins of Early Soviet State Violence.* London: Routledge, 2012.

Jansen, Robert. *Revolutionizing Repertoires: The Rise of Populist Mobilization in Peru.* Chicago: University of Chicago Press, 2017.

Kantor, Harry. *The Ideology and Program of the Peruvian Aprista Movement.* New York: Octagon Books, 1977.

Keller, Renata. *Mexico's Cold War: Cuba, the United States, and the Legacy of the Mexican Revolution.* Cambridge: Cambridge University Press, 2015.

Kersffeld, Daniel. "La Liga Antiimperialista de las Américas: Una construcción política entre el marxismo y el latinoamericanismo." *Políticas de la Memoria* 6/7 (Summer 2006–7): 143–148.

Klaiber, Jeffrey. "The Popular Universities and the Origins of Aprismo, 1921–1924." *Hispanic American Historical Review* 55, no. 4 (November 1975): 693–715.

———. *Religion and Revolution in Peru.* Notre Dame, Ind.: University of Notre Dame Press, 1977.

Klaren, Peter. *Modernization, Dislocation, and Aprismo: Origins of the Peruvian Aprista Party, 1870–1932.* Austin: University of Texas Press, 1973.

———. *Peru: Society and Nationhood in the Andes.* New York: Oxford University Press, 2000.

Lazitch, Branko. *Biographical Dictionary of the Comintern.* Rev. ed. With Milorad M. Drachkovitch. Stanford, Calif.: Hoover Institution Press, 1986.

Levine, Robert. *Father of the Poor: Vargas and His Era.* Cambridge: Cambridge University Press, 1998.

López Jiménez, Sinesio. "Configuraciones de partidos y coaliciones del APRA: Los desplazamientos del APRA hacia la derecho." *Clio: Historia y Actualidad del Perú y el Mundo,* June 4, 2010. http://clioperu.blogspot.com/2010/06/el-sistema-politico -tripartito-la.html.

Luna Vegas, Ricardo. *Mariátegui, Haya de la Torre y la verdad histórica.* Lima: Retama Editorial, 1978.

Macías-González, Victor M., "Las amistades apasionadas y la homosociabilidad en la primera mitad del siglo XIX," *Historia y Grafía,* 31 (2008): 19–48.

Manrique, Nelson. *Usted fue Aprista: Bases para una historia crítica del APRA.* Lima: Fondo Editorial de la Pontificia Universidad Católica del Perú, 2009.

Masterson, Daniel M. *Militarism and Politics and Latin America: From Sánchez Cerro to Sendero Luminoso.* Westport, Conn.: Greenwood, 1991.

McClintock, Cynthia. "Populism in Peru: From APRA to Ollanta Humala." In *Latin American Populism in the Twenty-First Century,* edited by Carlos de la Torre and Cynthia J. Arnson, 203–37. Washington, D.C.: Woodrow Wilson Center Press, 2013.

McGee Deutsch, Sandra. "Gender and Sociopolitical Change in Twentieth-Century Latin America." *Hispanic American Historical Review* 71, no. 2 (May 1991): 259–306.

McNicoll, Robert Edwards. "Intellectual Origins of Aprismo." *Hispanic American Historical Review* 23, no. 3 (August 1943): 424–40.

Melgar Bao, Ricardo. "Cominternismo intelectual: Representaciones, redes y prácticas político-culturales en América Central, 1921–1933." *Revista Complutense de Historia de América* 35 (2009): 135–59.

———. "Exile in the Andean Countries: A Historical Perspective." In *Exile and the Politics of Exclusion in the Americas*, edited by Luis Roniger, James Naylor Green, and Pablo Yankelevich, 87–101. Portland, OR: Sussex Academic, 2012.

———. *Redes e imaginario del exilio en México y América Latina: 1934–1940*. Buenos Aires: Librosenred, 2003.

———. "Redes y espacio público transfronterizo: Haya de la Torre en México (1923–24)." In *Redes intelectuales y formación de naciones en España y América Latina (1890–1940)*, edited by Marta Elena Casaús Arzú and Manuel Pérez Ledesma, 65–105. Madrid: Ediciones Universidad Autónoma de Madrid, 2005.

———. *Vivir el exilio en la ciudad 1928: V. R. Haya de la Torre y J. Mella*. Mexico City: Ed. Taller Abierto, 2013.

Miller, Francesca. *Latin American Women and the Search for Social Justice*. Hanover, N.H.: University Press of New England, 1991.

Molinari Morales, Tirso. *El fascismo en el Perú: La Unión Revolucionaria, 1931–1936*. Lima: Universidad Nacional Mayor de San Marcos, 2006.

Mothes, Jurgen, "José Carlos Mariátegui und die Komintern." In *The International Newsletter of Historical Studies on Comintern, Communism and Stalinism* 3, no.7, 83–100.

Murillo Garaycochea, Percy. *Historia del APRA 1919–1945*. Lima: Enrique Delgado Valenzuela, 1976.

Nugent, David. *Modernity at the Edge of Empire: State, Individual, and Nation in the Northern Peruvian Andes, 1885–1935*. Stanford, Calif.: Stanford University Press, 1997.

Oliva Medina, Mario. *Dos peruanos en Repertorio Americano: Mariátegui y Haya*. San José: Universidad Nacional de Costa Rica, 2004.

Pakkasvirta, Jussi. ¿*Un continente, una nación? Intelectuales latinoamericanos, comunidad política y las revista culturales en Costa Rica y Perú (1919–1930)* San José: Editorial de la Universidad de Costa Rica, 2005.

Pareja Pflucker, Piedad. *Aprismo y sindicalismo en el Perú, 1943–1948*. Lima: Ediciones Peru, 1980.

Parker, David. *The Idea of the Middle Class: White-Collar Workers and Peruvian Society, 1900–1950*. University Park: Pennsylvania State University Press, 1998.

Pearcy, Thomas Lee. "Panama's Generation of 31." *Hispanic American Historical Review* 76, no. 4 (November 1996): 691–719.

Perrone, Fernanda. "Biographical Sketch of Frances Grant." *Inventory to the Papers of Frances R. Grant*, Special Collections and University Archives, Rutgers University Libraries, April 2000. http://www2.scc.rutgers.edu/ead/manuscripts/grantf.html.

Pike, Frederick. *The Modern History of Peru*. London: Weidenfeld and Nicolson, 1967.

———. *The Politics of the Miraculous in Peru: Haya de la Torre and the Spiritualist Tradition*. Lincoln: University of Nebraska Press, 1986.

Pita González, Alexandra. *La Unión Latino Americana y el Boletín "Renovación": Redes intelectuales y revistas culturales en la década de 1920*. Mexico City: El Colegio de México and Universidad de Colima, 2009.

Planas, Pedro. *Mito y realidad: Haya de la Torre*. Lima: Centro de Documentación Andina, 1985.

Portocarrero Maisch, Gonzalo. *De Bustamante a Odría: El fracaso del Frente Democrático Nacional, 1945–1950*. Lima: Mosca Azul, 1983.

Radcliffe, Sarah. *"Asi es una mujer del pueblo": Low-Income Women's Organizations under APRA, 1985–1987*. Working Papers No. 43. Cambridge, UK: Center of Latin American Studies, University of Cambridge, 1988.

Ravines, Eudocio. *The Yenan Way*. New York: Charles Scribner's Sons, 1951.

Rebaza Acosta, Alfredo. "La Revolución de Trujillo." In *Trujillo 32*, 2:9–138. Trujillo: Trinchera de Mansiche, 1978.

Rebolledo, Antonio. "Reseña: Haya de la Torre: El indoamericano." *Revista Iberoamericana* 2, no. 3 (1940): 263–65.

Reedy, Daniel. *Magda Portal: La pasionaria peruana; biografía intelectual*. Lima: Ediciones Flora Tristán, Centro de la Mujer Peruana Flora Tristán, 2000.

Renique, José Luis. *Incendiar la pradera: Un ensayo sobre la revolución en el Perú*. Lima: Estación la Cultura, 2015.

Ribeyro, Julio Ramón. *Cartas a Juan Antonio*. Lima: Jaime Campodónico, 1996.

Roberts, Kenneth M. "Parties and Populism in Latin America." In *Latin American Populism in the Twenty-First Century*, edited by Carlos de la Torre and Cynthia J. Arnson, 37–60. Washington, D.C.: Woodrow Wilson Center Press, 2013.

Schlesinger, Arthur, Jr. "Left Out." Review of *Harold Laski: A Life on the Left*, by Isaac Kramnick and Barry Sheerman. *Washington Monthly*, November 1993, 44–47. http://www.unz.org/Pub/WashingtonMonthly-1993nov-00044.

Schwartzberg, Steven. *Democracy and U.S. Policy in Latin America during the Truman Years*. Gainesville: University of Florida Press, 2003.

Sessa, Leandro. "Los exiliados como 'traductores': Las redes del exilio aprista en la Argentina en la década de los treinta." *Trabajos y Comunicaciones*, 2da época, no. 40 (2014), http://trabajosycomunicaciones.fahce.unlp.edu.ar/.

Slaughter, Jane, and Robert Kern. *European Women on the Left: Socialism, Feminism, and the Problems Faced by Political Women 1880 to the Present*. Westport, Conn.: Greenwood, 1981.

Sobrevilla, Natalia. *The Caudillo of the Andes: Andrés de Santa Cruz*. Cambridge: Cambridge University Press, 2011.

Soto Rivera, Roy. *Víctor Raúl: El hombre del siglo XX*. 3 vols. Lima: Instituto "Victor Raúl Haya de la Torre," 2002.

Stein, Steve. "The Paths to Populism in Peru." In *Populism in Latin America*, edited by Michael Conniff, 97–116. Tuscaloosa: University of Alabama Press, 1999.

———. *Populism in Peru: The Emergence of the Masses and the Politics of Social Control*. Madison: University of Wisconsin Press, 1980.

Taracena Arriola, Arturo. "La Asociación General de Estudiantes Latinoamericanos de Paris (1925–1933)." *Anuario de Estudios Centroamericanos* 15, no. 2 (1989): 61–80.

Taylor, Lewis. "The Origins of APRA in Cajamarca, 1928–1935." *Bulletin of Latin American Research* 19, no. 4 (October 2000): 437–59.

Unruh, Vicky. *Performing Women and Modern Literary Culture in Latin America* Austin: University of Texas Press, 2006.

Valderrama, Mariano, Jorge Chullen, Nicholas Lynch, and Carlos Malpica. *El APRA: Un camino de esperanzas y frustraciones*. Lima: Ediciones Gallo Rojo, 1980.

Vasconcelos, José. *La raza cósmica*. Madrid: Agencia Mundial de Librería, 1925.

Vega Centeno, Imelda. *Aprismo popular: Cultura, religion y política*. Lima: Tarea, 1991.

Villanueva, Víctor. *El Apra en busca del poder*. Lima: Editorial Horizonte, 1975.

———. *El APRA y el ejercito*. Lima: Editorial Horizonte, 1977.

———. *Ejército peruano: Del caudillaje anárquico al militarismo reformistas*. Lima: Librería Editorial Mejía Baca, 1973.

———. *La sublevación aprista del 48: Tragedia de un pueblo y un partido*. Lima: Editorial Milla Bartres, 1973.

Wallace Fuentes, Maria Yvonne. "Becoming Magda Portal: Poetry, Gender, and Revolutionary Politics in Lima, Peru 1920–1930." PhD diss., Duke University, 2006.

———. *Most Scandalous Woman: Magda Portal and the Dream of Revolution in Peru*. Norman: University of Oklahoma Press, 2017.

Weaver, Kathleen. *Peruvian Rebel: The World of Magda Portal*. University Park: Pennsylvania State University Press, 2009.

Werlich, David. *Peru: A Short History*. Carbondale: Southern Illinois University Press, 1978.

Whitney, Robert. *State and Revolution in Cuba: Mass Mobilization and Political Change, 1920–1940*. Chapel Hill: University of North Carolina Press, 2001.

Wilson, Fiona. *Citizenship and Political Violence in Peru: An Andean Town, 1870s–1970s*. New York: Palgrave Macmillan, 2013.

Yankelevich, Pablo. *Miradas australes: Propaganda, cabildeo y proyección de la Revolución Mexicana en el Rio de la Plata, 1910–1930*. Mexico City: Instituto Nacional de Estudios Históricos de la Revolución Mexicana, 1997.

———. *La revolución Mexicana en América Latina: Intereses politicos e itineraries intelectuales*. Mexico City: Instituto Mora, 2003.

Zaïtzeff, Serge I. "El diáologo espistolar entre Carlos Pellicier y Germán Arciniégas." *Cuadernos Americanos* (Mexico), no. 82 (July–August 2000): 40–48.

Zegarra, Margarita. "María Jesús Alvarado y el rol de las mujeres peruanas en la construcción de la patria." In *Mujeres, familia y sociedad en la hisotira de América Latina, siglos XVIII–XXI*, 541–72, edited by Scarlett O'Phelan and Margarita Zegarra. Lima: Centro de Documentación sobre la Mujer, Pontificia Universidad Católica del Perú, Instituto Francés de Estudios Andinos, 2006.

Index

Acción Democrática, 2, 5, 8
Alexander, Robert, 5, 8
Allende, Salvador, 119, 188
Alva Castro, Luis, 89, 124, 162
Alvarado, María Jesús, 169–70, 176
Amauta, 31
American Civil Liberties Union 148
American Federation of Labor and
   Congress of Industrial Organizations (AFL-CIO), 95, 112, 114, 119
American Popular Revolutionary
   Alliance (APRA), 2; anti-
   communism of, 114; civilizing
   mission of, 134–35; coalition
   government, as, 53, 76–79, 112;
   comedores populares, 144; Comité de
   Defensa, 82; Communism, distinct
   from, 8, 29; Communism, labeled
   as, 73, 87; Communist attacks on,
   32–34; *congresos postales*, 47, 129,
   145; Constituent Assembly (1978),
   89, 162; continentalist claims, 129,
   189; *convivencia* (1956–62), 85–86,
   122, 201; criticism from the Left
   of, 3; departure from, 138, 143, 145,
   156, 196–97; dissolution, danger
   of, 41, 56, 116; elections and, 43, 58,
   63, 74, 76, 79, 81, 84, 87–88, 104,
   186; expulsion of congressional
   delegation (1932), 44, 61–62; First
   National Convention of Aprista
   Women, 166, 193; foundational
   mythology of, 25, 121, 128–29;
   founding of, 13, 23, 26, 28–29, 91,
   97–98, 142; government amnesty
   of, 44; government attacks on,
   43–44; Víctor Raúl Haya de la
   Torre and, 1, 13, 29, 32, 34, 36,
   40–1, 43, 56–57, 66, 75, 79, 85, 132,
   141–142, 144, 159, 180; ideological
   shifts of, 2, 78, 92, 109, 196, 199,
   203; insurgent wing in, 9, 51, 54,
   82; International Executive
   Committee, 130–31; international
   party, 13–14, 16, 35, 37, 44–45, 47,
   62, 65, 73–74, 101, 112–13, 139;
   labor unions, control of, 58, 78,
   112, 143–44, 173, 176; legal status
   of, 16, 47–48, 77, 122, 152, 161,
   193–94; longevity of, 2, 5, 10,
   125–26, 144, 164; male-dominated
   hierarchies in, 11; martyrs of, 61,
   104, 136–37, 196–97; middle-class
   support for, 58, 78; military and,
   51–53, 58–61, 65–70, 73–77,
   79–80, 82–84, 86–89, 114, 134, 162,
   202; military organization, as, 29,
   34, 53, 55, 89, 131, 148; military
   organization, within, 82–83,
   88–89, 139; National Assembly of
   Aprista Labor Unions, 78;
   National Executive Committee,
   132; opposition party, as, 88;
   outlawed party, as, 44, 62, 74, 76,
   80, 101, 116, 182; Partido del
   Pueblo, 16, 44, 201; party congresses, 25, 59, 81, 101, 141, 171, 173,
   195, 197; party discipline, 77, 127,
   133–35, 137–39, 144; party
   headquarters, 43, 49, 57, 62, 114,
   124–25, 133, 144–45, 161, 173–74,
   184, 192–93, 202, 204; party
   leaders, 47, 52, 62–63, 76, 83–84,
   126, 129, 131–32, 134, 145, 161, 174,
   184, 193, 195–96, 201; party loyalty,
   136; party organization, 11, 126,

Greenland, 160

Guatemala: APRA section in, 143; Víctor Raúl Haya de la Torre, articles published in, 99; Víctor Raúl Haya de la Torre, expulsion from, 41, 56, 100; Víctor Raúl Haya de la Torre in, 7, 48, 92, 138; Liga Antiimperialista de las Américas, 18; U.S. treatment of, 93, 103

Guevara, Che, 3, 7

Gunther, John, 150; *Inside Latin America*, 150

Gutierrez Sánchez, Tomás, 134

Hacia la mujer nueva (Portal), 166, 175, 177

Halperín, Tulio, 6

Hamas, 55

Hatzky, Christine, 32

Haya de la Torre, Agustín "Cucho," 62–63

Haya de la Torre, Víctor Raúl, 8–9, 11–13, 18, 24, 25, 26, 33, 34, 41, 46, 50, 60, 104

—critics of: criticism by former Apristas, 156–57; criticized by party leaders, 126–27, 132; duality of, 2, 201, 203

—early years: popular universities and, 19, 142–43; Protestantism and, 20, 23, 134; student activist and leader, as, 4, 12, 19, 21–22, 140–41, 180, 20; University Reform Movement and, 12, 140–41; YMCA and, 18, 19–20, 25

—later years: Constituent Assembly and, 49, 89, 124, 162–63; death mask, 183; distance from Peruvian politics, 16, 48–49, 85, 121, 123, 129, 159, 202; elder statesman, as, 49, 89, 124, 129, 161–62, 202; Villa Mercedes, 124, 161, 205

—party building and: cult of personality, 10, 125–26, 129, 146, 148–49, 152–56, 163; discipline, 34, 61, 130, 133–35, 138, 155; exile, criticism of, 46, 128, 136, 191; hagiographies of, 27, 152–56; institution builder,as, 3, 10, 33, 127, 131, 202; loyalty to the party, demand for, 137; male-dominated social hierarchies and, 11, 167; organization, 126, 129–30, 138; propaganda, 3, 6, 28, 57, 66, 75, 99, 109–10, 114, 118, 120, 132, 144; sensualism, objection to, 128, 136, 191, 202

—personality and personal life: celebrity status, 12, 21, 48, 118, 146–50, 158–59; charming personality, 81, 92, 204; death, awareness of, 102, 122, 129, 148; exile and travel abroad (*see names of specific countries*); family background of, 18; financial assistance received, 28, 97, 192; financial difficulties, 35–36, 123, 151, 156–57; health problems, 27, 124; hiding, 4, 21, 44–46, 101–3, 106–7, 116, 129, 133, 135, 150, 183, 190, 201; imprisoned, 52, 63, 65–66, 70, 133, 135, 146, 175, 179, 187; homosexuality, alleged, 5, 42, 87, 126, 128, 156–58, 160–61, 167, 183, 191–92, 202–4; messianic leader, as, 2; mythical figure, as, 126, 138, 145, 150–51, 163; Nazism, witnesses, 41; spiritualism, 61, 75–76, 137; teacher, as, 140, 161, 202; transnational networks and, 5, 8, 17, 19, 22–24, 97–98, 119

—Peruvian politics and: elections, 7, 42, 57–58, 60, 74, 87, 101, 122–23, 132, 184, 186; kingmaker, as, 75, 112, 116; labor movement and, 58, 79; military and, 9, 51–53, 58–59, 62, 74, 77, 79–80, 82–84, 86–89, 107, 122, 202; military coup, support of, 52–53, 70, 75–77, 83; paths to power, 7, 9, 50–52, 70, 81, 131; political asylum, 46, 116–19, 158–59; political violence and, 7, 9,